The Struggle for Equality

The quest for equality in the public sphere by religious minorities in India remains highly contested. For the Muslims, the largest religious minority, it continues to define the community's politics more than seven decades after Independence. The United Progressive Alliance (UPA) government's (2004–2014) policies on religious minorities—the Muslim community in particular—provide a test case for examining *why* a government committed to a radical new approach for equality of opportunity for religious minorities was unable to deliver on its promises. The author focuses on probing the deeply entrenched systemic reasons that help explain the UPA's lack of success. Drawing on empirical sources that include official data, parliamentary proceedings and commission reports, the book discusses in detail the underlying modes of institutional resistance to UPA policies that rendered them ineffective or non-implementable, especially against policies targeted at disadvantaged Muslims.

It presents a rich, comprehensive, and nuanced understanding of the policy process in India. Significantly, it is an understanding that locates the role of history and institutions in continuing to shape policies for religious minorities.

Heewon Kim is a British Academy Postdoctoral Fellow in the Department of Religions and Philosophies, SOAS, University of London. Her research focuses on religion and politics in modern India, with particular reference to the post-1947 management of religious diversity, India's Muslim community, and the post-9/11 state responses to demands from religious minorities for equal opportunities.

The Struggle for Equality
India's Muslims and Rethinking the UPA Experience

Heewon Kim

CAMBRIDGE
UNIVERSITY PRESS

314 to 321, 3rd Floor, Plot No.3, Splendor Forum, Jasola District Centre, New Delhi 110025, India

Cambridge University Press is part of the University of Cambridge.

It furthers the University's mission by disseminating knowledge in the pursuit of education, learning and research at the highest international levels of excellence.

www.cambridge.org
Information on this title: www.cambridge.org/9781108416108

© Heewon Kim 2019

This publication is in copyright. Subject to statutory exception and to the provisions of relevant collective licensing agreements, no reproduction of any part may take place without the written permission of Cambridge University Press.

First published 2019

Printed in India by Shree Maitrey Printech Pvt. Ltd., Noida

A catalogue record for this publication is available from the British Library

ISBN 978-1-108-41610-8 Hardback

Cambridge University Press has no responsibility for the persistence or accuracy of URLs for external or third-party internet websites referred to in this publication, and does not guarantee that any content on such websites is, or will remain, accurate or appropriate.

To my parents

Contents

List of Tables and Figures	ix
List of Abbreviations	xi
Acknowledgements	xv
Introduction	1
1. Opening Up the 'Black Box' of Public Policy: Towards an Institutional Analysis of India's Policies on Religious Minorities	16
2. Constitution-Making, Equality of Opportunity and Religious Minorities: Reassessing the Critical Juncture	39
3. The UPA in Power: The New Equal Opportunities Framework, Religious Minorities and the Limits of Change	65
4. UPA, Muslims and Public Sector Employment: Assessing the Record	93
5. UPA, Muslims and Service Delivery	127
6. UPA, Muslims and the Communal Violence Bill	171
Conclusion	195
Appendix	208
Bibliography	210
Index	236

Tables and Figures

Tables

2.1	'Competing equalities': SCs, STs, OBCs and religious minorities	48
2.2	Muslim employees in government sector employment	60
2.3	Percentage of Muslims in senior civil service posts	61
3.1	A summary of the UPA's policy initiatives on religious minorities	69
4.1	Central government and departments with high recruitment of minorities, 2006–2013	115
4.2	Central government and departments with medium recruitment of minorities, 2006–2013	117
4.3	Central government and departments with low recruitment of minorities, 2006–2013	119
5.1	Some of the main recommendations of the *SCR* and *RMCR* on education, finance and infrastructure	130
5.2	The multitude of schemes and initiatives for minorities under the UPA	133
5.3	States and political parties in distribution of scholarships (mid 2007–mid 2014)	144
5.4	Provision of PSL to minority communities	150
5.5	Degree of implementation in provision of PSL against targets to religious minorities (2007–2014) by state	151
5.6	Proportion of minorities in 121 MCDs as per Census 2001	158
5.7	Share of minority in total minority population in MCD	161
5.8	Budget allocation by the Union government for minorities in the Eleventh Five-Year Plan	162
5.9	Fund utilisation by the Union government for minorities in the Eleventh Five-Year Plan	165

Figures

1.1	Stages of the policy process	20
1.2	UPA and Muslims: actors and institutions	26
1.3	A summary of the analytical approach: institutional policy analysis	33
3.1	MoMA and organisational dependence: ministries and other structures	86
5.1	PSA in 121 MCDs by scheduled banks	155

Abbreviations

AIADMK	All India Anna Dravida Munnetra Kazhagam
ANHAD	Act Now for Harmony and Democracy
BJD	Biju Janata Dal
BJP	Bharatiya Janata Party
BPL	below poverty line
BSF	Border Security Force
BSP	Bahujan Samaj Party
BSUP	Basic Services to Urban Poor
CISF	Central Industrial Security Force
CPI	Communist Party of India
CPI (M)	Communist Party of India (Marxist)
CRPF	Central Reserve Police Force
DI	diversity index
DMK	Dravida Munnetra Kazhagam
DoPT	Department of Personnel and Training
EOC	Equal Opportunity Commission
IAS	Indian Administrative Service
IAY	Indira Awaas Yojana
ICDS	Integrated Child Development Service
IFS	Indian Foreign Service
IHSDP	Integrated Housing and Slum Development Programme
IIM	Indian Institute of Management
IIT	Indian Institute of Technology
INC	Indian National Congress
IPC	Indian Penal Code
IPS	Indian Police Service
ITI	Industrial Training Institute
JD (U)	Janata Dal (United)
JMM	Jharkhand Mukti Morcha

JNNURM	Jawaharlal Nehru National Urban Renewal Mission
LSD	*Lok Sabha Debate*
MCD	minority concentration district
MGNREGS	Mahatma Gandhi National Rural Employment Guarantee Scheme
MNF	Mizo National Front
MoMA	Ministry of Minority Affairs
MPPGP	Ministry of Personnel, Public Grievances and Pensions
MP	Member of Parliament
MSDP	Multi-Sectoral Development Programme
MSJE	Ministry of Social Justice and Empowerment
NAC	National Advisory Council
NCBC	National Commission for Backward Classes
NCM	National Commission for Minorities
NCMP	National Common Minimum Programme
NCSC	National Commission for Scheduled Castes
NCST	National Commission for Scheduled Tribes
NDA	National Democratic Alliance
NGO	non-governmental organisation
NHRC	National Human Rights Commission
NIC	National Integration Council
NMDFC	National Minorities Development & Finance Corporation
NPF	Naga People's Front
NRDWP	National Rural Drinking Water Programme
OBC	Other Backward Class
PDP	(Jammu and Kashmir) People's Democratic Party
PIB	Press Information Bureau
PMO	Prime Minister's Office
PM's 15PP	Prime Minister's 15-Point Programme
PSA	priority sector advances
PSL	priority sector lending
RBI	Reserve Bank of India

RJD	Rashtriya Janata Dal
RMCR	*Ranganath Misra Commission Report*
RSD	*Rajya Sabha Debate*
RSS	Rashtriya Swayamsevak Sangh
SAD	Shiromani Akali Dal
SC	Scheduled Caste
SCR	*Sachar Committee Report*
SDF	Sikkim Democratic Front
SEBC	Socially and Educationally Backward Class
SGSY	Swarnajayanti Gram Swarozgar Yojana
SJSRY	Swarna Jayanti Shahari Rozgar Yojana
SP	Samajwadi Party
SRC	socio-religious category
SSA	Sarva Shiksha Abhiyan
SSB	Sashastra Seema Bal
SSP	Sikkim Sangram Parishad
ST	Scheduled Tribe
TMC	Trinamool Congress
UIDSSMT	Urban Infrastructure Development Scheme for Small and Medium Towns
UIG	Urban Infrastructure and Governance
UPA	United Progressive Alliance
VHP	Vishwa Hindu Parishad

Acknowledgements

This book emerged out of my experience in a northern city in India, where I spent the scorching hot summer of 2006. One ordinary day, my friends and I were heading to a restaurant in the city centre for lunch. When we had almost reached the city centre, two policemen came to us, stopped one of my friends and started asking him a couple of questions. I had no idea why this particular guy was picked out from our group. But the tone and atmosphere of the conversation was enough for me to feel that he was being interrogated. A few minutes later, when I overheard the word 'passport' from their conversation, my friend turned furious and started arguing with the police. After my friend came back to us, we had a very long conversation lasting a whole afternoon. It was only then that I realised, in my group of friends, he was the only Muslim man with Islamic clothing, a cap and a beard. The stories he shared made me raise questions about things I had never considered before. It lingered in my mind for the next several years. That conversation became a trigger for my PhD research.

This book is the result of my research project that began in 2010 but the real journey seeking to find an answer to the interplay of religion, people, politics and humanity began much earlier. In the course of writing this book, I have incurred many debts to scholars, officials, librarians and others. My greatest debt, however, is to my PhD supervisor, Gurharpal Singh, who has provided support in countless ways in finalising this project. Discussions with him have immeasurably improved the readability of my work. Thank you for having pushed me to do my best, Gurharpal. You pushed me to do better, to improve myself, and test my limits as a researcher. I appreciate your tremendous support and help in completing this project.

Finishing this book would have been all the more difficult were it not for the generous funding I received from the Faculty of Arts and Humanities (SOAS), a Jordan Travel Grant from the Department of the Study of Religions (SOAS), a fieldwork grant from the Graduate School (SOAS), the British Academy, and the Aga Khan University Institute for the Study of Muslim Civilisations. Not only financial support but also fellowship at these institutions provided me with a rich academic environment from which I have drawn much intellectual stimulation. A big thank you to my colleagues and friends for their feedback, cooperation and friendship.

This research has made extensive use of libraries and collections in the UK and India. I acknowledge here the courtesies extended to me by the librarians at SOAS library (special thanks to Jiyeon Wood), the British Library, Senate House library, University of Birmingham library, Jawaharlal Nehru University library, Nehru Memorial Library, Central Secretariat Library, Parliamentary Library, and the Amity Institute of Advanced Legal Studies library in Noida. During my stay in India, I was privileged to have a fellowship at the Centre for Studies of Social Systems, Jawaharlal Nehru University, New Delhi.

This book would not have been possible without the cooperation and support of interviewees in India. I acknowledge here with profound gratitude the access which politicians, academics, civil servants, NGO activists and journalists gave me and enabled me to share their insights into the policy process. I would like to thank the following people for their support and encouragement: Justice Rajinder Sachar, Professor Zoya Hasan, Professor Surinder S. Jodhka, Professor Dipankar Gupta, Dr Abusaleh Shariff, Mr Wajahat Habibullah, Professor Amitabh Kundu, Ms Farah Naqvi, Ms Vrinda Grover and Mr Asaduddin Owaisi. I owe special thanks to the academic and jurist Professor Tahir Mahmood for giving so generously of his time: he not only inspired me with his courage and dedication in elaborating an insightful and progressive interpretation of the Constitution of India but also enriched my knowledge and understanding of the role of the judiciary since 1947. No less significant were my friends in the UK, India and Korea – too many to mention here by name. I thank especially those in India who provided generous and willing aid during my fieldworks. Vasant mummy (sister Hye), Minjung Kim, Parvathy Poornima, Jawed Alam Khan, a big thank you! I also would like to thank Cambridge University Press for enabling me to publish this book. Special mention goes to Qudsiya Ahmed and Aniruddha De at the Press for their support and patience throughout the publication process.

Last, but by no means least, my deepest appreciation goes to my family. This book would not have been completed without the moral support, sacrifices, prayers, patience and love from my parents, brother, sister-in-law and two nephews. In particular, I wish to thank my loving nephews – Junho and Yeonho – who provide unending inspiration. My late grandparents would have been truly delighted with publication of this book. Through this painful but enjoyable journey not only have I grown academically, but also personally. I dedicate this book to my parents, to whom I owe everything.

District-wise Concentration of Muslim Population in India, 2001

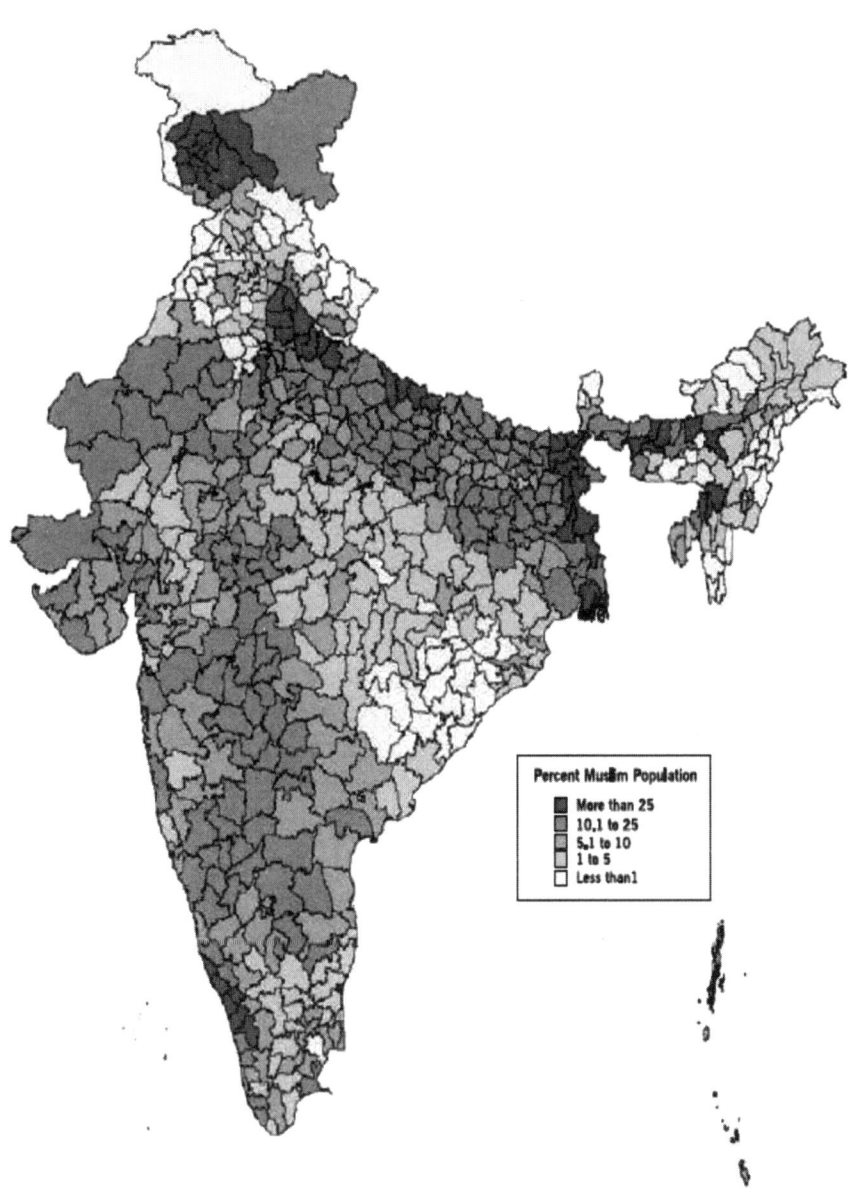

Source: Prime Minister's High Level Committee (2006: 32).

Introduction

One of the most remarkable features of states' responses to 9/11 was the near uniformity of approach towards Muslim minority communities across the globe. The dramatic impact of the attack on the World Trade Center in New York and the subsequent 'War on Terror' were accompanied by policies that appeared to pathologise Muslim minority communities around the discourses of terror, identity politics and self-imposed isolation (Kepel 2004; Roy 2004; and Modood 2005). Increasingly constructed in the language of Huntington's *Clash of Civilisations* (1996), these policies posited Muslim minorities as 'the enemy within'. 'Europe', admitted the distinguished French scholar Gilles Kepel, has 'emerged as the primary battlefield' (2004: 241) between the values of Enlightenment and Islam. Helmut Schmidt, the former chancellor of Germany, opined that 'a peaceful accommodation between Islam and Christianity is possible only in authoritarian states' (in Klausen 2005: 3). In many Western states this 'clash of civilisations within' was attributed to multiculturalism, a political creed that had allegedly undermined collective citizenship by fostering identity politics. Thus, in the aftermath of the 7 July 2005 (7/7) bombings in central London, British public opinion appeared to agree on the need to reform multiculturalism to remove its apartheid aspects (Wolff 2005).

Polemicists blamed this state of affairs on public policies and practices that encouraged the social and political isolation of minority immigrant communities. The events of Madrid on 11 March 2004 and London on 7 July 2005 gave further impetus to the critics of multiculturalism. However, political and administrative decision-makers, including security experts, were obliged to address the realities of diverse societies to keep jihadis and Islamophobes at bay while recognising the need to confront the segregationist aspects of multiculturalism. This response was matched by political strategies, almost universally across the West, designed to build 'social cohesion' and promote integrationist values. While the securitisation of Muslim minority communities reflected the hard edge of this policy, state-led efforts to examine causes of Muslim underachievement and disadvantage mirrored the 'softer' integrationist intent (Fekete 2004 and Samad 2013). Almost all states in

Europe have adopted policies that include a mixture of these approaches, with the initial emphasis on securitisation being displaced by a renewed policy interest in disadvantage and discrimination suffered by Muslim minorities (Klausen 2005).

A similar process has been taking place in developing countries as well. In African countries with large Muslim communities such as Nigeria and Tanzania, state policies have been characterised by both securitisation and the need to tackle concerns of identity and underdevelopment. In Asia, where Muslim minorities traditionally have been subject to violence, post-9/11 many states have recognised that securitisation can only be legitimised if accompanied by realistic efforts to confront underdevelopment and long-standing issues of (mis)recognition. Thus, in India, the post-9/11 response to the country's Muslims was distinguished, on the one hand, by the central government of the Bharatiya Janata Party (BJP)–led National Democratic Alliance condoning pogroms against Muslims in Gujarat in 2002, which cost 2,000 lives and displaced a further 150,000 (Z. Hasan 2006), and, on the other, efforts of the NDA's successor, the Congress-led United Progressive Alliance (UPA), to overcome the 'development deficit' suffered by the country's largest minority community.

Against the backdrop of the Indo-Pakistan Kargil war (1999), the mobilisation of India's forces against Pakistan following an attack on the Indian Parliament by Islamic militants (2001), and the pogroms in Gujarat (2002), the election of the UPA government in 2004 marked a turning point. Committed to 'preserve, protect and promote social harmony', its National Common Minimum Programme (NCMP) promised 'to provide full equality of opportunity, particularly in education and employment for Scheduled Castes (SCs), Scheduled Tribes (STs), Other Backward Classes (OBCs) and religious minorities' (Government of India 2004). These promises, moreover, were backed by Congress' efforts to rebuild its relations with minorities, especially the Muslim community, through 'affirmative action for all religious and linguistic minorities'. Drawing on the model of reservations in employment and education in Kerala and Karnataka, the party was determined 'to adopt this policy for ... Muslims and other religious minorities on a national scale (INC 2004). For the first time since Independence, it appeared the concerns of India's Muslims had found a receptive political audience.

India's Muslims

India's 172 million Muslims, constituting 14.2 per cent of the total population, are the largest religious minority, followed by Christians (2.3 per cent) and Sikhs (1.7 per cent) (Ministry of Home Affairs 2011b). India has the third largest Muslim population in the world (after Indonesia and Pakistan), and is home to some of the oldest communities since the birth of the faith. However, this legacy is bittersweet: Indian Muslims carry the burden of being stigmatised as 'outsiders', and more importantly, in recent times, as the 'children of India's Partition' (Gayer and Jaffrelot 2012: 2). This weight has been difficult to endure since Independence because Muslims have had to demonstrate their loyalty to the new nation and to bear the brunt of a resurgent Hindu Right, notably since the 1980s. As a recent high-powered committee concluded, Muslims in India 'carry a double burden of being labelled as "anti-national" and as being "appeased" at the same time' (Prime Minister's High Level Committee 2006: 11, hereafter *Sachar Committee Report* [*SCR*] after its Chairman). Negotiating this unpropitious environment has not been easy, and set against the background of domestic and global developments, the community has often felt, and has been viewed by many, as being under siege. 'The Muslims of India', writes Glazer, 'are thus a unique minority, unique in their size, unique in their relation to a foreign nation which is seen as the permanent and unchanging enemy of India, unique in their history as a once dominant group that is now reduced to one that has lost power, property, and dominance' (Glazer 2007: 184).

Central to understanding the dilemmas facing the community today are its social and political challenges. Although its leaders like to project the idea of a monolithic and historic community, India's Muslims have lost their historic status as a dominant, cohesive and privileged elite under the Mughal and British Raj. Today, they are increasingly differentiated by language, caste, region and social stratification, and resemble the economically and socially disadvantaged groups within Hindu society. Large sections are among the most deprived groups in India. Decades of identity politics since Independence have given way to more prosaic concerns about development and jobs, and while SCs, STs and OBCs have witnessed a general improvement in their social development, the continued social exclusion of Muslims casts a deep shadow over the 'success' of India's democracy.[1]

---

[1] For an analysis of the 'success' of India's democracy, see Kohli (2001).

Geographically, India's Muslims are concentrated in the northwest, north, east and west coasts, and the central region around Hyderabad (see map on page xvii). These geographical divisions are significant for a community that also tends to be divided by language and regional histories, with states in the south more integrated into the local economy and society. Apart from Jammu and Kashmir and Lakshadweep, Muslims are everywhere a minority in the states in which they live. In 2001, more than 60 per cent of the Muslim population was located in the three states of Uttar Pradesh, Bihar and West Bengal—states that are also among the least developed (*SCR* 2006: ch. 4). Muslims also tend to be more urbanised than other Indians, with 35.7 per cent of the community living in cities, according to the 2001 Census.[2] However, as Gayer and Jaffrelot (2012: 11) observe, 'urban Muslims are comparatively poorer than rural Muslims, in contrast to the situation prevailing for most of the other communities'. The social and economic condition of Muslims in India today is most problematic in the 'cow belt', the north and east of India where the legacy of Partition politics still looms large.

In the early 2000s, when the popular media regularly associated Muslims with terrorism and jihadi attacks (Indian Parliament, Mumbai, New Delhi), a High Level Committee established by the Prime Minister, Manmohan Singh, to examine the socio-economic and educational condition of India's Muslims (subsequently known as the Sachar Committee after its Chairman and its report the *Sachar Committee Report*, or *SCR*), found strong evidence of a community mired in underdevelopment. Nearly 70 years after Independence, Muslims performed badly on almost all indicators of socio-economic development. Overall, the status of the majority of the community was only marginally above SCs and STs and below the Hindu OBCs. Only 8 per cent of the community's urban population was found to be working in the formal sector compared to a national average of 21 per cent; 68 per cent maintained a lowly existence in the informal sector, working in casual employment in industries that were declining, or were adversely affected by

---

[2] The 2011 Census (Ministry of Home Affairs 2011b) shows that community concentration is strongest in the states of Assam, West Bengal and Kerala, and the proportion of the Muslim community living in an urban setting increased to 39.9 per cent. Since the UPA's motivation for policymaking for disadvantaged religious minorities was based on the findings of the 2001 Census, here we provide the figure from the 2001 Census data but also recognise the change in the 2011 Census.

economic liberalisation. Almost a third of the community's population was below the poverty line, with average expenditure of urban Muslims at 800 rupees per month (approximately 8.85 pound sterling) in 2004–2005—the same as Dalits (at the bottom of the Hindu caste system) and Adivasis (tribal populations), and half of that of upper caste Hindus. This status was further confirmed by findings that the male Muslim literacy rate (67.6 per cent) was only 1 per cent above that of Dalit men (66.6 per cent) at a time when literacy rates among Dalits were improving rapidly as a result of reservations in education and employment. Surprisingly, the popular perception that the community's educational performance was being thwarted because of madrasa education was shattered by the revelation that only 4 per cent of Muslims actually attended madrasa schools. Nothing, however, was more striking than the overwhelming under-representation of Muslims in the state sector: at all levels in public sector employment, in institutions of public representation and in non-official bodies, the community was significantly under-represented if not at times completely unrepresented. While the representation of excluded and minority groups in state and national legislatures was increasing, that of the Muslim community was declining (Gayer and Jaffrelot 2012: 1–6; SCR 2006: chs 3, 4, 5 and 8).

The systematic underdevelopment of the Muslim community since 1947 is further reflected in its social structure. Socially, it has been divided into three categories. At the apex are the *ashraf* ('noble') who claim descent from central Asia and represent the elites. Significant sections of the *ashraf* migrated to Pakistan, leaving the community's leadership severely depleted. They also include high-caste Hindus, such as Kshatriyas, who converted to Islam during Mughal rule. Below the *ashraf* are the *ajlaf* ('commoner'), converts from Hinduism of middle and lower castes, often identified with such occupations as weaving, tailoring and hair-dressing, who form the bulk of the community. The lowest social group are the *arzal* ('degraded') who share the same occupations and life-patterns as the former untouchables (SCs). Caste is present in Muslim society but the status of 'each non *Ashraf* "caste" (*zat*, equivalent to *jati* among Hindus) varies according to their lineage, ethnicity, traditional occupation and physical proximity to higher "castes"' (Gayer and Jaffrelot 2012: 7).[3] Taken together, the *ajlafs* and *arzals* in the OBC category

---

[3] Caste or caste-like formations are almost universal across South Asia and cut across all faith communities (see Dumont 1972). The tensions between the sociological reality of caste and the egalitarian precepts of some of the faiths—

constitute nearly 40.7 per cent of Indian Muslims (Gayer and Jaffrelot 2012),[4] and the social condition of these groups both approximates to the most disadvantaged groups in Indian society and is reinforced by disadvantage arising from religious discrimination, periodical communal violence and uncertain employment patterns. The social exclusion of these groups, and the absence of substantive equality of opportunity for disadvantaged Muslims, is one of the major challenges facing Indian democracy today.[5]

It is important to recognise that India's Muslims can no longer be constructed as a homogenous community defined primarily by religious identity.[6] The levels of social and political differentiation within the community, as we shall see in subsequent chapters, has proceeded at a rapid pace. Particularly noteworthy is the increasing political mobilisation of Dalit Muslims, for example, the *pasmanda* movement in Bihar, which seeks to access the reservations accorded to SCs and STs. What is interesting about these mobilisations is that they are rooted among the *ajlaf*s and *arzal*s, the most disadvantaged and deprived sections of India's Muslims, and aim to secure the public goods for development (reservations and equal proportion of state services) accorded to their Hindu, Buddhist and Sikh counterparts.

Equality of opportunity, the Indian state, minorities and Muslims

The UPA's efforts to provide 'full equality of opportunity' for minorities, especially Muslims, need to be seen in its historical and contemporary dimensions. The Indian Constitution, like in most liberal democracies, bars any discrimination on the grounds of religion, race, caste, descent and place of birth and recognises that equality of treatment is a precondition of effective citizenship. Procedural equality in the operation of state structures and their

---

Buddhism, Christianity, Islam and Sikhism—are, as we shall see in subsequent chapters with reference to India's Muslims, at the core of the politics of equality.

[4] The reference here is to the proportion of Muslims falling into the OBC category and the data from National Sample Survey 61st round (2004–2005) (Gayer and Jaffrelot 2012). Not all backward communities are covered under the OBC category.

[5] As we shall see in Chapter 1, the debate about the 'development deficit' within the Muslim community is increasingly framed within the discourse of social exclusion.

[6] This point is made most forcefully in Suroor (2014).

interface with citizens is firmly specified. However, the Constitution recognises the principle that equality of opportunity is, for some groups, dependent on the recognition of their cultural rights (for example, personal laws and dress code). This was an important concession, presaging a later debate in Western liberal democracies that equality of opportunity is subject-dependent (see Mahajan 1998 and Kelly 2002).

However, for minorities[7] (non-Hindu religious groups) the framing of equality of opportunity in the Constitution was qualified by two major considerations that created a structural imbalance. First, historic minority rights relating to reservations in legislative assemblies, employment and state services were dramatically curtailed, with the result that minorities could no longer make political claims based on religious identities (see Bajpai 2011).[8] Second, reservations in legislatures, employment and education were introduced for SCs and STs to address the concerns of socially and economically disadvantaged lower castes. The provision of protective equality for SCs was to be limited to Hindu caste groups only. Religious communities (Buddhist, Christian, Muslim, Sikh) which professed an egalitarian creed but had social groups with similar status to SCs were excluded.[9] Although subsequently the remit of reservations would be expanded through the category of OBCs, particularly at the state level, and thrown open to non-Hindu communities, the Constitution institutionalised a form of path dependence that minorities, notably Muslims, have found difficult to reverse.[10]

Since Independence this framework of equality of opportunity has not matched the aspirations of some of the minorities. Muslims in particular have struggled to assert procedural equality in the face of discrimination, violence and regular stigmatisation as the Indian nation's 'other'. Simultaneously, they have witnessed the transformation in the social and developmental status of

---

[7] The Constitution of India provides a vague definition of 'minorities'. Here and subsequently it is taken to mean non-Hindu groups.
[8] This work is discussed in Chapter 1.
[9] However, Sikh SCs were brought under the reservations net in 1956 and Buddhist SCs in 1990.
[10] 'Distinctive and separate strategies', notes Zoya Hasan (2009a: 5), 'were followed for different groups. The Constitution and state made a basic distinction between the cultural rights of minorities and group rights for communities that were discriminated on the basis of caste. While minorities were located in the framework of religion, disadvantaged castes were removed from this realm and located in the framework of social justice.'

backward communities that now stands on the cusp of surpassing them in terms of socio-economic indicators. Naturally, therefore, Muslim groups have raised demands for a 'full equality of opportunity', a radical conception of the term which, in contrast to the procedural or liberal approach outlined above, privileges the 'equality of outcome'. 'The absence of fair distribution is', for the radical approach, '*ipso facto*, evidence of unfair discrimination' (Mason 1990: 51). Typically, this approach aligns itself with reservations and quotas as the surest way of delivering outcomes—in contrast to positive, or affirmative, action that is often associated with the 'liberal' conception of equal opportunities.[11] As we shall see in subsequent chapters, in India both for policymakers and campaign groups, radical or substantive equal opportunities offer the tantalising prospect of building new (and old) vote-banks.

Defining the puzzle of UPA, equal opportunities and Muslims: a paradigm shift or political pragmatism?

The election of the UPA government in May 2004 was followed by a raft of policy initiatives aimed generally at minorities but even more specifically at Muslims. These measures came on the heels of high-powered commissions or committees that investigated the conditions of the minorities, or were charged with examining new, alternative approaches to the existing framework of equality of opportunity with lessons drawn from comparative experience. The most notable of these committees was the Sachar Committee which

---

[11] The terms 'reservation', 'affirmative action' and 'positive action' are often, misleadingly, used interchangeably. Affirmative action was first used in the United States in 1961, under the Kennedy government, to refer to policies that recognised race, colour, religion, gender, sexual orientation or national origin in order to benefit an under-represented group. Affirmative action may, but does not normally, include reservations and quotas. It is generally aimed at combating discrimination and using promotional policies to ensure a more representative presence of excluded minorities. Such measures can include advertising in minority press, targeting, codes of practice, monitoring, training against bias in recruitment and service delivery, and pro-active measures. Reservations are fixed quotas for preferential selection. Such quotas are mandatory and are often seen as compensation for past injustices inflicted on a particular social group. Positive action is the British variation of affirmative action but does not include the use of quotas. For our purposes, the radical approach is used interchangeably with substantive equality. See Levy (2000) and Heredia (2012).

single-handedly focused the discourse of Indian Muslims on 'identity', 'security', and 'equity'. The *SCR* and other policy initiatives included the creation of new institutions such as the Ministry of Minority Affairs (MoMA), new draft legislation to tackle communal violence, the use of executive discretion to implement affirmative action to enhance Muslim employment in the public sector, and improved service delivery to Muslim communities. It also included the recommendations made by the National Commission for Religious and Linguistic Minorities, also known as the Ranganath Misra Commission after its Chairman, that reservations in employment and education should be implemented for disadvantaged Christians and Muslims. At one level these policy measures sought to create an even playing field within the framework of 'competing equalities' (see Galanter 1984).[12] At another, it was also distinguished by an effort to transcend these 'competing equalities' to create a new overarching framework of equality of opportunity along Western, especially British, lines as the United Kingdom merged its different regimes of discrimination and disadvantage (gender, disability and ethnicity) into the Equality and Human Rights Commission under the Equality Act (2010). This new approach, adapted to Indian requirements and allied to the needs of minorities, according to some analysts, represented a 'paradigm shift' in policy thinking (Khaitan 2008). Such a shift also held the promise of a new deal for minorities, the possibility that they too would realise the full potential of Indian citizenship.

Yet, within three years of the UPA's election, most of these policy initiatives were put on the back burner. While publicly the Congress-led coalition still professed commitment to these policies, its allegiance was more tactical, symbolic and performative. What accounts for this about-turn? Why was the momentum lost? Was this simply another example of failed 'vote-bank politics', a poor effort to rebuild the Congress' traditional relationship with Muslims? Or was the government's record more the outcome of enduring historically institutionalised resistance to a policy change that would place

---

[12] The term 'competing equalities' is used by Galanter to refer to the policies of compensatory discrimination in India—in the judicial tendency to resolve disputes among compensatory discrimination policies and the norms of equality with reference to SCs, STs and OBCs. In this research we operationalise the term 'competing equalities' with reference to equal, but different, opportunity frameworks for religious minorities (procedural equality) and SCs/STs (protective equality) in the Indian political system.

minorities, especially poor Christians and Muslims, on par with India's other disadvantaged communities?

This book focuses on the institutionalised opposition to UPA policies that rendered them ineffective or, sometimes, non-implementable. Its central argument is that we cannot understand the UPA's reluctance to implement the new initiatives generated by its policy process mainly through the calculus of political incentives, the trade-off between action and votes. Political explanations are important in assessing how the Congress-led UPA acted, or did not act, but provide a partial account. Most importantly, we need to recognise the structural factors that constrained the government's actions. A more comprehensive account of the UPA's policies on minorities, but particularly Muslims, therefore, would recognise the deeply embedded historical institutional opposition to a policy change that would accept India's largest religious minority as an integral part of the system of reservations and affirmative action. This opposition emanated from three significant constituencies. First, it came from the institutionalised SC, ST, and OBC regimes and lobbies that view themselves as the guardians of these caste groups' interests, and as such, saw provisions for minorities as encroaching upon their rights because of the potential threat to dilute their existing institutional structures and legal provisions of reservations. Second, it was rooted in state structures (civil service and judiciary), which since Independence have become accustomed to treating minority demands as religiously defined, and therefore, beyond the realms of public policy in a secular state. This institutional resistance, which intersects with the majoritarian view of minorities, acted as a powerful constraint on policy change. Finally, it was articulated most forcefully by the BJP and the allied forces of *Hindutva*, but not without significant representation within Congress as well. This constituency viewed itself as the custodians of the Constitution but the thrust of its resistance was to protect the ideological construction of caste as it applied to disadvantaged Hindu caste groups. Locating itself as the firm defender of the constitutional settlement, this opposition rejected the claims of religious identity as a marker of social and economic disadvantage. In short, the combined opposition of these three major institutional forces undermined the ability of the UPA to implement its new initiatives.

This book substantiates the above argument by developing an institutional policy analysis. Our perspective combines two distinct approaches to the subject. First, it is located firmly within neo-institutionalism, the argument that institutions matter and shape patterns of behaviour of political actors and outcomes (see Pierre, Peters and Stoker 2013). Neo-institutionalism, however, is a broad church with many competing and contradictory schools of thought. Central to the analysis is the need to situate and understand the role of core institutions; how, for instance, the constitutional settlement after Independence created a framework of reservations in which the distinction between caste and religion became solidified. We examine how this division between caste and religion became institutionalised after 1950 with deleterious consequences for religious minorities, especially Muslims. Accordingly, we borrow from historical institutionalism, especially its emphasis on the enduring impact of institutions, to provide the broad perspective for situating the comparative experience of minorities, particularly Muslims. Within historical institutionalism we highlight recurring behaviour and its outcomes through the use of the concept of path dependence. The existence of a critical juncture—the creation of particular institutional structures at a given point in time (in this case India's constitution-making)—followed by a chain of events (path dependence) generates 'increasing returns' to actors who benefit from existing institutional arrangements that make policy change more and more difficult. Policy changes that require a radical reassessment of existing arrangements often require another critical juncture. Thus, the main argument is that the distinction between caste and religion established at Independence in the provision of reservations for socio-economically disadvantaged castes has 'locked-in' a form of path dependence that has witnessed the increasing expansion of reservations for SCs, STs and OBCs since 1950, while on the other hand, the claims of disadvantaged religious minorities have become relatively marginalised because they are not considered to fully come within the framework of backward classes.

Historical institutionalism and the concept of path dependence provide the framework within which this book is located. However, it also concentrates on the UPA's policy process on minorities. Thus, in examining critically how these policies were implemented, we have drawn from public policy analysis the concept of the policy process (how policy is evolved, formulated, decided, implemented and evaluated) and policy sectors (key actors and structures).[13] We have used this framework to track the progress of particular policies aimed at increasing Muslim employment in the public sector, improving service

---

[13] Here we draw extensively on the work of Howlett and Ramesh (2003). This is reviewed in Chapter 1.

delivery to Muslim communities and creating model anti-communal violence legislation.

The book recognises the constraints of policy analysis in the Indian context, where access to decision-making and data is severely restricted. In order to minimise such problems, I conducted a number of in-depth interviews with key personnel who were integral to the policymaking process. These insights constitute the major new empirical findings of this research: indeed, for the first time, it sheds new light on why some policy options were pursued, others neglected and others still left in abeyance.

This hybrid approach has been developed because it enables us to undertake a detailed analysis of the UPA's policies on minorities from 2004 to 2014, and demonstrate the limits of policy change beyond those put forward by conventional political explanations. It does not, of course, preclude the possibilities of change, but my analysis suggests that the likelihood of transformative policy change is severely limited.

The form of historical path dependence on caste and religious minorities established at Independence has heavily circumscribed the limits of policy change. The policy process for any government in this area, for example the UPA, suggests that policy change is certainly possible but it needs to overcome a very high threshold of resistance from institutions and actors that have become the main beneficiaries of the constitutional settlement in this important policy sector. Neither electoral incentives nor the nature of the policy process under the UPA were the major determinants of the outcome of UPA policies on minorities; rather it was the in-built opposition from the three major constituencies identified above which were pre-eminent in determining their fate.

Finally, it is important to emphasise that this book is not about policy evaluation *per se*. While it reviews evaluation in the policy process with special reference to the two key areas—employment and service delivery (the communal violence bill was not legislated upon)—a systematic and comprehensive assessment of the impact of UPA policies in this area is beyond the remit of this work. Instead, the primary objective of this work is to better understand the institutional resistance to the UPA's policies, how they were stymied, and why they were difficult to implement. This resistance is explored both with reference to the nature of the policy process during the UPA government and the enduring influences of historical institutionalism that ultimately defined the possibilities of change.

Outline of the Book

No work can adequately cover the vast range of policy initiatives for minorities by the UPA government from 2004 to 2014. The UPA government itself, during its tenure, sedulously avoided a serious evaluation of these policies.[14] Taking as our point of departure the *SCR*'s emphasis on the Muslim community's need for recognition of its 'identity', to guarantee Muslims 'security' and to provide 'equity' in public services, this book examines detailed case studies of efforts to improve Muslim employment in the public sector, enhance the provision of public sector service delivery to Muslim communities across India and enact a model anti-communal violence law. These case studies are thus inevitably limited and detailed but, nonetheless, provide crucial fresh insights into the shortcomings of the policy process and confirmatory evidence of the broader pattern of institutional path dependence. These in-depth analyses will enable us to arrive at a better understanding of the underlying modes of institutional and political resistance to such policies, especially when directed towards Muslims.

Chapter 1 has three objectives. First, it offers a brief summary of the limitations of existing accounts in explaining why the UPA government was unable to establish a new architecture of equality of opportunity designed to address inequalities suffered by religious minorities, especially Muslims. Second, it develops a framework of institutional policy analysis, a new approach to the study of religious minorities in India which combines historical institutionalism (especially path dependence) with the policy process on the subject during the UPA government. Finally, it outlines the methodological approaches operationalised during the research to assess both the historical path dependent nature of the Indian state's policies on religious minorities and the UPA's policy process from 2004 to 2014.

It is necessary to locate the historical background to the framing of religion during constitution-making between 1946 and 1949 (a 'critical juncture') which created a long-term institutional pattern of public policy that persists to the present. Chapter 2 examines how the policymakers interpreted religious minority rights and constructed the idea of the Indian nation state

---

[14] In February 2013, the government announced the setting up of a high-powered committee to evaluate the implementation of *SCR*'s recommendations. The interim report was submitted to government in March 2014 (just before the end of UPA administration) but the final report was submitted in September 2014 when the new government led by the BJP came to power at the centre.

that marginalised the political claims of religious minorities. In contrast, development of social policy was largely framed in terms of reservations for socio-economically disadvantaged Hindu caste groups. In brief, the chapter will outline the contrasting forms of historical institutionalisation that have resulted from this policy in the competing forms of path dependence access to state goods (employment, service delivery and socio-economic programmes) among socio-economically similar groups (broadly Hindu and non-Hindu). It will also illustrate how this institutionalisation has created powerful lobbies that make policy change difficult.

Chapter 3 sets the context for more detailed case studies of policies which provide the empirical core of the book. It reviews the efforts of the Congress-led UPA government (2004–2014) to implement new policies and practices to improve the social and economic conditions of religious minorities after 9/11 and the Gujarat riots. The chapter will identify the key elements of the UPA's new equal opportunity framework and provide an overview of the UPA policy initiatives on religious minorities, the innovations and institutions created to effect change (some of them borrowed from comparative and Indian provincial level experience) and the persistent modes of resistance to such policy change—political, within the state structures and from institutionalised socio-economically disadvantaged caste lobbies. It will reflect on how in response to this opposition the UPA ultimately opted for symbolic or performative policy implementation. It will also demonstrate how the Hindu majoritarian sentiment and the decisions made by the constitution-makers in narrowly circumscribing the rights of religious minorities in a secular state impacted on the effectiveness of the UPA's policies that were implemented.

In Chapter 4 a detailed case study is undertaken of Muslim employment in central government during the UPA administration. Both the *SCR* and the *Ranganath Misra Commission Report (RMCR)*—as well as several previous surveys—acknowledge the gross under-representation of Muslims in public sector employment. This chapter explores the key decisions made by policy actors, the debates in both houses of Parliament as well as at the executive level and the public controversy around reservations for minorities, particularly disadvantaged Christians and Muslims. Through these debates, it aims to explain how the high-profile commitment to increase Muslim representation in national public sector employment and implement reservations for religious minorities remained largely unrealised. The chapter also critically assesses the utility and validity of employment monitoring data provided by the government and the serious limitations in developing appropriate policy instruments to effect change in this critical area.

Traditionally poor service delivery to socio-economically disadvantaged religious communities was identified by the *SCR* as one of the key drivers of the development deficit. In Chapter 5 detailed case studies are undertaken of service delivery better targeted at religious minorities in three sectors with special reference to the Muslim community: education (scholarships, a recipient-led initiative), finance (a highly institutionalised and regulated sector) and the Multi-Sectoral Development Programme (a broad area-based development programme aimed at minorities). The chapter assesses the effectiveness of these policies in delivering better service to disadvantaged religious communities such as Muslims, especially in north India. It presents new evidence to demonstrate how these policies were thwarted by institutionalised opposition, resulting in poor formulation, the use of inappropriate policy instruments, and the creation of confusing and overlapping executive structures for implementation and evaluation. The chapter also reviews persistent patterns of policy formulation and implementation that have fostered a conservative mode of policymaking by key institutions and policy actors. These selected policy case studies illustrate how policy path dependence and institutional opposition to more targeted service delivery for religious minorities, notably Muslims, contributed to undermining the UPA government's objectives.

The UPA's efforts to legislate a model anti-communal violence bill were at the heart of its strategy to provide security to religious minorities by increasing the penalties for perpetrators of violence and negligent state officials. Chapter 6 is a critical assessment of the draft bills produced in 2005 and 2011. It highlights how the UPA's efforts to produce 'top-down' legislation were frustrated by the institutionalised opposition from political, administrative and judicial institutions and how such efforts were, in contrast, supported by a civil society network that sought to build political support for these bills. This chapter will also make an assessment of the UPA's inability to steer the passage of these bills through Parliament, situating this outcome within the broader context of the traditional post-conflict management practice of the Indian state.

The conclusion will reassess the UPA's record in light of the findings of the *Post-Sachar Evaluation Committee Report* (MoMA 2014). It will also reflect on the policies of the BJP-led NDA (since 2014) on religious minorities and how the current discourse on minorities can be better understood within the long-term path dependent approach to the subject by the Indian state.

1

Opening Up the 'Black Box' of Public Policy

Towards an Institutional Analysis of India's Policies on Religious Minorities

Introduction

The election of a Congress-led UPA coalition government in 2004 surprised most analysts, and the appointment of Manmohan Singh as Prime Minister was symbolic of a new approach towards India's religious minorities. For some, the UPA's policies, institutional innovations and executive decisions in its first term represented a 'paradigm shift' in how equality of opportunity is understood in India (Khaitan 2008). This shift marked a dramatic break, especially for religious minorities, who had disproportionately suffered social exclusion and discrimination. The *SCR*, for example, by recognising the social and economic marginalisation of India's Muslims highlighted the 'development deficit' suffered by the community since Independence. The *RMCR*, probably the most radical official document on India's minorities since 1947, drew a pointed reference to 'inequalities' which excluded disadvantaged religious minorities, such as Christians and Muslims, from reservation in employment and education. In brief, these and other initiatives appeared to suggest that the UPA government would forge a new social contract with India's religious minorities.

The purpose of this book is to explain the UPA's failure to translate its manifesto commitments for religious minorities into effective policies. The UPA's shortcomings, it argues, are similar to the experience of *all* governments in India in implementing public policy in this area, especially towards Muslims. This weakness is not the reluctance of leadership, or an inability to formulate appropriate policies, but to secure broader legitimacy for such policies within the Indian political system and overcome historically institutionalised opposition to such policies from important political and institutional constituencies that see such change as a threat to the established constitutional arrangements. To explain the UPA's experience, this work is located within a historical and institutional context of how the rights of religious minorities since 1947 have been framed, how they were institutionalised and how they have evolved in a path-dependent way that militates against substantive policy change. Combining historical causation with institutional policy analysis, this book aims to bring new insights to the understanding of the UPA's policy performance and to the approach of governments of all political hues to religious minorities, particularly Muslims.

Existing Literature and Arguments

Because in its last four years the UPA government was paralysed by corruption scandals, a systematic evaluation of its policies and record on religious minorities has largely evaded serious analysis. Existing scholarship on the subject provides useful insights into aspects of the policy process but falls significantly short of providing meaningful explanations.

First, reviews of UPA I and II performance, naturally, place a great deal of emphasis on the exigencies of managing a political coalition. These, it is suggested, placed significant constraints on the Congress' autonomy for action (Wilkinson 2012). More recently, a case has been made that Manmohan Singh's reforming zeal was frustrated also by the Congress hierarchy (Baru 2014). Despite these constraints, however, the government was able to undertake major initiatives in energy, social and economic policy. The utility of coalition politics as an explanatory variable, therefore, is clearly limited. Second, some scholars have drawn attention to the ideological differences between the UPA and the NDA to account for the former's performance (Sáez and Singh 2012). However, such perspectives, while providing an overarching review of the UPA government's policies, mostly overlook the policy process as well as the legislative, executive and judicial contexts in which the policy outcomes were determined. Third, for some, normative political theory is a more relevant point of departure for interrogating the shifting terrain of equal opportunities and anti-discrimination policies in contemporary India, including the UPA government (Bajpai 2011; Verma 2012). The development of what Bajpai calls 'group differentiated rights' for socio-economically disadvantaged castes and classes at Independence is seen as intimately connected to how the concept of social justice has evolved with reference to equality of opportunity and anti-discrimination; the exclusion of poor Christians and Muslims from this framework and the UPA's failure to create a level playing field was because of a reluctance to develop appropriate 'legitimising vocabularies' (Bajpai 2011: 23). Arguably, along with 'legitimising vocabularies', the role of institutions and embedded opposition forces in shaping policies and their outcomes is equally if not more important. Fourth, public policy analysts have scrutinised the UPA's record in office with notable stress on policy implementation and evaluation (Centre for Equity Studies 2012; Council for Social Development, India 2013; Khan 2012; Shariff 2012). While this literature is extensive, it has two major weaknesses: it does not satisfactorily cover the whole dimensions of the policy process (Figure 1.1) or develop a more nuanced appreciation of the nature of the ideological and institutional resistance to UPA policies beyond general references. Fifth, some aspects of the UPA's policies have been covered by the burgeoning field of Muslim community studies (Abdelhalim 2016; Afzal 2014; Alam 2010; Ansari 2006; Engineer 2010; Gupta 2011; Jairath 2011; Khalidi 2010; Rehman 2016; Shaban 2012, 2016; Sikand 2006; Suroor 2014). This field covers a wide range of challenges facing Indian Muslims today—madrasa education, inter-religious and intra-Muslim relations, conflict in Kashmir, Muslim women and Islamic law, Dalit Muslims, communalism, political exclusion, declining political and army representation, and anthropological exploration of Islam among different sectarian traditions. Muslim community studies deals with rich and emerging subject areas. However, its main shortcoming is the over-emphasis on community particularism or ethnographic analysis: most offer incomplete insights into how the state has responded to the community's demands or lack a comprehensive coverage of the UPA experience. Finally, the last decade saw a renewed focus on India's Muslims following the *SCR*'s findings of a significant 'development deficit' among the community and renewed interest in the concept of social inclusion (Gayer and Jaffrelot 2012; Z. Hasan 2009a; Mahajan and Jodhka 2010). For example, Hasan, in addressing the plight of poor religious minorities (Christians and Muslims), recognises the need to not only interrogate the founding principles of reservations that created a permanent cleavage by excluding non-Hindus, but also alert us to some of the reasons why the Congress-led UPA government, despite its official rhetoric, was prepared to pursue policy change 'only up to a point'. Hasan's work is especially insightful because it combines a radical egalitarian conception of equality of opportunity for poor religious minorities with a need to explain the 'paradoxes of inclusion and exclusion' and the 'inbuilt biases of the policies and institutions that maintain and create power inequalities in India today' (Z. Hasan 2009a: 12). This book aims to further develop Hasan's insights by combining a policy-based approach to the UPA's initiatives on religious minorities (with special reference to Muslims) with historical institutionalism to better understand the broader context since 1947 within which the Indian state reproduces recurring patterns of policy outcomes.

Public Policy Studies and the Policy Process

The discipline of policy studies emerged after the Second World War with a 'multi-disciplinary', 'problem-solving' and 'explicitly normative' approach in areas traditionally neglected by political science (Howlett and Ramesh 2003: 2–3). For Dye, public policy is 'whatever governments choose to do or not to do' (Dye 2008: 1). This definition recognises that the principal 'agent of public policy-making is a government' (Howlett and Ramesh 2003: 5). It also draws attention to the fact that governments need to act to change, or maintain, the *status quo* and take negative or 'non-decisions' (ibid.). Indeed, decision-making, or non-decisions, involves a range of actors and institutions that need to be engaged at various levels of the political system. In this respect public policy is 'a relatively stable, purposive course of action followed by government in dealing with some problem or matter of concern' (J. E. Anderson 2006: 7). Clearly, public policymaking thus involves many governmental and societal actors and institutions but this descriptive approach fails to account for *why* governments take particular decisions over others.

The UPA's policies on Muslims can be examined in terms of the 'policy process, that is, the stages of policy evolution from inception to execution. Political decision-making requires agreement of policy actors at several points in the policy process. Therefore, analysing the policy outcome within the formal policy process enables us to understand: (*a*) how the policy actors who propose a new legislation design their strategies within the institutional constraints, (*b*) how the interest group(s) in opposition create(s) veto points in the decision-making process (Immergut 1992)[1] and (*c*) how the institution ultimately shapes and determines the fate of the proposed policy.

There is an implicit understanding of a 'policy cycle' or 'process' that unfolds in a set of sequential stages. Figure 1.1 outlines the core stages of this process.

---

[1] According to Immergut, a constitution provides strong 'veto opportunities by setting forth procedural rules that establish a division of power amongst elected representatives'. Throughout this book, we will see how the limited understanding of rights of religious minorities established during the constitution-making is reproduced by the Hindu Right and others.

Figure 1.1 Stages of the policy process

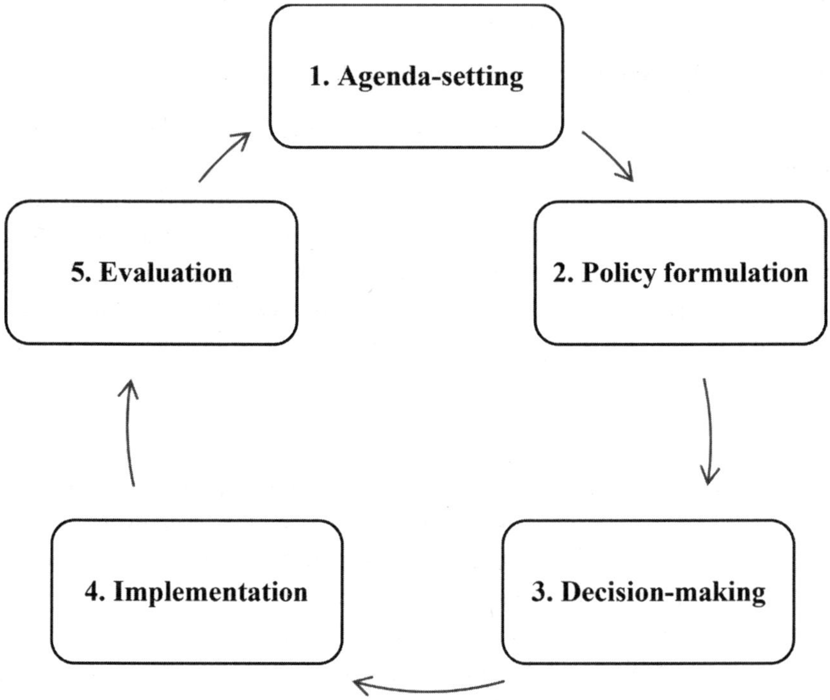

```
        1. Agenda-setting
       ↗                ↘
5. Evaluation         2. Policy formulation
   ↑                        ↓
4. Implementation  ←  3. Decision-making
```

Source: Howlett and Ramesh (2003: chs 5–9).

The initial stage is identified as 'agenda-setting' when a policy issue or a problem is recognised by the government. Agenda-setting for public policy is highly contentious, driven by, among other things, the politics of pre-election manifestos, the nature of the regime, historical institutional legacies, economic management, ideological differences and patterns of social mobilisation (Howlett and Ramesh 2003: 120–141). Hence, prior to the 2004 elections, the 2002 Gujarat pogrom against Muslims was to have a profound impact on the UPA's policymaking.

Agenda-setting is followed by 'policy formulation', a stage at which policy options are produced within government and 'involves assessing possible solutions to policy problems or ... exploring the various options available for addressing a problem' (ibid.: 143). Inevitably, the choice of policies determines their outcome. These can be heavily influenced by substantive constraints (specific to the problem itself) or procedural constraints (institutional, constitutional, budgetary and organisational). Crucial to policy formation is the role of the state and policymaking actors. Subsystems—'policy networks', 'iron-triangles' and 'advocacy coalitions' (ibid.: ch. 6)—are also critical variables in this process. In a developing society such as India, however, although these elements exist and are increasingly important, the state continues to be the main actor. Well-established mechanisms of 'top-down' expert commissions, as will be shown in Chapter 3, were at the core of policy formulation. Policy networks for minorities as an advocacy coalition became more fully engaged after the agenda-setting stage. Significantly, *how* policies were formulated would eventually influence their outcome.

'Decision-making' involves 'authoritative' and 'non-authoritative' actors operating within the framework of governance in a political system. Typically, 'only those politicians, judges, and government officials actually empowered to make authoritative decisions in the area in question can participate with both "voice" and "vote" at this stage of the policy cycle' (ibid.: 163). Decisions can be 'negative' (opposed to the policy), 'positive' (supportive of the policy) or 'non-decisions' (deliberate inaction) (ibid.: 165). While negative decisions move through agenda-setting and policy formulation to decision-making, and terminate at that stage, non-decisions can filter out policy options throughout the policy cycle—agenda-setting, policy formulation, decision-making and implementation. Lukes (2005: 39) has drawn our attention to the importance of non-decisions both as indicators of non-action but also, importantly, as examples of agenda-setting power. Non-decisions are determined by the constraints under which key policy actors operate. As Forester argues, public policy operates under a range of institutional (subsystems) and constitutional constraints.[2]

Critical to understanding these decisions as 'positive', 'negative' and 'non-decisions' are the institutional parameters outlined above and the political constraints of operating within a coalition government. Coalition politics, especially the need for support of national and regional parties, notably caste-based parties like the Bahujan Samaj Party (BSP), the Samajwadi Party (SP), and class-based parties, the Communist Party of India (CPI) and

---

[2] What politicians and administrators do 'depends on the situations in which they work. Pressed for quick recommendations, they cannot begin long studies. Faced with organisational rivalries, competition and turf struggles, they may justifiably be less than wholly candid about their own plans. What is sensible to do depends on the context one is in, in ordinary life no less than public administration' (Forester 1984: 23).

the Communist Party of India (Marxist) (CPI[M]), as this book will show, influenced the decision-making process. Equally significantly, if not more importantly, class, caste and regional groupings within the Congress were influential in determining *what* decisions were taken. When policies were targeted specifically at Muslim OBCs and SCs, decision-making processes included potential national and state level trade-offs (see Chapter 4).

The penultimate stage in the 'policy cycle' is 'implementation' when decisions are translated into action (Howlett and Ramesh 2003: 185–204). Here, the emphasis is on the effectiveness of implementation, the methods used and the policy instruments drawn upon. Implementation is contingent on administrative structures or quasi-government organisations, and can be 'top-down' or 'bottom-up'. Whatever the approach used, it faces the principal–agent problem, that is, the discretion given to 'agents' by decision-makers who have indirect control over them. The relationship is normally defined legally. However, 'the administrators have their own understanding, ambitions, and fiscal and knowledge resources that may come in the way of policies being implemented as originally conceived by decision-makers' (ibid.: 191). Agent autonomy might be increased if, as in the case of service delivery of the UPA's policies, complex inter-organisational coordination is required, or if the problem needs innovative solutions, or even more so if the target group is diverse and complex. As a consequence, a great deal of discretion can be placed in the hands of civil servants. In a federal system like India, where the execution of policy takes place mostly at the state level, with political formations opposed to those at the centre, political and administrative discretion between the 'principal' and the 'agents' can be very wide. It is precisely because of this discretion that the appropriate 'policy instruments' (the tools government uses to put policy into effect) need to be employed. These instruments can be substantive (where there is state involvement in the production of goods and service delivery) or procedural/regulatory (where there is an effort to manipulate subsystem behaviour). In reality, most public policy problems utilise a combination of these approaches (ibid.: 200–202). As Howlett and Ramesh conclude, 'the choice of policy instruments is shaped by the characteristics of the instruments, the nature of the problem at hand, governments' past experience in dealing with the same or similar problems, the subjective preference of the decision-makers, and the likely reaction to the choice by affected social groups' (ibid.: 201).

The problems of 'implementation', the gap 'between policy and implementation, between passing legislation nationally and seeing it executed at the local level, is a little understood black box in Indian public policy' (Sáez and Singh 2012: 149). However, in some areas of social policy, especially vis-à-vis SCs and STs, policy instruments have had a higher degree of effectiveness than policies directed towards religious minorities (Z. Hasan 2009a: 41–74). Surprisingly, the UPA was reluctant to draw on the rich 'tool-box' of public policy instruments used for disadvantaged castes, and in contrast, its policies on Muslims tended to be highly 'top-down', 'overlapping', 'confusing', 'poorly funded' and with a great deal of 'agent discretion', that is, leeway to local officials to interpret policy implementation according to their priorities. Lacking adequate feedback and monitoring mechanisms, moreover, these policies and initiatives had limited accountability both to the target groups (members of the poor Muslim community) and within the administrative structure itself. According to critics, the emphasis on voluntarism and 'general initiatives' rather than targeted redistributionist policies, which are generally acknowledged to have much more impact on improving the 'development deficit', compounded policy ineffectiveness (Centre for Equity Studies 2012: 39–50). Critics view these policies as essentially 'tokenistic', 'symbolic' measures designed to placate the Muslim vote. For others, for example the policy advocacy networks for minorities, these shortcomings can be overcome by borrowing from comparative public policy experience in different social sectors in India and the states.

The final stage of the policy process is 'evaluation', an assessment of how a policy has fared (Howlett and Ramesh 2003: 207–224). Often, this is posed in terms of 'success' or 'failure'. Modes of evaluation can be administrative, to check for 'value of money', technical monitoring of processes and efficiency-centred. Judicial evaluation often arises as a result of review by courts. In India, for instance in the last decade, the rise of public interest litigation (PIL) has led to the reassessment of a number of flagship anti-poverty programmes. Policy evaluation, therefore, is a 'struggle over scarce resources or ideologies' as much as a 'part of a process of learning in which policies develop and change on the basis of assessments of past successes and failures and conscious efforts to emulate successes and avoid failures' (ibid.: 224).

As we shall see in this book, one of the striking features of UPA policies on Muslims in areas of employment and service delivery was the absence of effective monitoring and evaluation. This shortcoming was apparent in the reluctance to develop effective monitoring mechanisms within the programmes themselves and the unwillingness to establish legislative scrutiny through Parliament. The MoMA, which had general oversight of these programmes, was found wanting in being able to undertake such regular evaluation and to provide feedback on the policy process. In short, effective evaluation of policies was sorely missing. Such was the criticism from non-governmental organisations (NGOs) and advocacy coalitions about these shortcomings that in February 2013 the Minister of Minority Affairs, K. Rahman Khan, was compelled to announce that the UPA government would appoint a 'high-power committee to review and assess the implementation of Justice Rajinder Sachar Committee's recommendations and Prime Minister's 15-Point Programme' (Ali 2013).

To sum up, the policy process, or cycle, is a useful heuristic device for understanding UPA policies on religious minorities and Muslims in particular, because a decade after the process began, with the election of the first UPA government in 2004, the cycle reached its final stage. This stage is an appropriate point of departure to critically examine policies that make the agenda, why and how they are formulated, the critical decision taken to implement and not implement some of the policies, and the process of implementation itself. A comprehensive evaluation of *all* these policies is outside the remit of this book which is focused primarily on understanding the institutional resistance to these initiatives and historical causation to it. However, to demonstrate the coherence of the policy process in the field of employment and service delivery, a limited assessment of evaluation is undertaken using available data, including the findings of the Post-Sachar Evaluation Committee. Before we proceed to examine these dimensions with case studies, it is necessary to outline the institutions and actors involved in this process, the methodological approach taken and the case for understanding public policy for religious minorities within a historical and institutional framework.

Policy Actors and Institutions

The policy process outlined above operates within the context of key policy actors and institutions. Key actors operate within an institutional framework in which there are 'formal or informal rules and conventions, as well as ethical, ideological, and epistemic concerns [that] help to shape actors' behaviour by conditioning their perception of their interests and the probability of these interests being realised' (Howlett and Ramesh 2003: 53). The actors' 'assumptive worlds' or 'mental models' that 'provide both an interpretation of the environment and a prescription as to how that environment should be structured' (Denzau and North 1994: 4) are critical in shaping appropriate solutions and are influenced by normative views about 'the nature of society and the proper role of government' (Klein and Marmor 2006: 893). If institutions are heavily biased towards a particular policy path, key actors are likely to adopt a conservative, gradual and instrumentalist approach, or seek to operate within the 'rules of the game'. As we shall see in subsequent chapters, UPA policy implementation, especially by the national and state administrations, was heavily compromised by the institutional actors' beliefs about policies and attitudes towards Muslims.

The institutional analysis of the UPA's policies undertaken here is limited to interactions between institutions and actors, pressure groups and 'the constitutional arrangements within which governments operate, the rules of the game, and the bureaucratic machinery at their disposal' (ibid.). Thus, in India, these key actors are the elected officials of the executive (government), the Opposition (in the legislature and political parties), appointed officials (bureaucrats), the judiciary, interested groups, NGOs and the media. These actors operate, moreover, within an institutional context, or a subsystem that is vertically divided between the structure of governance at levels of the union and the states. While the quality of governance and policy implementation—at the national and state levels—varies enormously across the Indian states (Kohli 2006), the national and state level institutions are remarkably uniform in their structure and operational practices. Furthermore, this uniformity is reinforced by the existence of all the various arms of the Indian civil services, such as the Indian Administrative Service (IAS), Indian Police Service (IPS) and Indian Foreign Service (IFS), that provide the country with its 'steel-frame'. Figure 1.2 illustrates this policy context.

The interaction between institutions and actors took place within the formal system of governance, but the media and some NGOs were to play a key role in shaping policy. Equally important was the role of two other institutions. The judiciary, for instance, both at the national and regional levels, played a critical role because some of the policy initiatives of the UPA on religious minorities were challenged in courts. Finally, the UPA as a coalition government had to engage in a 'complex process of bargaining, negotiation, and political calculations' before investing 'administrative capacity and political capital' (Klein and Marmor 2006: 899) in some of the policies. This bargaining included important calculations at the national and state levels about the potential loss of support from other disadvantaged groups such as the SCs, STs and OBCs. The ever-present threat and capacity of the BJP to

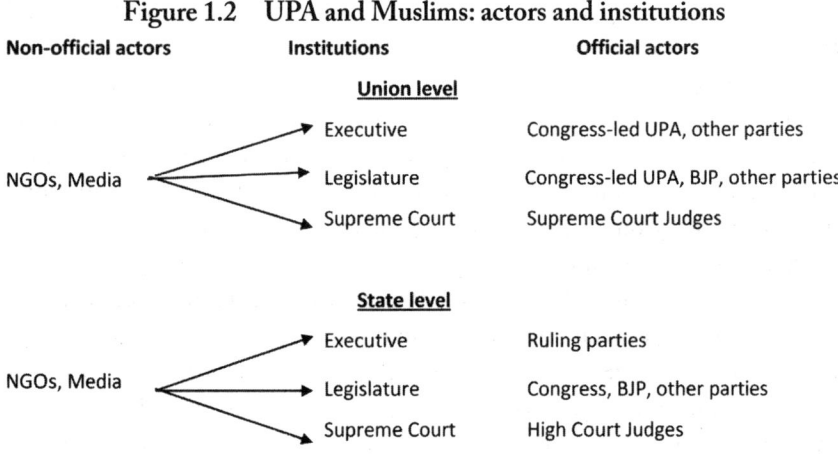

Figure 1.2 UPA and Muslims: actors and institutions

Source: Author.

mobilise against pro-Muslim policies was to prove a powerful constraint to the UPA's capacity for action.[3]

Studying Institutions

Thus far largely a descriptive account of the policy process has been outlined. It is now necessary to outline the analytical approach of the work. The main objective is to develop a historical sense of how national policy on religious minorities, especially Muslims, became institutionalised after 1947, and has proven difficult to change, and how it aligns with the formal policy process during the UPA administration. Consequently, the emphasis is on institutional policy analysis in which 'institutions' are, in a narrow sense as defined above, structures around which actors (agents) act, but also the embodiments of historical institutionalism—a methodological orientation that privileges institutions over individuals in shaping behaviour and outcomes.

---

[3] The institutional framework for this research is primarily at the national level with some need for consideration of policy at the sub-national (state) level. It is recognised, however, that while sub-national institutional structures in India are uniform, institutional histories and the configuration of social and religious groups, especially in southern states, which were less influenced by the spectre of Partition, have produced a more benign form of institutional path dependence of religious minorities, especially Muslims, that is at variance with the experience at the national level and that of Hindi-speaking states in the north. The point is further developed in Chapters 4, 5 and 6.

Approaches to public policy divide along familiar methodological lines (Howlett and Ramesh 2003: 20–48): deductive (for example rational choice theories, class analysis and actor-centred neo-institutionalism) that 'developed largely on the basis of the application of general presuppositions, concepts, or principles to specific phenomena' (ibid.: 20–21) and inductive (for example sociological individualism, group theories and socio-historical neo-institutionalism) that developed 'generalisations only on the basis of careful observation of empirical phenomena and subsequent testing of these generalisations against other cases' (ibid.: 21). As the focus of this work is on the UPA's performance against historically embedded constraints framed during constitution-making, historical institutionalism is an appropriate point of departure.

Peters has characterised the institutionalist approach as one in which

> institutions are the variable that explains political life in the most direct and parsimonious manner, and they are also the factors that themselves require explanation. The basic argument is that institutions *do* matter, and that they matter more than anything else that could be used to explain political decisions. (2005: 164, emphasis in original)

By 'institutions', Peters refers to both structural features such as formal institutions, for example the bureaucracy, executive, legislature and legal framework, and informally shared norms that ensure stability over time (ibid.: 8). Krasner, on the other hand, offers a much broader definition. 'An institutionalist perspective', according to him, 'regards enduring institutional structures as the building blocks of social and political life. The preferences, capabilities, and basic self-identities of individuals are conditioned by these institutional structures' (Krasner 1988: 67). Despite these differences, most institutionalists view institutions as an independent variable with public policy as the dependent variable. Or, in other words, public policy and the policy process are determined by institutions rather than vice versa.[4] Although Peters

---

[4] Institutionalism comes in many forms, but common to all its sub-schools is that it 'purports to explain human behaviour—be it of individuals, small groups, organisations, nation-states or international federations–in terms of institutions. Institutionalists believe that orderly behaviour is extraordinary, because so many factors (biological and social) would seem to predict selfish behaviour that would result in chaos ... This relationship can be *constraining* in nature, as an institution defines parameters of (in)action and labels alternative forms of behaviour as deviant. But an institution also has an *enabling* effect. It helps to make sense of

acknowledges that some schools of institutionalism consider institutions as a dependent variable, or both dependent and independent variables, yet most species of institutionalism 'have at their centre a more or less clear conception of institutions acting rather autonomously in making policy' (Peters 2013: 16). We concur with Peters that institutions are an independent variable and the policy process a dependent variable, but our understanding of institutionalism is historically located and tied to the policy process to develop a new framework of institutional policy analysis.

Historical Institutionalism and Path Dependence

Historically, institutions can have an enduring impact on political behaviour. Recently, Acemoglu and Robinson's *Why Nations Fail* (2012) has provided a seminal account of how decisions taken over time by almost identical polities have led to very contrasting patterns of institutional evolution and path dependence, that is, the self-reinforcing reproduction of institutions and institutional behaviour. In seeking to address the question as to why nations fail, Acemoglu and Robinson claim it is the quality of the institutions that 'influence behaviour and incentives in real life' (ibid.: 43). Political institutions, according to the authors, 'are a key determinant of the outcome of this game' (ibid.: 79). By political institutions Acemoglu and Robinson mean both the constitutional framework of governance and the 'power and capacity of the state to regulate and govern society' (ibid.: 42). They also include in this definition how 'political power is distributed in society, particularly the ability of different groups to act collectively to pursue their objectives or to stop other people from pursuing theirs' (ibid.: 42–43; see also Pierson 2016).

For Acemoglu and Robinson, there are two ideal types of political and economic institutions: those that are inclusive, plural and based on a degree of political centralisation, and those that are exclusive, extractive and limited. The former, they maintain, have led to the emergence of democratic and pluralist nations and state-building in the West; the latter have created extractive and exclusive political and economic polities in Asia and Africa. Such outcomes were determined by different decisions and choices made by political leaders at a 'critical juncture' when the existing relations between political and economic institutions were realigned. A critical juncture, according to Acemoglu and

---

a situation, providing guidance in deciding between various courses of action. An institution aligns task perceptions and partially determines the way in which employees use their discretion' (Boin and Kuipers 2013: 46–47, emphasis in original).

Robinson, is a major historical turning point that accentuates 'institutional drift' between polities because the small difference that sometimes exists between them can lead to path dependence that can become self-reinforcing through a feedback loop, or 'increasing returns'.

Why Nations Fail neatly encapsulates the essence of historical institutionalism and its associated concept of path dependence which holds that particular policies and choices made at a critical juncture can have a persistent and enduring impact over time. The idea of path dependence has been expounded at length by Pierson:

> The notion of path dependence is generally used to support a few key claims: Specific patterns of timing and sequence matter; starting from similar conditions, a wide range of social outcomes may be possible; large consequences may result from relatively 'small' or contingent events; particular courses of action, once introduced, can be virtually impossible to reverse; and consequently, political development is often punctuated by critical moments or junctures that shape the basic contours of social life. (2000: 251)

Path dependence theorists, thus, emphasise the long-term impact of decision-making and institution building. The creation of institutions at India's Independence designed to tackling caste disadvantage, for example, maintain a form of path dependence dedicated to reservations for these groups into which institutions and actors have become 'locked-in', producing a positive 'feedback loop' or 'increasing returns' that have subsequently been reinforced by the initial direction of change and are increasingly difficult for any government to reverse. Path dependence, in other words, is reproduced by increasing returns to actors and institutions established during the critical juncture. The high costs of switching to alternative policies militate against any change of path dependence. As Pierson notes, 'the probability of further steps along the same path increases with each move down that path ... [because] the costs of exit — of switching to some previously plausible alternative—rise' (ibid.: 252).

Path dependence has been criticised for being over-deterministic. The idea of 'increasing returns' over time also begs the question of 'diminishing' or 'constant returns'. In response, Mahoney and Schensul have drawn attention to reactive sequences in which the emergence of particular institutions can influence actions by triggering responses, sometimes unintended (Mahoney and Schensul 2006).[5] Similarly, Thelen suggests that if institutions are locked into a

---

[5] Reactive sequences are characterised by 'backlash processes that *transform*

particular trajectory, this often overlooks the degree to which they are contested, notwithstanding the costs involved in such contestation (Thelen 1999).[6]

Path dependence theorists have sought to address some of these concerns related to agency, structure and choice. First, they identify a critical juncture as 'a major event or confluence of factors [disrupting] the existing balance of political or economic power in a nation'. Often these distinct legacies affect 'a whole set of societies' (Acemoglu and Robinson 2012: 106). Critical junctures arise as a result of pre-existing cleavages, but mark a radical transformation to new institutional arrangements. This transition is not pre-determined but is characterised by a range of possible options, the choice of which is impossible to predict; whilst the duration of critical junctures can vary, their end point is marked by the creation of new stable institutional arrangements (Mahoney 2000; Pierson 2000).

The constitution-making process in India (1946–1949) is, thus, an ideal exemplar of a critical juncture. At the time of the formation of the Constituent Assembly, few would have anticipated the final draft of the Constitution. Even allowing for the official policies of the Indian National Congress (INC) and the Muslim League, in 1946 it would have been difficult to foresee the Partition, let alone the permanent removal of the long-established rights of religious minorities that were seen as the cornerstone of the constitution-making process. Nor would it have been possible to predict in 1946 that social justice would be defined primarily within the framework of reservations for socially disadvantaged castes. In this sense, Partition was a game changer, and constitution-making a critical juncture that set the template for post-Independence India.

Second, in addition to critical junctures, path dependence scholars recognise contestational junctures. Whereas the former 'give rise to particular paths of institutional development', the latter represent major challenges to the system (Javid 2012: 45). Whereas the former are exceptional events, contestational junctures arise as a result of mobilisation by new actors and institutions, and have the potential to be transformed into critical junctures, but more often than not in the short-term result in reinforcing the existing

---

and perhaps *reverse* early events ... [in] a chain of tightly linked reactions and counter-reactions' (Mahoney 2000: 526–527; emphasis in original).

[6] Space precludes a more detailed assessment of the responses to these criticisms. For institutional evolution and change that entails 'layering and conversion' under 'increasing returns', see Pierson and Skocpol (2002) and Thelen (2003).

institutional arrangements.[7] As we shall see in Chapter 2, India's constitutional settlement around caste has been contested at a number of junctures, principally by the Mandal debate (1990), and the gradual mobilisation of religious minorities, initially in the south, but increasingly in the north. This mobilisation culminated in the UPA's promise in the 2004 general elections to provide better equality of opportunity to religious minorities, including affirmative action.

Analytical Approach: A Summary

Institutions have always been central to the study of modern South Asian history and politics.[8] Moore, in his path-breaking comparative essay *Social Origins of Dictatorship and Democracy* (1967), drew attention to how the institutional structures of social life in India interacted with those of governance in creating a relatively conservative political settlement that is not conducive to rapid social change. Working within institutional economics in the 1980s, Bardhan highlighted how the post-1947 settlement has produced rent-seeking behaviour by what he calls the 'proprietary classes' (industrial capitalist, rich farmers and professionals) and how they had captured the regime of state-based planning (Bardhan 1984, 1988). Rudolph and Rudolph in their seminal work on the Indian state, *In the Pursuit of Lakshmi* (1987), propounded a powerful argument that the inherent centrism of Indian politics affords the state a great deal of institutional autonomy in negotiating what they have called 'command' and 'demand' politics. Jalal in her masterful survey of *Democracy and Authoritarianism in South Asia* (1995) drew attention to the common institutional legacies of South Asian states that have both nurtured democracy and forms of political closure. At the sub-national level,

---

[7] Those who are excluded have attempted to reverse the existing order through means of war, revolution or democratic mobilisation. Institutions therefore do not just generate positive feedback but they also 'generate grievances through political exclusion ... [and] actors who are aggrieved but not co-opted are an important source of pressure for institutional change' (Schneiberg and Clemens 2006: 218). Such junctures have the potential to be transformed into critical junctures. Institutional conversion takes place by the mobilisation of the previously excluded groups who subvert existing institutions into new ones. But as indicated earlier such efforts more often than not result in reinforcing the existing institutional arrangements.

[8] For public policy literature, see Mathur (2013) and Mathur and Björkman (2009).

Kohli in his research on poverty eradication among Indian states has noted the importance of institutional arrangements in explaining the variance in policy outcomes (Kohli 2006). More recently, scholars have operationalised historical institutionalism to interpret the Indian political structures created by the electoral system to consolidate large majorities in the first-past-the-post electoral system (Wilkinson 2004), the role of the military in Pakistan politics (Aziz 2007), the persistence of landed elites in Pakistani Punjab (Javid 2012), and in 2016 a major international conference panel was devoted to the subject of historical institutionalism and the concept of path dependence in South Asia.[9]

The increasing interest in the application of historical institutionalism in South Asian Studies is underpinned by how and why 'history matters' when it comes to explaining the different factors and processes that trigger and underlie institutional development over time, the choices actors make under the constraints imposed by particular historical contexts, and how these choices can have an impact on subsequent outcomes. Path dependence analysis thus offers new perspectives on the emergence and maintenance of unique institutional configurations. It also explains institutional variation across time and space, emphasising the role played by initial conditions, critical junctures, timing, and sequence in structuring institutional development (see Figure 1.3).[10]

This book addresses the puzzle of the UPA which came to power with an agenda of promoting better equality of opportunity for religious minorities, particularly disadvantaged Muslims, but was frustrated in its objective. It examines why the UPA's policies faced such political and institutional resistance despite commanding widespread support. It does so by focusing on three case studies. Empirically, we have to 'pry open the black box of policy change' (Boin and Kuipers 2013: 43) by examining the policy process on the subject—of how the issue came on the agenda, policy formulations, decision-making, (non)implementation and evaluation. This essentially descriptive approach needs to be tethered to a theoretical approach that elucidates the role of actors and institutions in order to account for recurring patterns of behaviour and outcomes. Thus, institutionalism, which privileges the role of

---

[9] See the panel 'Rethinking the Role of Institutions in South Asia: Historical Institutionalism and Path Dependence', European Conference on South Asian Studies, Warsaw, 27–30 July 2016.

[10] In Figure 1.3, the analytic structure of path dependent process is borrowed from Mahoney (2001: 113).

Figure 1.3 A summary of the analytical approach: institutional policy analysis

1. The issue: How to understand UPA's failure to implement its policies for religious minorites, especially Muslims

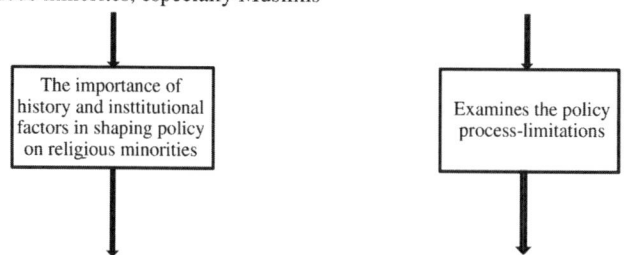

2. Historical institutionalism: 'institution matter','history matters'-India's constitution-making and minority right as a 'critical juncture' defining the limits of these rights and creation of institutions to manage them.

3. Path dependence: main institutions created at critical junctures lock-in a form of path dependence producing 'increasing returns' and making policy change prohibitive.

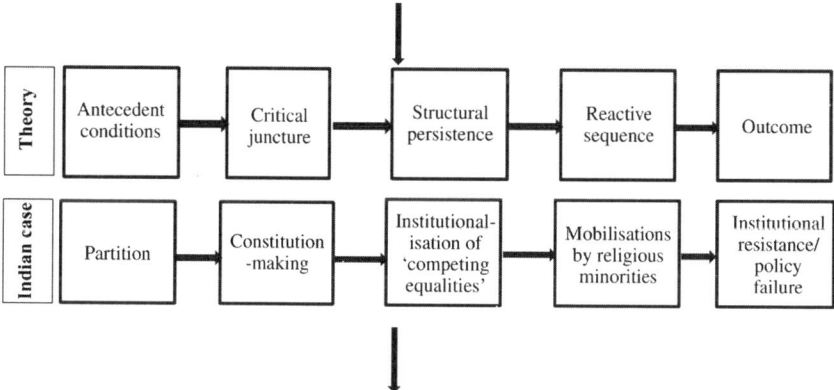

4. 'Institutional policy analysis' combines the formal policy process, historical institutionalism and its associated concept of path dependence: contextualising the UPA experience.

Source: Author.

institutions in explaining these outcomes, provides a necessary bridge for this research because the relevant policy process on the subject appears to be heavily shaped by bureaucratic design, incremental change and historical legacies. Institutional structures in India, broadly interpreted, both at the national and state levels, appear to have played an independent role in determining the fortunes of UPA policies on religious minorities.

Our institutional policy analysis approach focuses primarily on the performance of the UPA governments from 2004 to 2014. But in order to understand this experience historically, it is also necessary to draw on historical institutionalism and its analytical framework, path dependence. These perspectives, we argue, enable us to make better sense of recurring patterns of government performance and explain why the framework for minority rights established at Independence remains firmly in place. An institutional policy analysis approach recognises that in understanding UPA policies on religious minorities, history casts a permanent shadow over the present. Consequently, historical institutionalism and its focus on path dependence have defined the parameters within which the policy process can operate, shape, influence, and ultimately determine policy outcomes. In concurrence with writings of institutionalists, therefore, we acknowledge that institutions are the independent variable and the policy process the dependent variable.

Research Questions

The policy process under the UPA identified a range of policy areas on which action was needed to address the 'development deficit' suffered by religious minorities. This work focuses on three areas that were identified by the *SCR* as requiring special attention: public sector employment, service delivery and security.

Public sector employment has been selected because the experience of quotas and affirmative action policies, both in India and elsewhere, demonstrates that under-representation of minorities in the public sector is often associated with direct and indirect institutional discrimination (Ball and Solomos 1990; Sowell 2004). Overcoming this under-representation is a necessary condition for creating effective equality of opportunity. Surveys have regularly highlighted the under-representation of Muslims in public sector posts and undertakings at all levels (Wilkinson 2012: 71–72). This status has remained unchanged since Independence, a finding confirmed further by the *SCR* and the *RMCR*. Comparative and Indian experiences indicate that these policies, if appropriately designed, implemented and monitored, can have a transformative impact.

Similarly, in service delivery the issue is whether all citizens are treated equally or suffer unequal outcomes in the provision of public sector goods, such as housing, education, social services and basic infrastructure facilities. Studies have demonstrated that excluded cultural, ethnic, racial and religious minorities often suffer from unequal outcomes (Jenkins and Solomos 1987). The need for public services to cater for all, including minorities and excluded public groups, has led to a redesign of public policy, for instance in special provisions for SCs and STs. The UPA, as we shall see, was committed to a raft of new initiatives to improve service delivery for India's Muslims.

For minorities facing discrimination and victimisation, the provision of effective anti-violence and discrimination legislation is a necessary prerequisite of civil engagement.[11] Most countries have generic legislation against such violence and discrimination, but since the multicultural turn in public policy, this has been accompanied by legislation that both outlaws particular types of discrimination—based on religion, caste, race and ethnicity—and prohibits hate crimes against such 'protected categories'. In India, specific legislation exists for acts of violence against SCs and STs (Scheduled Castes and Scheduled Tribes [Prevention of Atrocities] Act [1989]). Yet, despite the high levels of communal violence against religious minorities, notably Muslims, the state has been reluctant to create a specific legislative framework that tackles communal violence, or inaction and non-compliance during such violence by official functionaries. The UPA's commitment to introducing such model legislation, therefore, marked a distinctive break.

The evaluation of UPA's performance on these three fronts is undertaken within a set of six interlinked questions:

1. What were the political considerations that led the UPA to adopt policies to promote substantive equality of opportunity for religious minorities, especially Muslims?
2. How were these policies formulated? Did they mark a radical break with previous experience of the Indian state? To what extent, if at all, did they represent a 'paradigm shift'?
3. What were the institutional innovations introduced to facilitate the new policies?

---

[11] The example of the United Kingdom is instructive. For an overview of the developments since 1945, see Solomos (2003).

4. What factors frustrated UPA administrations' efforts to improve the representation of Muslims in public sector employment in national administration and public sector undertakings?
5. What factors thwarted the UPA administrations' efforts to improve service delivery for Muslim communities identified as suffering a significant 'development deficit'?
6. Why did the UPA struggle to provide a new model legislative framework against communal violence?

A Note on Methodology

The study of religious minorities in a secular state poses a host of problems: most such states, including India, have been reluctant to collect data on religious minorities (Singh 2011). Traditionally, there has been hyper-sensitivity about such information. In 2006, for instance, efforts to ascertain the representation of Muslims in India's armed services led to a major controversy (Dhar and Dikshit 2006). Indeed, the 'control' of this data, and at times its deliberate misrepresentation on grounds of confidentiality, or breach of state secularism, has created major difficulties for a comparative assessment of public policy (see Chapter 4). Although the work of the Sachar Committee marked a major turning point, significant gaps still remain in the availability of comprehensive data on religious minorities at the national and regional levels.

To overcome some of these difficulties this work uses a mixed methods approach. It draws heavily on qualitative methodologies (documentary analysis of a broad range of official publications such as government and judicial records and secondary studies). The reports of expert groups on religious minorities and national commissions (Sachar Committee, Ranganath Misra Commission, Equal Opportunity Commission [EOC], diversity index [DI], National Commission for Minorities [NCM], National Commission for Scheduled Castes [NCSC], National Commission for Scheduled Tribes [NCST], and National Commission for Backward Classes [NCBC]) have been used extensively. These are further supplemented by Parliamentary Debates and relevant judicial cases. All sources have also produced significant quantitative data that has been drawn upon where relevant. Finally, to fill the gaps in publicly available data and to obtain informed insights into policy formation and implementation, in-depth interviews were conducted in Delhi with 39 'key' informants. These were individuals identified as having played a major role in the conception, formulation and implementation (and non-implementation) of the core policies under consideration. They comprised politicians, civil servants, academics, journalists and public intellectuals. Interviewees were identified from a preliminary analysis of official documentation and reputational analysis for engagement with this subject area, and further interviewees were identified through snowballing during fieldwork. Efforts were made to ensure the interviewees were representative and did not constitute a skewed sample. The definition of 'key' policy informants includes individuals from a cross-section of the Indian political spectrum (Congress, BJP, CPI, SP and All India Majlis-e-Ittehadul Muslimeen) as well as religious groups.[12]

Conclusion

This chapter has outlined analytical approaches and methodologies used in this book. It has argued that the limited explanatory value of existing accounts on the UPA's failure to transform its agenda on religious minorities into legislation suggests that there is a need to go beyond the formal policy process. A policy process approach, one that incorporates historical institutionalism, what we term 'institutional policy analysis', offers a more analytically relevant point of departure. Thus, institutional policy analysis provides new insights into policymaking during the UPA's tenure. But the UPA's performance also becomes more meaningful if it is situated within the historical pattern of the Indian state's policies on religious minorities, especially those aimed directly

---

[12] Interviews were conducted at the interviewee's place of work or residence during the initial fieldwork in New Delhi between January and April 2013. Prior to the interview, based on the interviewee's biographical material, a semi-structured questionnaire was prepared. In the main, interviews were in-depth, and on several occasions the respondents agreed to follow-up interviews. Some interviews were completed via Skype, telephone, email exchanges and during the second fieldwork in New Delhi in April 2014. Prior to the beginning of the interview, all interviewees were asked whether they consented to both the interview and to being quoted. Where possible, it was decided to tape-record the interview, but notes were also taken. Some of the interviewees requested that certain sections of the interview be excluded; hence those parts have been omitted. Some quotes were provided only on condition that they would not be attributed to the respondent. Following interviews, where possible, the transcriptions were cross-checked with the respondents. To control against bias in the interviewee's account, where relevant, the data have been triangulated with other sources, including other interviewees who could corroborate the claims.

at Muslims. For this reason, we need to extend the temporal scope of the work to include the institutional framing of issues pertaining to religious minorities since 1947. In sum, the core argument of the work is that historical institutionalism and the associated concept of path dependence defined, shaped and outlined the parameters of the UPA's policy process from which it found difficult to escape.

Seen in this broad perspective, the two UPA administrations thus marked a major contestational juncture in the pursuit of better equality of opportunity for religious minorities. Ostensibly, this juncture had the potential to establish a new pattern of path dependence for religious minority rights in India. However, as we shall see in subsequent chapters, institutional resistance to this change frustrated such a development. To understand this result, we have adopted research methodologies that focus both on documentary analysis but also include extensive in-depth interviews with the principal *dramatis personae*, the 'key' policy informants at the heart of the policy process.

2

Constitution-Making, Equality of Opportunity and Religious Minorities
Reassessing the Critical Juncture

Introduction

Constitution-making between 1946 and 1949 marked a fundamental rupture with the regime of rights of religious minorities under the colonial state: it was a critical juncture which created a template for how these rights were to be defined within a new framework of equality of opportunity. Unsurprisingly, India's religious minorities have struggled to work within a secular framework that has denied political claims to religious identities, with the result that some minorities, especially Christians, Muslims and Sikhs have, arguably, suffered disadvantage and discrimination on issues of security, identity and underdevelopment. Drawing on historical institutionalism and its associated concept of path dependence, this chapter provides an overview of how this settlement has evolved since 1947. First, it outlines the framework of equality of opportunity established at Independence and reviews the institutional framework that has emerged to support 'competing equalities' among socio-economically disadvantaged caste and non-caste groups. It then briefly reviews some of the contestational junctures—the early 1980s, 1990s and 2000s—when some of the minorities mobilised and challenged this settlement. Finally, with reference to the findings of the *SCR* that some religious minorities, particularly poor Muslims, suffer systematic discrimination and disadvantage, this chapter discusses the official recognition by the UPA that a new approach was required to redefine equality of opportunity in twenty-first century India.

Constitution-Making as a Critical Juncture: Redefining Minority Rights

India is a religiously and ethnically diverse society and home to major world traditions: Hindus (79.8 per cent), Muslims (14.2 per cent), Christians (2.3 per cent), Sikhs (1.7 per cent), Buddhists (0.7 per cent), Jains (0.4 per cent) and Zoroastrians (no data). Hindus constitute the overwhelming majority, with 172.2 million Muslims being the second-largest faith tradition (Ministry of Home Affairs 2011b). This religious diversity is overlaid with enormous linguistic and cultural diversity. Politically, accommodating such diversity was a major challenge faced by the framers of the Constitution.

The dominant view articulated by the Congress during the Constituent Assembly Debate was that separate political representation of religious communities under British colonial rule had resulted in the partition of the country and the creation of Pakistan. Although more Muslims chose to remain in India than to move to the new state of Pakistan, anxieties persisted about their future in a Hindu-dominated society. Foremost among these were questions of safeguarding religious liberty and protection against cultural homogenisation. If equality was to be realised, then minority communities needed assurances about their cultural practices, and though the principle of equality before the law was extremely important, by itself it was insufficient to ensure equal access to social and public goods.

In the late nineteenth century, the British colonial government introduced many special provisions for minorities or backward groups (Bajpai 2011: 31–32). These included provisions for special representation in the legislatures and quotas in the public services. Over time, these provisions were extended to include Christians, Muslims, Sikhs and Depressed Classes. In the constitution-making process, events and the hegemonic nationalist discourse were to play a major role in shaping minority rights (ibid.: 70–75).[1] Indeed, the provincial legislative elections (1945–1946) and the Partition resulted in an overwhelming majority of Congress members in the Constituent Assembly (Austin 1966: 9, 1999: 5): many were upper caste, accounting for a quarter of the assembly while constituting only 5 per cent of the population (Chiriyankandath 2000: 5). As Austin argues, 'the Constituent Assembly was a one-party body in an essentially one-party country. The Assembly was the Congress and the Congress was India' (1966: 8–9).

The discourse on minorities in the Constituent Assembly changed dramatically after Partition. The *Minority Rights Sub-Committee Report* tabled by Sardar Patel in August 1947 proposed legislative reservations for Christians, Muslims and SCs for an initial period of 10 years. But against

---

[1] For contrasting interpretations of the role of religion and secularism in defining minority rights in the Constituent Assembly Debate, see Bhargava (2010) and Copland (2010).

the backdrop of communal violence, mass migration and unparalleled human suffering, the dominant mood in the Constituent Assembly opposed political safeguards for minorities on the basis of religion because these were seen as a potential threat to the political unity and integrity of the country (Bajpai 2011: 76–80). Nationalists claimed that group identities, such as caste, creed and religion, would continue to divide society. As such, they were determined to privilege individual citizenship over these identities. Representation based on religion was considered antithetical to the ideal of a secular state. Moreover, it was argued, such representation would ultimately lead to the isolation of minorities and sharpen communal differences in which citizens would remain permanently alienated from one another (Bhargava 2002). Accordingly, efforts were made to persuade minority representatives to forego the claim for separate representation (Chiriyankadnath 2000: 13), and as Chiriyankandath notes, 'Sardar Patel and K.M. Munshi were instrumental in getting rid of separate electorates and reserved seats for religious minorities' (ibid.: 10). Austin is also adamant that the Assembly's Hindu majoritarian outlook dissuaded the minorities from their position: 'There can be little doubt that Patel, despite his belief that the minorities must make their own decisions on such issues and not be simply out-voted by caste Hindus, quietly and privately put a great deal of pressure on the minorities to relinquish special privilege' (Austin 1966: 151).

For the political leadership of the minority communities, a combination of factors persuaded them to accept the *fait accompli*. Demoralised by the leadership of Jinnah and the violence of Partition, Muslim leaders had little choice but to accept the new reality in which the 'secular democratic state' promised the best chance of security (Chiriyankandath 2000: 13). The pressure to 'disavow reservation' was also imposed on Christian leaders 'from Patel, [and] exercised by K.M. Munshi' (Austin 1966: 149). Equally, Sikh political representatives came under similar pressure but ultimately refused to sign the Constitution (Bajpai 2011: 53–54; Chiriyankandath 2000: 12). Indeed, in the final report of the Advisory Committee on Minorities (1949), the abolition of reservation on religious lines was justified in terms of 'the foundations of a true secular democratic State' (Chiriyankandath 2000: 13). Nehru welcomed the report as 'a historic turn in our destiny' (Constituent Assembly Debates [Proceedings] 1949: 329). The only exception was reservations for SCs and STs. This was considered necessary to compensate for past discrimination and included quotas in education, government employment and legislatures (Bajpai 2000: 1837).

Despite this agreement, the Hindu majoritarian sentiment in the Constituent Assembly was not a negligible force. Early drafts of the *Minority Rights Report* wanted to 'explicitly [refer] to the SCs as a "section of the Hindu community"' (Chiriyankandath 2000: 16). Furthermore, leading figures were deeply concerned about the 'lack of reference in the Constitution to a distinctly Hindu identity or to central tenets of Brahminical Hinduism such as the notion of *dharma*, [which] left the majoritarians dissatisfied' (ibid.: 10). Although Hindu majoritarians were a powerful lobby, they had to ultimately compromise with secularists led by Nehru. These innate but enduring tensions within the Constituent Assembly led to the ambiguous accommodation of secular and majoritarian sentiments as well as special group rights for SCs and STs[2]—tensions that would subsequently be exploited by the Hindu Right and the BJP.

Religious Minorities, Equality of Opportunity and the Constitution

The starting point for an understanding of the framing of equality of opportunity is the making of the Constitution of India. In essence, the Constitution embraces a dual conception of equality: one based on the generic principle of non-discrimination and another rooted in protective equality for seriously disadvantaged groups. These two approaches represent 'competing equalities', ones that are historically rooted in the Indian social formation and are products of historical evolution (Galanter 1984: esp. chs 2 and 3).

As a modern, secular text, the Indian Constitution recognises individual rights associated with liberal democracy. As a corollary, it established a strong

---

[2] 'It was not surprising', as Chiriyankandath notes, 'that the form of secularism that found expression in the Constitution was ambiguous. Leaders like Sardar Patel, Rajendra Prasad and K. M. Munshi were sensitive, if not openly sympathetic, to the majoritarian sentiments voiced by a number of Congressmen in the Constituent Assembly. They knew that these predilections were widely shared, especially among the upper caste Hindi-speaking members ... The result was that the Constitution sought to do several things. It made some allowance for the role played by religion, especially Hinduism, in Indian life. It also gave statutory recognition to minorities, thereby implicitly accepting the existence of a majority. It sought to foster a common civic identity but then compromised this by the provision of reserved seats in legislatures to Scheduled Castes and Scheduled Tribes' (Chiriyankandath 2000: 20).

principle of non-discrimination: Articles 15 and 16 prohibit the state from discriminating on the grounds of religion, race, caste, descent, place of birth or any of them generally, in the state's actions. More specifically, they prohibit discrimination 'relating to employment or appointment to any office under the State' (MoMA 2007: 4–5, hereafter *Ranganath Misra Commission Report* [*RMCR*], after its chairman) The principle of non-discrimination is further enshrined in procedural equality embedded in Articles 14–16 that commit the state to combat discrimination. Non-discrimination was thus one of the 'core principles guiding the development of a democratic nation state in India' (Verma 2012: 69). Articles 15 and 16 extend the equality guaranteed by providing for redress against discrimination. The slight difference between the two is that the former prohibits discrimination by the state against citizens, while the latter is restricted to public employment. Article 15 concentrates on the process through which a burden is imposed on an individual; it assumes a finite list of disfavoured criteria—race, religion, sex—and prohibits making allocations to or decisions about individuals based on those criteria.[3] As an extension of the non-discrimination clause, Article 16[4] guarantees equal opportunity for all citizens in employment under the state: it implies that all public offices and resources are available to all on the basis of the principle of non-discrimination.

Alongside the principle of non-discrimination, which is an essential requirement of liberal democracy, the Constitution also recognises the need for positive discrimination for disadvantaged groups. Article 15 permits the state to make 'any special provisions for women, children [and] any socially, educationally backward class of citizens' and SCs and STs. Article 16 (4) further enables the state to make provisions for reservations in appointments of posts in favour of 'any backward class of citizens which, in the opinion of the State, is not adequately represented in the services under the State'. Whereas the former provision has become the bedrock of affirmative action in employment and education (and reservation of seats in the legislatures)

---

[3] Article 15 (1) states: The State shall not discriminate against any citizen on grounds only of religion, race, caste, sex, place of birth or any of them.

[4] Article 16 states: (1) There shall be equality of opportunity for all citizens in matters relating to employment or appointment to any office under the State; (2) No citizen shall, on grounds only of religion, race, caste, sex, descent, place of birth, residence or any of them, be ineligible for, or discriminated against in respect or, any employment or office under the State.

for SCs and STs, since 1950, the latter article, especially at the level of states, has justified the extension of reservations (employment and education) to OBCs. Quotas in legislatures, public employment and education for the SCs and STs were intended to protect them from the practices of exclusion and discrimination. In addition to these measures, the state committed itself to undertaking development initiatives to bridge the gulf between the SCs and STs and the rest of society. Over the years, the scope of these policies has been expanded to cover an ever-widening range of governmental schemes and programmes (Z. Hasan 2009a: 42–47).

To recapitulate: Indian constitution-making was a new critical juncture that redefined the template of minority rights in post-Independence India. It established a pattern of institutional path dependence which 'locked in' minority rights into secular, universalistic and nationalist discourses in which communitarian representation was considered anathema in a modern liberal democracy. The presence of diverse and historically distinct religious, linguistic and cultural communities within the polity was recognised with assurances that minority cultures and identities would be protected and treated equally. Yet, while the dominant nationalist discourse was opposed to political rights for religious minorities, it accepted that reservations were necessary to address the 'backwardness' of lower castes and tribes (Bajpai 2011: 168). It is also important to acknowledge that provision for affirmative action was constructed largely in response to the political claims of former untouchable castes.

Partition and the creation of Pakistan severely circumscribed the claims of minority rights which were limited to the cultural and linguistic sphere—such as personal law, the right to set up educational establishments and official recognition for languages (Z. Hasan 2009a: ch. 2). The project of democratising Hindu society resulted in the re-designation of SCs and STs—who, before the Government of India Act (1935), were loosely defined as 'Depressed Classes'— as a part of the majority (Hindu) community. Equally disadvantaged and poor religious minorities such as Buddhists, Christians, Muslims and Sikhs, on the other hand, were excluded from these provisions as the criteria for reservations were defined primarily with reference to caste, tribe and backwardness. They were also deemed to be outside the remit of these provisions because of the egalitarian precepts of these faiths. The Constitution, in taking an ideological construction of caste that identified it with Hinduism—as opposed to a sociological one—created a sharp boundary between Hindus and non-Hindus while excluding equally disadvantaged groups among Buddhists, Christians, Muslims and Sikhs because such claims were seen to *reinforce* religious group rights. In short, the Constitution in rejecting the political claims of religious minorities, recognising the cultural and linguistic rights of all minorities, and in introducing affirmative action provisions for SCs and STs, set up the project of democratising Hindu society. The last measure did not just create a structural imbalance in the equality of opportunity for disadvantaged minorities. As Weiner has noted, the Government of India would consistently refuse 'to extend reservations to religious groups on the grounds that it would be divisive'. Such opposition, however, would strike 'many Muslims as discriminatory, given the government's willingness to grant benefits to caste, tribal, and linguistic groups' (Weiner 1997: 487).

Institutionalisation of Caste and 'Competing' Equalities of Opportunity after Constitution-Making

The constitution-making process thus 'marked a moment of containment of group rights' (Bajpai 2011: 15). At the same time, however, a new cleavage defined by caste between the 'majority' and the 'minorities' was created. Henceforth, group rights and affirmative action provisions attached to them would be defined primarily with reference to victimised socio-economically disadvantaged Hindu caste groups. These differences would subsequently become further institutionalised as the scope of reservations was extended to include OBCs, and national and state level institutions emerged to oversee the executive administration of these policies.

In the period after Independence, this structural imbalance would manifest itself, on the one hand, in the demands from SCs, STs and OBCs to increase the scope of reservations, and demands from the socio-economically disadvantaged religious minorities, on the other, that their exclusions from these provisions on grounds of religion was a form of discrimination. The criteria for SCs and OBCs were clearly defined by the overarching emphasis on caste within the Hindu tradition, and when this was challenged, the courts continued to err in favour of the hegemonic understanding of these categories.[5] One notable variation from this norm was the practice of reservation for OBCs at national and state levels. At the national level the criteria for OBCs were

---

[5] The Supreme Court held that 'the caste to which a Hindu belongs, is essentially determined by birth and that if a Hindu is converted to Christianity or another religion, which does not recognise caste, the conversion amounts to a loss of the said caste' (*Mrs. S. Yasmine vs The Secretary* on 13 June 2013).

only established by the Mandal Commission (1978), which conceded that religious communities like Muslims also had 'backward classes' that should be given reservation. But in the pre-Mandal period, states' interpretation of the OBCs criteria was largely influenced by history, tradition and regional peculiarities, so that some states like Karnataka and Kerala included Muslims under this category (Yadav and Singh 1994: 136–150). However, even these breakthroughs were unable to make significant progress in changing the hegemonic discourse: the rise of the Hindu Right in the 1980s and 1990s, together with mobilisation of Dalit communities after the implementation of the Mandal Commission recommendations (1990),[6] at the national level further weakened the case for considering the interests of socio-economically disadvantaged religious minorities (Jenkins 2003: ch. 6). The need to radically revise this framework of equality of opportunity for religious minorities, especially India's Muslims, was dramatically illustrated by 9/11, the Gujarat riots in 2002 and the mobilisation of India's religious minorities.

Institutionalised Regimes of 'Competing Equalities'

Before reviewing the religious minorities' mobilisations against the foundational settlement, it is necessary to outline the institutional framework that has evolved to administer these policies and how it reinforces patterns of path dependence. Table 2.1 compares the relative position of SCs, STs, OBCs and religious minorities. It contrasts the national provision for these groups of reservations in legislatures (and local bodies after 1993), employment, education, specific provisions for service delivery, group-specific anti-discrimination legislation, parliamentary oversight (for example committees), and executive oversight (Ministries/National Commissions). To appreciate this process of institutionalisation of different regimes, we need to keep four developments in mind.

First, the constitutional consensus on special measures for SCs and STs is reflected in the clear institutionalisation of these provisions. Although reservations for these groups had a 10-year sunset clause, they have been renewed every decade. In fact, the scope and meaning of reservations have been extended to include promotions, service delivery specifically targeted at SCs and STs, and pro-active legislation against caste violence (Dhavan 2008:

---

[6] In 1990, the Prime Minister V. P. Singh issued an order to implement the recommendations of the *Mandal Commission Report* (provision of 27 per cent quotas in government employment for OBCs) but due to severe opposition, the recommendation was not implemented until after 1992 (Hasan 2009a: 87–88).

xvii; Heredia 2012: 182–183). These provisions have also been backed by strong executive and legislative overview, both nationally and in the states. Whilst this process of institutionalisation has taken several decades, and has been re-enforced by path dependence, which has brought 'increasing returns' to political formations supporting it (Congress in the 1950s and 1960s, Dalit parties in the 1990s), it has created the normative ideal to which all reservation-seeking groups aspire.[7] In short, the position of the SCs and STs are the benchmarks of protective equality in the Indian political system.

Second, the Mandal Commission extended reservations and service delivery at the national level to OBCs. The commission, which reported in 1980, identified 3,743 backward castes/classes and estimated that these groups as a whole constituted 54 per cent of India's total population. As a result, it recommended a reservation of 27 per cent in both the government and the education sector for the OBCs listed (Backward Classes Commission 1991)—in addition to 22.5 per cent already reserved for SCs and STs. In the absence of a national directive, many states in the south had enacted legislations providing reservations for backward classes in education and in government (Gill 2006),[8] but the decision of the V. P. Singh government in 1990 to implement the Mandal Commission's recommendations nationally had widespread ramifications. At once, it crystallised the process of Dalitisation of Indian politics,[9] and further institutionalised a form of path dependence

---

[7] Thus, in 1992, in the *Indra Sawhney Etc. Etc vs Union of India and others, Etc* judgment, the Supreme Court placed a ceiling of 50 per cent on reservations. However, Tamil Nadu, which had 69 per cent reservations, persuaded the national government to pass the seventy-sixth Constitutional Amendment so as to place the state beyond legal challenge. Since then at least four other Constitutional Amendments have been passed to protect or enhance rights of SCs and STs (Heredia 2012: 181–182).

[8] While the Mandal Commission recognised the Muslim OBCs, there was limited recognition of Muslim OBCs at the national level. In contrast, reservations in states in the south have a longer history: in Kerala, religion-based reservations were introduced in the British colonial era (1936) and it was replaced in 1952 with communal reservation of 45 per cent (35 per cent to OBCs including Muslim OBCs and 10 per cent for SCs and STs). The share has increased to 50 per cent, with earmarking (Hardgrave 1965; *RMCR* 2007: 133; Yadav and Singh 1994: 136–150).

[9] The reference to 'Dalitisation' of Indian politics is primarily about setting the context of the UPA's policies. It is not intended as a wider engagement with the broader politics of India's SCs, STs and OBCs.

Table 2.1 'Competing equalities': SCs, STs, OBCs and religious minorities

Nature of provision at the national level	Scheduled Castes and Scheduled Tribes	Other Backward Classes	Religious minorities
Reservations in employment, education, legislatures	• SCs and STs get 15% and 7.5% reservation in case of direct recruitment • Reservations in national and state legislatures and local bodies • No reservation in promotion* • In government-funded higher educational institutes, reservation available at the same rate	• 27% reservation in case of direct recruitment • 27% reservation in central government-funded higher education institutions • No reservations in promotion • No reservations on the legislatures or local bodies	Sikh Dalits (1956), Buddhist Dalits (1990) included within scope of SC reservations
Specific provisions for service delivery	Planning Commission: from the 1st Five-Year Plan (1951–1956) to 12th Five-Year Plan (2012–2017); National Scheduled Castes Finance and Development Corporation (1989); National Scheduled Tribes Finance and Development Corporation (2001)	Planning Commission (Backward Classes Division); National Backward Classes Finance and Development Corporation (1992)	Planning Commission (Minorities Division); Maulana Azad Education Foundation (1989); National Minorities Development and Finance Corporation (1994); National Commission for Minority Educational Institutions (2004); Prime Minister's 15-Point Programme (2006)

(*Contd.*)

(*Contd.*)

Nature of provision at the national level	Scheduled Castes and Scheduled Tribes	Other Backward Classes	Religious minorities
Group specific anti-discrimination measures	Protection of Civil Rights Act (1955); The Scheduled Castes and Scheduled Tribes (Prevention of Atrocities) Amendment Act (1989)	No equivalent legislation	No equivalent legislation (except for protection for Buddhist and Sikh SCs)
Legislative Oversight	Committee on Social Justice and Empowerment; Committee on Welfare of SC/ST; Consultative Committee on Social Justice and Empowerment	Committee on Social Justice and Empowerment; Consultative Committee on Social Justice and Empowerment	Committee on Social Justice and Empowerment; Consultative Committee on Minority Affairs
Executive Oversight	Ministry of Social Justice and Empowerment (1998); Ministry of Tribal Affairs (1999)**; National Commission for Scheduled Castes (1978); National Commission for Scheduled Tribes (2003)	Ministry of Social Justice and Empowerment; National Commission for Backward Classes (1993)***	Ministry of Minority Affairs (2006); National Commission for Minorities (1992)

Source: Derived from Z. Hasan (2009a: 41–74); MoMA website; Government of India (2004); RMCR (2007: 74–76, 120–126, 140–141).

Notes: The 117th Constitutional Amendment Bill providing reservation in promotions to SCs and STs in government jobs was passed in Rajya Sabha in 2012 but failed to get approval of the Lok Sabha.

* Ministry of Welfare which existed at least from 1985 was renamed the Ministry of Social Justice and Empowerment in 1998, and the Tribal Development Division was enlarged to form a separate Ministry of Tribal Affairs in 1999.

** A bill seeking to grant constitutional status to the National Commission for Backward Classes was passed by Lok Sabha in April 2017 and pending in Rajya Sabha at the time of writing (February 2018).

around caste-based vote-bank politics that would transform the politics of the states in the north (for example Uttar Pradesh and Bihar) (Varshney 2000: 18–20). The rise of the OBCs in the states, and then nationally, began the gradual decline of the upper-caste, upper-class elites who dominated Congress party politics (Jaffrelot 2003).

Third, the emergence of OBCs as a distinct socio-economic category that is politically mobilised has created new forms of institutionalisation and path dependence in which 'increasing returns' arise and generate further demands for extending the scope of reservations. Regionally, Chandra has described this phenomenon as 'patronage politics' (Chandra 2004). Thus, the initial implementation of the Mandal Commission recommendations (termed Mandal I) included employment, but the UPA government widened this scope to embrace higher education (termed Mandal II), with increasing demands for group-specific service delivery.[10] As Table 2.1 indicates, the Indian state's response to 'competing equalities'—among SCs, STs, OBCs, and religious minorities—is to keep them separate and respond differentially to group-specific demands.

Fourth, both nationally and provincially, definitional disagreements about what constitutes an OBC have led to interminable judicial disputes. These cases are important for they determine who is represented on the OBC reservations list. While the Supreme Court has erred towards including 'caste' and 'class' in the definition, including a rejection of reservations for the 'creamy layer' (the socially and economically advanced OBCs who outperform other OBCs as well as economically disadvantaged upper caste in some states), nationally and at the state level, governments are more comfortable with the familiar category of caste. This modularity of caste with class in everyday public policy reinforces the normative ideal of 'caste' as a Hindu category that remains the 'most important unit of identification' (Z. Hasan 2009a: 113). At the same time, it places religious minorities in a difficult predicament: despite the existence of the criteria of 'class' their inclusion is more likely to be entertained if they articulate their case in the language of caste.[11]

---

[10] Interestingly, in response to a judicial judgment (P. A. Inamdar & Ors vs State of Maharashtra & Ors on 12 August 2005), under pressure from OBC parties in the coalition, the UPA passed the ninety-third Constitutional Amendment to extend reservations in higher education.

[11] As we shall see in chapter 4, this is precisely the case in West Bengal under Mamata Banerjee's Chief Ministership.

In contrast to the protective provisions for SCs, STs and OBCs, therefore, the position of religious minorities is somewhat anomalous, and reinforces a form of path dependence that aims to restrict religious minorities' claims to the cultural sphere, even for some of their most socially and economically disadvantaged sections. As we have seen earlier, during constitution-making, religious minorities' claims for political reservations were relegated to recognition of cultural difference within a multicultural polity; politically, their exercise of collective identity was restricted to the framework of individual rights. Given the national trauma over Partition and the construction of minorities in the nationalist discourse, the claims of minorities to special treatment, poor or otherwise, have not received a receptive political audience.

However, there has been some pragmatic accommodation. Sikhs and Buddhists were included as communities within the SCs (Sikhs in 1956, Buddhists in 1990), with the right to reservations in employment and education; they were also brought under the Protection of Civil Rights Act (1955) and the Scheduled Castes and Scheduled Tribes (Prevention of Atrocities Act) (1989). Extending this logic to similar caste groups among Christians and Muslims, however, has been firmly resisted (*RMCR* 2007: 132–133). Similarly, national legislative and executive institutions that oversee the interests of religious minorities have been poorly institutionalised, or sometimes have emerged as a result of external pressure.[12] The NCM, for instance, established in 1992 to monitor minority rights, still lacks a constitutional status.[13] Its remit to protect minority rights, monitor their representation in public employment and safeguard cultural rights has not been adequately fulfilled, with some of the annual reports yet to be tabled or discussed in Parliament.[14] It is regularly criticised by minorities as being a 'toothless tiger' for its inactivity, despite mounting evidence of violence against minorities and increasing discrimination and disadvantage among some minority sections (for example Christians and Muslims) (*Outlook* 2012a).

---

[12] Historically, India has been reluctant to recognise national minorities. India's NCM (1992) was formed in the same year when the United Nations adopted the Declaration on the Rights of Persons Belonging to National or Ethnic, Religious and Linguistic Minorities (1992). See ncm.nic.in.

[13] Providing constitutional status for the NCM was one of the UPA's promises. However, the government failed to fulfil this pledge.

[14] This fact was confirmed by the former chairmen of the NCM, Tahir Mahmood and Wajahat Habibullah, interviews, 12 February 2013, New Delhi, and 20 February 2013, New Delhi, respectively.

To recapitulate: the post-1947 institutionalisation of the constitution-making settlement has produced a form of path dependence that has accentuated the difference in religious minority and non-minority rights, especially for socio-economically disadvantaged castes. Whereas the nature and scope of reservations for SCs, STs and OBCs have been continuously extended, producing 'increasing returns' for political formations supporting such policies, most notably after Mandal I and Mandal II, similar demands from religious minorities remain constitutionally and politically difficult to negotiate. For minority rights, in contrast, the pattern of institutionalisation and path dependence restricts the extension of cultural rights into socio-economic or political rights. In the light of this trajectory, the assertion of minorities' citizenship rights has proved doubly problematic because minority rights are also often threatened by high levels of communal violence against minorities. Ironically, counter-violence is one way in which minorities have attempted to revise the constitutional settlement.

Minorities, Communal Violence and a Contestational Juncture: The 1980s, 1990s and 2000s

If racial, ethnic and religious violence against minorities is one indicator of their degree of political and social integration, then some of India's religious minorities remain poorly integrated.[15] Violence against religious minorities since Independence, particularly Muslims, has been endemic, with high rates of casualties in urban areas in the north. For other regionally concentrated minorities, such as Christians in the North-east, Muslims in Kashmir, and Sikhs in Punjab, this violence has taken on the form of ethno-regional struggles. While the causes of such violence are, undoubtedly, many and complex, Paul Brass argues that in many cities in northern India there exists an 'institutionalised riot system'—the presence of political parties, ideological context and partisan state actors and institutions that have in-built incentives to 'produce communal riots' in which Muslims tend to be the main victims. Both militant Hindus and those who have no connection with militant Hindu groups 'suffer from the presence in the very present of the evidence of Partition

---

[15] High levels of communal violence against religious minorities since Independence are one of the recurring features of Indian politics. See Brass (2003), Varshney (2002) and Wilkinson (2004).

and the imagined dangers of future partitions' (Brass 2003: 384). 'In every major city and town in north India', writes Brass,

> there are further symbols of that presence wherever there are large concentrations of Muslim populations. These Muslim concentrations are called 'mini Pakistans' ... [and] in turn are seen as the centres of riot production designed to intimidate Hindus and generate more and more Partitions, more and more violence on the Hindu body. (Ibid.)

Not unnaturally, high levels of violence have produced reactions from minorities too. The period from the 1980s to the 2000s saw the emergence of a new contestational juncture in which some minorities (Christians, Muslims and Sikhs) sought to revise the constitutional settlement but instead precipitated the rise of the Hindu Right.

Partition not only led to a division of India on religious lines, but also ethnic consolidation of displaced people and the growth of Hindu nationalism. Migration changed the demography of many localities, cities and sometimes provinces. The resettlement of large numbers of refugees in many parts of India provoked conflicts between the new arrivals and existing residents (Talbot and Singh 2009: 128–129). But in the 1950s and 1960s, generalised conflict was avoided because violent Hindu–Muslim riots had discredited Hindu nationalism and Muslim separatism, and the Congress' political accommodation of minorities deflected their religious and cultural demands.[16] Symbols of minority identity (Muslim Personal Law, Urdu and Aligarh Muslim University), perceptions of discrimination (Sikhs and the Punjabi Suba movement) and constraints on freedom of religion (Christians and conversion) would eventually lead to competing mobilisations by the minorities and the Hindu Right. This process can be dated from the general election of 1967: the gradual political decline of the Congress over the next 20 years, the formation of the Janata government (1977–1979), in which the

---

[16] Singh (2000: 45–48) has conceptualised this form of accommodation as 'hegemonic control' because it was not a bargain of equals but traded political support for protection and unequal encapsulation. He makes a distinction between the exercise of 'hegemonic control' and 'violent control' over religious minorities. The former is predicated on some degree of consent but which makes an overt contest for power 'unthinkable'; the latter arises when 'hegemonic control' breaks down and coercion is used to control the challenge to state power.

Bharatiya Jana Sangh was an important coalition partner, and the mobilisation of minorities—all were key signposts in this development.

By the early 1980s, some religious minorities, especially those in the border regions (Punjab, Jammu and Kashmir and the North-east), had begun to contest 'hegemonic control' with ethno-religious demands for self-determination. Thus, some political formations among Sikhs in Punjab, who had remained unreconciled to the Partition, continued to pursue sovereignty within the Indian Constitution, first, through the demand for Punjabi Suba (Punjabi-speaking state), and then the Anandpur Sahib Resolution (1973). The Dharam Yudh Morcha (1981) by the Shiromani Akali Dal (SAD) led to the storming of the Golden Temple by the Indian Army (1984), and a 10-year campaign by Sikh militants for a separate Sikh state of Khalistan. This violent rebellion was ultimately crushed by the use of overwhelming force (250,000 military and paramilitary personnel) but at the cost of nearly 30,000 lives and the suspension of normal governance in the state. In the event, the Indian state restructured Sikh politics but almost two decades after the return of normalcy, the ethno-religious demands of the Anandpur Sahib Resolution remain unaddressed.

Similarly, in Jammu and Kashmir, decades of failure to evolve a working political settlement for the management of the state with special status under the Constitution led to full-scale insurgency from the mid-1980s. By conservative estimates, almost 50,000 people were killed by militant or Indian security personnel and 150,000 Kashmiri Hindus fled the valley to settle in the Hindu majority region of Jammu (Bose 2003; Ganguly 1997). For the Hindu Right, the plight of these refugees became a potent symbol of violence against the nation. Again, the insurgency in Jammu and Kashmir was confronted by an overwhelming use of force which restored the familiar pattern of 'violent control' that has characterised governance in the state; although since 2002 and 9/11 the insurgency has subsided, the valley continuously relapses into cycles of violence interspersed with semblances of peace.

Christian majority states in the North-east also witnessed a significant rise in ethnic and religious violence in the 1980s. Some states like Nagaland have sustained a separatist movement dating from Independence that had oscillated between periods of sustained insurgency and a willingness to negotiate with the Indian state (Baruah 2010; Franke 2011). In others, for instance Manipur, the conflict was directed at new settlers, often Hindu and Muslim Bengali settlers. Both forms of conflicts, however, further provided ideological grist to the *Hindutva* mill in the construction of Christians as an alien community. Indeed, the regular efforts of Christian missionaries to exercise the right to conversion subsequently led to episodic violence (Odisha 2007–2008), attempts at reconversion (Gujarat) and pressure by BJP and Congress state governments to introduce Freedom of Religion Bills to restrict the right to convert to another faith.[17] In the early 2000s, the annual reports of the US Department of State on Freedom of Religion were highly critical of the violations of one of the basic fundamental rights in India.[18]

Yet the main mobilisation by a religious minority, and one which produced a massive counter-reaction, both within the Congress and the Hindu Right, was a defensive response by India's Muslims. A mass conversion of low caste Hindus to Islam in the south in 1981 provided political Hinduism with a popular symbol with which to attack Muslims and other religious minority groups (N. Subramanian 1999: 308). The Shah Bano case (1986), which led the Congress government to overturn a Supreme Court ruling restoring the *status quo ante* in favour of Muslim personal law, became the mainspring for the BJP's virulent campaign to construct a Hindu temple dedicated to the deity Lord Ram at the site of the Babri Masjid in Ayodhya—a mobilisation which saw the emergence of the BJP as a major national political force committed to ideological Hindu nationalism. The demolition of the Babri Masjid in Ayodhya by Hindu nationalist activists in December 1992 marked the climax of the mobilisation of the forces of *Hindutva*. This event was followed by the rise of the BJP to national governance (1996, 1998–1999, 1999–2004) and renewed efforts to build a Hindu nation.

Although Hindu nationalist efforts to pursue the *Hindutva* agenda at the national level during the BJP-led NDA period (1998–2004) were somewhat stymied by its coalition partners—who rejected the demands to abrogate Article 370 of the Constitution that gives special status to Jammu and Kashmir, repeal Muslim personal law and build a temple to Lord Ram at Ayodhya—these impulses were redirected to the state level (Spodek 2010). In Gujarat, communalisation began in earnest when the BJP assumed state power in 1998. In coordination with the Vishwa Hindu Parishad (VHP) and the Bajrang Dal, the BJP began to target Gujarat's religious minorities (*Communalism Combat* 2002).[19] In 1999, a bill against forced conversion,

---

[17] The adoption of the Freedom of Religion Act in the state of Gujarat in 2003 further stoked up communal passions (Osuri 2013).
[18] See US Department of State, www.state.gov/j/drl/rls/irf.
[19] In the first half of 1998 alone, there were over 40 recorded incidents of assaults on prayer halls, churches and Christian assemblies.

with the exception of conversion to Hinduism, was introduced to the state legislative assembly, even though the attempt was frustrated due to the subsequent public outcry (Concerned Citizens Tribunal—Gujarat 2002 2002: 149). Anti-Muslim violence in the state reached its climax on 27 February 2002, when a train carrying Hindu *karsevak*s (religious volunteers) was set on fire outside Godhra railway station, allegedly by a large Muslim mob. The state government promptly declared the incident an organised Islamic terrorist attack. In the ensuing violence, incited by a communalised media and government, Hindu mobs, unchecked and often with the support of the state administration, embarked on a four-day retaliatory massacre in which more than 2,000 Muslims were killed and over 150,000 were displaced (Z. Hasan 2006: 201–202). At the height of the violence, there were 125,000 refugees in camps. The Gujarat pogrom is the most serious example of ethnic cleansing of Muslims since Partition.

To summarise: the period from the 1980s to the 2000s witnessed the emergence of a contestational juncture that challenged how the rights of India's religious minorities had been framed at Independence. However, political mobilisation by Christians, Muslims and Sikhs in the borderland states evoked a violent counter-response in the form of a narrow, ideological vision of political Hinduism. Seventy years after Independence, minorities' citizenship rights continue to be mediated by the 'people'[20] in which some minorities, particularly Muslims, are regularly constructed as the 'other', becoming the targets of high levels of discrimination and violence.[21] Not unnaturally, for some religious minorities these shortcomings have impacted adversely on their identity, security and ability to develop economically and socially.

Religious Minorities and the Institutionalisation of 'Competing Equalities': The Case of India's Muslims

The argument made so far is that the institutionalisation of 'competing equalities' at Independence has created different forms of path dependence for minorities and non-minorities, and has also undermined minorities' citizenship rights because the assertion of these rights is all too often viewed

---

[20] For this important distinction between 'citizen' and 'the people', see (Gupta 2011: 29–31).
[21] The state's failure to tackle communal violence and its post-conflict responses will be examined in Chapter 6.

as undermining the national ideal. But not all minorities are equally affected: small and prosperous communities, such as Jains and Parsis, are among India's high achievers; others like Christians, Muslims and Sikhs, have varying levels of integration, and their socio-economic profile is different in regions in which they constitute a majority (North-east, Jammu and Kashmir, Punjab) (Mahajan and Jodhka 2010). Nonetheless, the pattern of institutionalised difference is most apparent among India's Muslims for whom insecurity, discrimination and exclusion from state-sponsored development, either through employment facilitated by reservations or targeted socio-economic development, have produced one of the most disadvantaged communities.

In 1983 the report of the High Power Panel on Minorities (henceforth *Gopal Singh Panel Report*) declared Muslims a socially and educationally backward community requiring special measures. It noted that Muslims were educationally worse off than most minorities and severely under-represented in the elite services—IAS (3.22 per cent), IPS (2.64 per cent) and IFS (3.14 per cent) (Z. Hasan 2009a: 264). But almost two decades later, the *SCR* noted a further deterioration in the community's status: on almost all indicators Muslims were as disadvantaged, if not more so, as the lowest caste groups who had benefited from reservations and targeted development policies. After the *Gopal Singh Panel Report*, central and state governments did little to correct this situation despite mass social and poverty alleviation programmes. The dominant policy discourse continued to ignore the exclusion of non-Hindu minorities on the assumption that policies designed to tackle exclusion are applicable only to historically oppressed groups (SCs, STs and from the 1980s onwards mostly Hindu OBCs). Even after Mandal, while public policies on the lower castes continued to be framed in the language of justice, equality and democracy, the concerns of minorities were seen mainly as matters of security and identity (ibid.: 9–10). A decisive break, however, appeared to take place with the formation of the first UPA government in 2004.

The dominant approach after 1950 towards religion's claim for public space was defined by secularism and development. Often, the state assiduously rejected such claims because of the assumed religious intent, with minority claims regularly stigmatised as 'communal', 'separatist' and encouraging 'fissiparous' tendencies (Singh 2000: 42). However, the *SCR* (2006) 'marked an important shift in the popular/political discourse on India's religious minorities' (Jodhka 2009: 297). By directly addressing the 'development deficit' among Muslims, it 'opened up new ways of talking about religious minorities' (ibid.). These 'new ways' included *inter alia* taking the socio-religious category (SRC) seriously, recognising the level of deprivation among some of these communities, especially Muslims, and developing new approaches to remedy this underdevelopment.

Despite the wealth of data available to the Planning Commission and other executive agencies, for political and ideological reasons it had not been disaggregated for religious minorities. As the *SCR* observed:

> While the perception of deprivation is widespread among Muslims, there has been no systematic effort since Independence to analyse the condition of religious minorities in the country. Despite the need to analyse the socio-economic and educational conditions of different SRCs, until recently appropriate data for such an analysis was not generated by Government agencies. (*SCR* 2006: 2)

One of the major achievements of the *SCR* was to use new data to examine the condition of SRCs. In doing so, it was a significant act of recognition within the secular establishment that disadvantaged communities exist among religious communities. This shift, from simple recognition to accepting SRCs as social categories deserving of targeted state policy programmes, acknowledged that the life chances of some communities were also determined by their religious identities.[22]

By identifying data on the social and economic development of religious communities, the *SCR* was able to demonstrate the scale of disadvantage suffered by some of India's Muslims. This included, among other things, very poor representation in state governance and employment, both at the national and state levels; a dismal provision for education, infrastructure and security in areas of Muslim settlement; extremely improvised support from financial services for Muslim corporations; and widespread perception of wholesale religious discrimination, resulting in ghettoisation and an inward-looking, identity-centred community.[23] Comparatively, on key performance indicators, such as education, most SRCs, including SCs and STs, recorded a noticeable improvement. However, similar evidence for developments within India's Muslim communities was difficult to find. As the *SCR* concluded:

---

[22] 'Indeed the proposals put forward by the Sachar Committee for amelioration of the Muslim population are premised on the assumption that religious identity be treated as a relevant category in the State policy and perspective on development' (Jodhka 2009: 298).

[23] For a detailed discussion of the findings, see *SCR* (2006: chs 3–9).

Our analysis shows that while there is considerable variation in the conditions of Muslims across states, (and among the Muslims, those who identified themselves as OBCs and others), the *Community exhibits deficits and deprivation in practically all dimensions of development. In fact, by and large, Muslims rank somewhat above SCs/STs but below Hindu-OBCs, Other Minorities and Hindu-General (mostly upper castes) in almost all indicators considered.* Among the states that have large Muslim populations, the situation is particularly grave in the states of West Bengal, Bihar, Uttar Pradesh and Assam ... In addition to the 'development deficit', the perception among Muslims that they are discriminated against and excluded is widespread, which exacerbates the problem. (2006: 237, emphasis added)

The *SCR*'s analysis of the Muslim community's disadvantage is wide-ranging. For reasons outlined earlier, our focus is on three dimensions of the post-*SCR* developments: public sector employment, service delivery and provision for enhanced security.

Muslims and Public Sector Employment

In terms of employment, the *SCR* recognised that the profile of the Muslim community was heavily biased towards the unorganised sector in urban areas. This sector had faced severe challenges following economic liberalisation, making Muslim livelihoods even more precarious. However, what was equally striking was the low level of Muslim employment in the public sector: the report noted 'Muslims' shares in employment in various [government] departments are abysmally low at all levels' (ibid.: 167). Table 2.2 highlights the level of significant under-representation of Muslim employment in government and public sector undertakings. In some of the largest undertakings, such as railways, banks, security agencies and state-level departments, it is well below the 14 per cent proportion of the community's share in the total Indian population. In no department or undertaking is it matched or exceeded. Employment, moreover, was concentrated in lower grades (C and D), with significant under-representation in senior positions.

Table 2.2 Muslim employees in government sector employment

Departments/ Institutions Reporting	Reported Number of Employees	Reported Number of Muslim Employees	Muslims as Percentage of Reported Employees
State Level Departments	4,452,851	278,385	6.3
Railways	1,418,747	64,066	4.5
Banks and RBI (Reserve Bank of India)	680,833	15,030	2.2
Security Agencies*	1,879,134	60,517	3.2
Postal Service	275,841	13,759	5.0
Universities**	137,263	6,416	4.7
All Reported Government Employment (Excludes Public Sector Undertakings)	8,844,669	438,173	4.9
Central Public Sector Undertakings***	687,512	22,387	3.3
States Public Sector Undertakings	745,271	80,661	10.8
All Public Sector Undertakings	1,432,783	103,048	7.2

Source: SCR (2006: 165).

Notes: *CRPF (Central Reserve Police Force), CISF (Central Industrial Security Force), BSF (Border Security Force), SSB (Sashastra Seema Bal—one of India's Central Armed Police Forces), and other agencies; **129 universities (central and state) and 84 colleges; *** Data from 154 public sector undertakings.

Table 2.3 indicates that there has only been a marginal change in the number of Muslims employed in senior service posts since 1980: only in the IPS the proportion increased slightly. Nor is the situation better in the states: 'in no state' did the employment of Muslims 'match their population share'. Even best performing states only matched 50–70 per cent of the proportion (ibid.: 171).[24]

---

[24] These included Karnataka, Tamil Nadu and, surprisingly, Gujarat.

Table 2.3 Percentage of Muslims in senior civil service posts

Name of Service / Year	1980	2006
Indian Administrative Service	3.2	3.0
Indian Police Service	2.6	4.0
Indian Foreign Service	3.1	1.8

Sources: Z. Hasan (2009a: 264); SCR (2006: 165).

The *SCR* concluded its section on employment by noting that a 'detailed analysis of Muslim presence in government employment' confirmed that a 'very small proportion of government/public sector employees are Muslims and on average they are concentrated in lower-level positions' (ibid.: 186–187).

Muslims and Service Delivery

The *SCR* noted that if Muslims are heavily under-represented in public and private sector employment, the community's 'development deficit' can also be attributed to poor service delivery—the provision of public sector goods and infrastructure. The report found the community lagging behind in all key human development indicators. In education, for instance, it found high levels of deprivation: 'From lower levels of enrolment to a sharp decline in participation in higher levels of education', the report concluded, 'the situation of Indian Muslims is indeed very depressing as compared to most other SRCs; in fact their situation seems to have worsened in relative terms' (ibid.: 243). The report recognised the centrality of improving the educational performance of the community, but noted with interest that the improvement in the educational background of SCs and STs, who had been able to 'catch up with Muslims', was most likely the result of specially targeted programmes to 'establish schools or improve infrastructure and provide incentives for enrolment'. In a telling phrase, the *SCR* noted that reservations for these groups have had an impact in 'providing the economic means to educate children and simultaneously increase the economic returns to education' (ibid.: 76).

In contrast, in the absence of such special programmes directed at the Muslim community, the clustering of deprivation—poor educational achievement, high levels of poverty and unemployment—was identified with poor service delivery. In large regions of the north, Muslim communities were more disadvantaged than most other communities: 'more than 1,000 Muslim-concentration villages in West Bengal and Bihar [did] not have any educational institutions; in Uttar Pradesh, this figure is 1,943' (ibid.: 143); 40 per cent of 'larger villages with a substantial Muslim concentration [did] not have any medical facilities' (ibid.: 150). While poor infrastructure was one of the common features Muslims shared with other poor communities, they were especially affected because this was combined with a discriminatory attitude, a general 'secular' development bias, and a pervasive insensitivity of the state and NGOs to the community's needs. As the *SCR* surmised, 'access to schools, health care, sanitation facilities, potable water and means of daily transportation are some of the basic facilities one can expect a state to provide for its citizens' (ibid.: 253). With the exception of Kerala, there was 'relatively low access to such facilities for Muslims across India' (ibid.).

Muslims and Insecurity

Although the *SCR* centred on the socio-economic conditions of the Muslim community, it recognised how insecurity had impacted their development. The report noted that Muslim identity had become increasingly 'problematic in public space', with growing marginalisation of shared common spaces. Perceptions of discrimination by Muslims were especially high in sectors such as employment, housing and education. Muslim women felt particularly vulnerable. In fact, the *SCR* noted that 'lack of a sense of security and a discriminatory attitude towards Muslims is felt widely' (ibid.: 13). It acknowledged that there was a variation in the intensity of feeling across the states, but 'communal tension or any untoward incident in any part of the country is enough to make Muslims fear for their safety and security' (ibid.). The Commission concluded that

> violent communal conflicts especially like some recent ones in a state [Gujarat], in which there is large-scale targeted sexual violence against Muslim women, has a spread affect even in regions of the country not directly affected by the violence. There is immense fear, a feeling of vulnerability ... The lack of adequate Muslim presence in the police force accentuates this problem in almost all Indian states as it heightens the perceived sense of insecurity, especially in a communally sensitive situation. (Ibid.: 14)

According to the *SCR*, this outcome was largely the failure of law enforcement agencies to control communal conflicts and the experience of state agencies in dealing with post-conflict situations in which Muslims were victims (ibid.). But the long-term impact of these developments was the further 'ghettoisation' of Muslim populations in areas of the community's concentration: 'Fearing for their security', the *SCR* observed, 'Muslims are increasingly resorting to living in ghettos across the country' (ibid.). The impact of insecurity had led to cumulative processes that had reinforced discrimination and disadvantage.

Increasing ghettoisation of the community implies a shrinking space for it in the public sphere ... Social boycott of Muslims in certain parts of the country has forced Muslims to migrate from places where they lived for centuries; this has affected their employability and means of earning a livelihood. Ghettoisation, therefore, has multiple adverse effects: inadequacy of infrastructural facilities, shrinking common spaces where different SRCs can interact and reduction in livelihood options. (Ibid.)

While some of these conclusions were undoubtedly drawn from the post-conflict experience of Gujarat, other independent studies have confirmed the trend towards ghettoisation as well (see, in particular, Gayer and Jaffrelot 2012).

Conclusion

This chapter has examined how minority rights were framed during constitution-making, India's critical juncture which marked a radical rupture with the colonial past and embodied the vision of a modern, secular India. Minority rights which had assumed political dimensions during colonial rule were severely curtailed while group rights were largely limited to socio-economically disadvantaged Hindu castes. Equally disadvantaged groups among religious minorities were largely excluded from the system of protective discrimination through reservations, though inroads into reservations were made over time by the dilution of the OBC category at the states' level. Nevertheless, this distinction institutionalised different forms of path dependence for socio-economically disadvantaged groups among religious minorities and the majority, giving rise to rival structures and institutions of regimes of 'competing equalities'.

The *SCR* was a major turning point in the post-Independence history of India's Muslims: it recognised, for the first time, the degree of discrimination and disadvantage ('development deficit') suffered by the community.[25] The

---

[25] The *SCR* findings were critiqued on ideological, methodological and legal grounds. One senior academic interviewed in Delhi agreed with the provision of reservation or special programmes for backward religious communities but insisted that these must be linked to discrimination. According to this interviewee, 'A discriminated group is denied equal opportunity because of caste and religious background. But that has to be proved. In the case of SCs, it is absolutely clear. But in the case of Muslims you have to prove statistically that they are discriminated against. If not, the general policy of economic intervention is enough. The SCR and RMCR have not referred to discrimination; they only focus on inequality that Muslims lag behind the

report acknowledged that this was determined, to some extent, by factors such as regional variations (the concentration of Muslims in some of the poorest states such as Uttar Pradesh, Bihar and West Bengal), the community's own assets and its cultural capital. However, official state policies, or the lack of those, had impacted disproportionately on the community's sense of identity, security and its overall development.

Implicitly, the *SCR* also acknowledged that India's critical juncture had institutionalised different forms of path dependence in terms of equality of opportunity between minority and majority disadvantaged groups because in key indicators (for example education) of progress, some minorities, such as Muslims, were at a lower level than SCs and STs. Whereas reservations provide 'increasing returns' to politically mobilised SCs, STs and from the 1990s onwards the OBCs, poor religious communities became further marginalised. Even the potential for greater inclusion of Muslims in the OBC category after Mandal had failed to provide a critical breakthrough: the recognition of these castes/classes remains politically contested, though more efforts have been made to implement the policy in some states (Kerala, Karnataka, Andhra Pradesh and Tamil Nadu) than others (*SCR* 2006: ch. 10).

From the 1980s to the early 2000s, one response to discrimination and unequal treatment by minorities, particularly in the borderland regions, was to mobilise around identity and ethno-nationalist demands that produced prolonged insurgencies and counter-insurgencies. These also generated a powerful counter-reaction in the rise of the Hindu Right and the Gujarat riots in 2002. These events appear to have changed some minority communities' political outlook from 'identity' to 'development,' and from the late 1990s onwards intersected with the Congress' efforts to rebuild its relationship with the minorities. Thus, the election of the Congress-led UPA government in 2004 marked the beginning of a new contestational juncture in which politically mobilised minority groups called for 'full equality of opportunity'. How the UPA responded to this challenge is examined in the next chapter.

Hindus. So, removal of disparity within the group itself is the independent objective of the government. But if that disparity is caused because of general neglect in the past, or because of discrimination, we don't know. In case of Dalits, we know the disparity is because of discrimination even in the present. Many studies conducted on this issue prove that SCs are discriminated. But how can you prove Muslims are discriminated?' (anonymised, interview, 19 March 2013, New Delhi). Political parties, particularly the BJP, as we shall see in subsequent chapters, opposed the report. For some incisive critiques, see Alam (2010) and Wilkinson (2007).

3

The UPA in Power
The New Equal Opportunities Framework, Religious Minorities and the Limits of Change

Introduction

The formation of a Congress-led UPA government after the Lok Sabha elections in 2004 marked a new contestational juncture in the efforts to establish a more substantive framework of equality of opportunity for India's religious minorities. Against the backdrop of 9/11, the rise of the BJP and *Hindutva* forces and the failure of the direct assertion of minority rights by ethno-religious communities from the 1980s to the 2000s, this new approach was distinguished by locating the concerns of religious minorities within national and international discourse on social exclusion. This debate highlighted the need to counter the negative implications of the securitisation of Muslim communities and to tackle their social and economic disadvantage. For the Congress, the change coincided with its reinvention as a social democratic party that was willing to come to terms with coalition governance. The new contestational juncture held the promise of redefining the constitutional settlement by addressing long-term demands of minorities, especially disadvantaged Muslims. Although this development gathered considerable momentum in the first few years of the UPA I's administration, by mid-2007 the political momentum behind these policies had largely dissipated. Thereafter, the familiar pattern of path dependence reasserted itself.

This chapter provides the background for more detailed case studies of policies on employment, service delivery and security in Chapters 4, 5 and 6. It gives an overview of the UPA's approach to minorities, with special reference to Muslims, by operationalising the framework of institutional policy analysis outlined in Chapter 1, particularly the policy process (agenda-setting, policy formation, decision-making, implementation and evaluation) and the role of key institutions and actors. It first reviews how change in policy occurred before the 2004 general elections. The process of policy formulation is then examined with reference to the *SCR* and *RMCR*. Of particular interest are how these reports and associated committees sketched out a new framework of equality of opportunity which promised to transform the foundational settlement. However, institutional and political factors combined to frustrate this outcome, with the consequence that the UPA's decision-making process ultimately produced a partial commitment to new policies that were poorly designed and ineffectually implemented.

Agenda-setting: UPA and the 2004 General Elections

Although the BJP-led NDA's (1998–2004) policies on minorities were Janus-faced—'to accommodate minority interests while trying to query the concept of minority itself' (Mitra 2005: 78)—state power was used to influence cultural policy and education (ibid.: 85). The events of 9/11, the Kargil war, the militants' attack on the Indian Parliament and the post-attack mobilisation against Pakistan were all skilfully exploited to equate Islam with violence. The narrative of Hindu–Muslim conflict, which is central to *Hindutva*, became entwined with the global 'clash of civilisations'. The 'clash within' (Nussbaum 2007) was overlaid by a meta-narrative of the 'War on Terror'. Thus, the Gujarat riots (2002) took place against the background of heightened global and domestic Indian Islamophobia, and in the post-conflict management, even the mild-mannered Prime Minister, Atal Bihari Vajpayee, could not resist highlighting the association between Islam and violence (Dasgupta 2002). The BJP at the national level tried to backtrack from this position, but the damage had been done.

The origins of the new UPA-period contestational juncture lie in developments during the 1990s. First, many low caste Christian and Muslim organisations became increasingly disenchanted with their community leadership's pursuit of identity politics. The implementation of the Mandal Commission recommendations led to the formation of the All India Backward Muslims Morcha which was founded in Bihar in 1994 to secure SC status for Dalit Muslims. Similarly, the Pasmanda Movement led by Ali Anwar Ansari sought to create an awareness of the socio-economic conditions of Muslims, especially those suffered by Dalit Muslims. It campaigned for access to reservations and affirmative action programmes for religious minorities and for better representation of Muslims in government structures (Ansari 2009: 8). The movement was unable to build a strong following across Bihar and among Muslims, but its mobilisation led to the passage of resolutions in state assemblies of Bihar (2000), Uttar Pradesh (2006) and Andhra Pradesh

(2009) that supported the inclusion of Dalit Christians and Muslims in the SC category (Kashif-ul-Huda 2009). Second, a number of significant court cases concerning the definition of OBCs indirectly bore down on the inclusion of religious minorities within this category, particularly in states in the south that were inclined to take an expansive definition (Z. Hasan 2009a: ch. 4). Third, some sections within the Congress began to recognise the transformative potential of granting reservations in employment and education to religious minorities (Christians and Muslims) within the OBC category, despite its historic opposition to the Mandal Commission's recommendations. Following three election defeats (1996, 1998 and 1999), the Congress reassessed its traditional refusal to participate in coalitions. Coming to terms with the regionalisation of Indian politics also required building an agenda for coalition governance with parties that had spearheaded Mandalisation. In 2003, the party decided upon a clear preference for coalition alliances with like-minded secular parties.

In this context, minorities, especially Muslims, featured prominently in the party's election campaign. Substantive equality of opportunity for SCs, STs, OBCs and religious and linguistic minorities was to be the core of the party's agenda on minorities (INC Manifesto 2004). The party's 2004 election manifesto stated:

> The Congress believes in affirmative action for all religious and linguistic minorities. The Congress has provided for reservations for Muslims in Kerala and Karnataka in government employment and education on the grounds that they are a socially and educationally backward class. The Congress is committed to adopting this policy for socially and educationally backward sections among Muslims and other religious minorities on a national scale ... The Congress will adopt all possible measures to promote and maintain communal peace and harmony, especially in sensitive areas. It will enact a comprehensive law on social violence in all its forms and manifestations, providing for investigations by a central agency, prosecution by Special Courts and payment of uniform compensation for loss of life, honour and property. (Ibid.)

The BJP was criticised for having damaged social harmony—sponsoring the Gujarat riot, glorifying violence against missionaries and encouraging communal organisations (VHP/Bajrang Dal) to spread hate (ibid.). Vajpayee was attacked for not displaying consistency and clarity on major national issues such as Ayodhya, the preservation of secularism, relations with Pakistan, and Jammu and Kashmir (ibid.). The Congress boldly claimed that the 2004 Lok Sabha elections were 'a clash of sharply competing values, of diametrically opposite ideologies', and offered an opportunity to 'consolidate all forces subscribing to the fundamental values of our Constitution' (ibid.).

The UPA's NCMP, agreed upon by all parties that supported the alliance after the elections, including the Communists who gave outside backing, provided the broad framework of governance. It committed the administration

> ... to preserve, protect and promote social harmony and to enforce the law without fear or favour to deal with all obscurantist and fundamentalist elements who seek to disturb social amity and peace, [and] *to provide for full equality of opportunity, particularly in education and employment for Scheduled Castes, Scheduled Tribes, OBCs and religious minorities.* (Government of India 2004, emphasis added) [1]

In brief, both the Congress manifesto and the UPA's NCMP were committed to a new approach towards equality of opportunity for minorities. The real test was whether the UPA could deliver.

Policy Formulation

The process of policy formulation, as with other stages in the policy process, is difficult to delineate into a discrete stage. Nonetheless, because of the highly contentious nature of the subject matter it did correspond with the policy

---

[1] The NCMP promised to: reverse the communalisation of education under the NDA, especially in higher education; implement the Places of Worship (Special Provisions) Act, 1992; encourage negotiation for a settlement on Ayodhya; 'enact a model comprehensive law to deal with communal violence and encourage each state to adopt that law to generate faith and confidence in minority communities'; 'promote modern and technical education among all minority communities [for] social and economic empowerment of minorities'; establish a National Commission to address the socially and economically backward sections among religious and linguistic minorities, with reserved places in education and employment; provide adequate funding for the National Minorities Development Corporation; provide Constitutional status to the Minorities Commission; restructure the National Integration Council and ensure that it met twice a year; 'strive for recognition and promotion of Urdu language under Article 345 and 347 of the Constitution'; and 'take the strictest possible action, without fear or favour, against all those individuals and organisations who spread social discord, disturb social amity, [and] propagate religious bigotry and communal hatred' (Government of India 2004: 6–11).

process outlined in Chapter 1 (see Figure 1.1). At the core of this process was the need to establish sound empirical evidence for policy change while drawing on familiar patterns of institutional innovation. Accordingly, policy formulation was undertaken within the conventions of Indian policymaking which include 'top-down' expert commissions and committees, and engagement with emerging policy networks, such as the network of civil society activists and Muslim communities, academics and politicians. As such, it was heavily influenced by substantive constraints (defined by the problem itself) and procedural constraints (institutional, constitutional and organisational). The core framework of policy formation was provided by reports of four expert groups: the *Sachar Committee Report* (2006), the *Ranganath Misra Commission Report* (2007), a report by the expert group on Equal Opportunity Commission (2007) and a report by the expert group on Diversity Index (2008). These initiatives are summarised in Table 3.1.

Table 3.1   A summary of the UPA's policy initiatives on religious minorities

Policy initiatives	Specific measures taken
Affirmative action for minorities	· Sachar Committee Report (2006) · Ranganath Misra Commission Report (2007) · Prime Minister's 15-Point Programme (2006) · Executive action to monitor and target employment of minorities in national government service (Office Memorandum, 2011)
New institutions	· Ministry of Minority Affairs (2006) · Introduction of a bill to give constitutional status for National Commission for Minorities (2004) · National Commission for Minority Educational Institutions (2004)
Anti-religious discrimination	· Expert group report on Equal Opportunity Commission (2007) · Communal Violence Bills (2005/2011)
Promotion of diversity	· Expert group report on Diversity Index (2008) · National Commission for Minority Educational Institutions Act (2004)

Source: Ministry of Minority Affairs, National Common Minimum Programme.
Note: This table excludes promotional policies.

The Sachar Committee was set up following a notification from the Prime Minister's Office (PMO) on 9 March 2005. Its rationale was that because of the

> lack of authentic information about the social, economic and educational status of the Muslim community of India which comes in the way of planning, formulating and implementing specific interventions, policies and programmes to address the issues relating to the socio-economic backwardness of this community, [the] Government has constituted a High Level Committee to prepare a comprehensive report covering these aspects. (*SCR* 2006: v)

More specifically, the terms of references required the committee to examine the locations in which Muslims live, their pattern of livelihoods, socio-economic development, 'relative share in public and private sector employment', and whether it was 'in proportion to their population in the various states' and if not, what were the 'hurdles' (ibid.: 3). The Committee was also to ascertain the share of Muslim OBCs in public sector employment at the centre and the states. Although no specific interventions were identified, the Committee's finding would enable the 'government to address relevant issues relating to the social, economic and educational status of the Muslim community' (ibid.). The Committee was to be chaired by Rajinder Sachar, a distinguished jurist with a track record in human rights, and included academics and public activists. It was to report within 15 months.

Prior to the formation of the Sachar Committe, on 29 October 2004, the government also set up a National Commission for Religious and Linguistic Minorities (or the Ranganath Misra Commission, after its chairman). This commission was charged with three specific tasks: to address the issue of developing criteria for 'socially and economically backward sections among religious and linguistic minorities'; to recommend measures ... 'including reservation in education and government employment' for the welfare of these groups; and to suggest 'necessary constitutional, legal and administrative modalities required for the implementation of its recommendations' (*RMCR* 2007: 1). But, unlike the Sachar Committee, this commission was not formally constituted until March 2005, had its terms of reference extended and, despite an initial reporting deadline of six months, belatedly submitted its final report in May 2007.

Mainly because of its terms of reference, the work of the Ranganath Misra Commission was deeply contested. Formally, commissions in India have legal autonomy from the government in power; they are regarded as independent and objective, and therefore their recommendations are respected. Although many governments use a commission to delay policymaking, or defer decision-taking, they rarely invite controversy over its composition. However, appointments to the Ranganath Misra Commission were highly politicised. According to one member, Tahir Mahmood, he initially declined to join but was prevailed on to do so by the Prime Minister because he knew that as a former Chairman of the NCM Mahmood supported reservation for minorities.[2] Apparently, the Prime Minister informed Mahmood: 'I am not a law man. Recommending reservation needs support with legal grounds; that is why I set up this commission and that is why I nominated you to this commission.'[3] Whereas Mahmood's appointment appear to have been strategically driven to make the case for minorities, the appointment of Asha Das, a retired former secretary of the Ministry of Social Justice and Empowerment (MSJE), well-known for her BJP sympathies, as an additional member-secretary of the Commission in May 2005 counterbalanced his influence. She was appointed only after the Commission's work had commenced, and her appointment remains shrouded in mystery. Who recommended this dissenting member to be added to the Commission, on what grounds the decision was made, and whether there was any strong difference between the Prime Minister and other decision-makers

---

[2] As Chairman of the NCM, Professor Tahir Mahmood had recommended that reservations should be introduced for minorities. The NCM 'recommended that (1) as even fifty years after Independence there are serious imbalances and inequalities in respect of the representation of Minorities in all public employments, top priority should be given to the adoption of measures to rectify this situation and ensure the Minorities their due share in the National resources and their management, (2) in all public employments under the Central Government there must be at least 15 per cent representation of the Minorities – with a breakdown of 10 per cent for the Muslims and 5 per cent for the other Minorities taken together; and that this should be ensured by adopting suitable measures and issuing mandatory guidelines to all government departments, public sector undertakings and the concerned recruiting authorities, (3) the wholly vague provision for "special consideration" to be given to Minorities in recruitment to public service, found in the Prime Minister's 15-Point Programme for Minorities, be clarified to specify that it means weighting and relaxation of prescribed requirements as are available to the Scheduled Castes and Tribes' (National Commission for Minorities 1999: 40). Remarkably, these recommendations mirror almost exactly the recommendations of the *RMCR*.

[3] Tahir Mahmood, interview, 20 February 2013, Noida.

over her appointment, or whether it was a calculation on the part of the UPA to forestall a backlash against the recommendations, are questions that remain unanswered.[4] Whatever the intentions, Asha Das frustrated the Commission's work, opposed its main recommendations and ultimately submitted her own dissenting note. Her efforts to continuously prolong the Commission's tenure when the Chair was seriously ill were eventually thwarted in March 2007.

UPA I and a new framework of equality of opportunity for religious minorities with special reference to Muslims

The four reports of expert groups—the *SCR*, the *RMCR*, EOC, DI—mark a major landmark in the development of equal opportunities discourse in India. Together, it has been suggested, they represent a 'paradigm shift' in how to address the challenges of delivering equality in twenty-first century India (Khaitan 2008). Combining specific (directed at minorities) and general (directed at redefining the framework of equality of opportunity) measures, the recommendations of these reports recast the framework of 'competing equalities' with a perceptible shift from the focus on national integration, which had characterised the earlier construction of religious minorities, to justice and equality. This change was made possible by the new discourses of social inclusion, diversity and anti-discrimination, and was most evident in the desire to shift the debate with reference to India's Muslims from the politics of 'identity' to the politics of 'development' and 'social exclusion'. The core elements of this framework included: (*a*) recognising religion as a category of social exclusion, (*b*) creating a level playing field for religious minorities on a par with SCs, STs and OBCs, (*c*) ensuring that service delivery reflects the principle of proportionality and (*d*) institutionalising the better monitoring of equality of opportunity and promotion of social diversity.

Religion as a Category of Social Exclusion

As noted earlier, the Sachar Committee was formed because of 'lack of authentic information about the social, economic and educational status of the

---

[4] It was suggested by some of those interviewed that the appointment of a member-secretary to the Commission was deliberately designed to frustrate the Commission's recommendations. While there is no written documentary evidence to support this inference, the subsequent actions of the member did contribute to the delay in the *RMCR* becoming public.

Muslim community of India' (*SCR* 2006: v). This outcome was the result of institutional resistance by the secular state against the recognition of religious communities as communities that had social and economic characteristics. In the political language of the foundational settlement, religion as a category was non-negotiable beyond cultural and linguistic rights. As a consequence, despite widespread perception of deprivation and discrimination among religious communities, notably Muslims, there was no analysis by government agencies of the socio-economic and educational conditions of the minorities (ibid.: 2). Therefore, much of the initial work of the *SCR* centred on disaggregating such data to establish the comparative position of Muslims vis-à-vis other communities. With the disaggregated data, to overcome the development deficit, the *SCR* proposed two types of measures: specific programmes aimed at enhancing affirmative action through better educational, infrastructural and self-help provision and support by private and public sector undertakings aimed at the Muslim community, and general initiatives that went beyond the conventional conceptual tool-box of the Indian approach to disadvantage. First, it proposed the creation of a National Data Bank for transparent, generally accessible and relevant data on SRCs so their engagement in public and private programmes could be better evaluated. Second, an autonomous Assessment and Monitoring Authority was proposed that would highlight areas of concern for further development. Third, to enhance the legal basis for providing equal opportunities, the *SCR* recommended constituting an EOC. Finally, to promote diversity and arrest religious ghettoisation, the Committee proposed the construction of a DI that would measure diversity in critical areas such as employment in the public and private sectors and housing. The degree of organisational diversity would become the new marker of willingness to embrace diverse, plural and equal opportunities-driven modern India (ibid.: ch. 12).

Religious minorities and SCs, STs and OBCs—a new level playing field

In addition to the approaches to ensure better equality of opportunity and promotion of diversity, a key feature of the new framework was to erase the structural barriers between religious minorities and SCs, STs and OBCs in the recognition of protective equality. By creating a level playing field in which religious minorities would be included in the protective and developmental provisions of reservation and affirmative action in employment and service delivery, the framework sought to end the existing anomaly. Potentially, this proposal challenged the very essence of the constitutional settlement.

The *RMCR*'s main proposal extended protective equality enjoyed by SCs, STs and OBCs to religious minorities. To this end, the Commission opted for the criteria of socio-economic backwardness that has been applied to the majority (Hindu) community to ensure 'no discrimination whatsoever between the majority community and minorities' (*RMCR* 2007: 148–149) and argued that 'the criteria applied for this purpose to the majority community— whatever that criteria may be—*must be unreservedly applied also to all the minorities*' (ibid.: 149, emphasis added). The logical extension of this principle was that

> all those social and vocational groups among the minorities who but for their religious identity would have been covered by the present net of Scheduled Castes should be unquestionably treated as socially backward, irrespective of whether the religion of those other communities recognises the caste system or not. (Ibid.)

To be consistent with this recommendation, which de-linked caste from religion, there was a need to delete paragraph 3 of the Constitution (Scheduled Caste) Order (1950), 'which originally restricted the Scheduled Caste net to the Hindus and later opened it to Sikhs and Buddhists' but still excluded Christians, Jains, Muslims and Parsis (ibid.: 154, 156–168).[5] In making caste religiously neutral, moreover, the Commission was insistent that a change in an individual's religion, for example conversion to Christianity or Islam, should not affect his or her SC status. In short, the constitutional logic of restricting reservations to former Hindu SCs was now to be extended to religious minorities, including the followers of those religions that officially proclaimed an egalitarian creed.

By making caste religiously neutral, the *RMCR* opened up the possibilities of reservations in central and state employment for religious minorities. Given the extent of under-representation of some religious minorities in public employment, especially Muslims, the Commission suggested that 15 per cent 'of posts in all cadres and grades under the Central and State governments should be earmarked' for Muslims (10 per cent) and other minorities (5 per cent). It argued such a provision was consistent with Article 16(4) of the Constitution, which provides the enabling provision for reservations for

---

[5] This recommendation was strongly opposed by Asha Das in her dissenting note in which she argued against granting the SC status to disadvantaged Muslims and Christians.

SCs and STs.[6] In the event this proved difficult to implement, the *RMCR* recommended that 8.4 per cent of the 27 per cent OBC quota be reserved for religious minorities, with 6 per cent earmarked for Muslims and 2.4 for non-Muslims (*RMCR* 2007: 153).

In addition, the *RMCR* proposed a raft of legal and institutional measures which included: firm protection for minority rights to education; the need for statutory status for the judicial enforcement of the Prime Minister's 15-Point Programme (PM's 15PP) for minorities; a Parliamentary Committee on constitutional policy for minorities; a national committee for monitoring the educational and economic development of minorities; the establishment of state-level Minorities Commissions and Welfare Departments in all states and Union Territories; and the decentralisation of all minority-related schemes to the district-level with corresponding structures for minority representation (ibid.: 154–155).

Proportionality in Service Delivery

Another basic dimension of the new approach was that the principle of proportionality should apply in public sector service delivery. In the development of equal opportunity policies in the US and the UK, it became axiomatic that services provided by the state and parastatal organisations should be beyond direct and indirect discrimination, and service budgets should be proportionally allocated to target groups, such as black and ethnic minorities, to reflect their proportion in the population (Ball and Solomos 1990). In India, the principle of proportionality had been conceded to some degree for SCs and STs in the five-year plans—notwithstanding the problems associated with inadequate allocation of funds, non-utilisation, and implementation and administrative bottlenecks. But this principle was not extended to religious minorities because of concerns that any special treatment for these groups would contravene the Constitution.

Although the case for a sub-plan for minorities in the Eleventh Five-Year Plan (2007–2012) was rejected, the proposals which emerged from the *SCR*, *RMCR* and other related initiatives recognised the principle of proportionality within the limits of executive and legislative action. Hence,

---

[6] This article stipulates: 'Nothing in this article shall prevent the State from making any provision for the reservation of appointments or posts in favour of any backward class of citizens which, in the opinion of the State, is not adequately represented in the services under the State.'

the PM's 15PP, re-launched in January 2006, was the flagship measure at the centre of this drive, with the specific aim of improving equal opportunities for religious minorities by ensuring an equitable share in economic activity and employment, improving their living conditions, and preventing and controlling communal riots. This initiative drew on resources allocated to other programmes. Where possible, it aimed to ensure that 15 per cent of the total outlay was earmarked for minorities. In 2007–2008, the newly created Ministry of Minority Affairs identified 90 minority concentration districts (MCDs) for a Multi-Sectoral Development Programme (MSDP) 'to address the "development deficits" specially in education, employment, sanitation, housing, drinking water and electricity supply' (PIB 2008a).

The case for proportionality was also made for some of the high-profile UPA government programmes aimed at poverty reduction (see Table 5.2). Monitoring data available for some of these programmes indicated that take-up by religious minorities, notably Muslims, was below the mean (*RMCR* 2007: ch. 7), and in seeking to correct this imbalance through better distribution and monitoring, the case was also made for extending this approach to the activities of public sector units, banks and private contractors dependent on official contracts. In following this approach, these recommendations were building on the existing policies of leveraging change by using the state sector.

Institutionalising Equality of Opportunity and Promotion of Social Diversity (Equal Opportunity Commission and Diversity Index)

A further innovation in creating a level playing field for religious minorities was the proposal to create an EOC and a DI. Both proposals emerged from the recommendations of the *SCR*, but their origins were to be found in the experience of the Western societies in responding to competing social disadvantages on race, ethnicity and gender. Some of these countries (for example UK), like India, were faced with multiple, competing and overlapping institutions for promoting equality that required integration within a singular overarching framework (Equal Opportunity Commission 2008; Khaitan 2008).

In order to face these complex challenges of disadvantage and discrimination, often around the existence of multiple axes of deprivation, new thinking was needed on 'how to handle the interaction effects of more than one axis of disadvantage' (Equal Opportunity Commission 2008: 12). The expert group which examined this subject proposed an EOC with a focus on eradicating discrimination against 'deprived groups' identified by an objective deprivation index defined by 'sex, caste, language, religion, disability, descent, place of birth, residence, race or any other' grounds (Government of India 2008: 8). The EOC was to be the executive body that would initially focus on two domains: education and employment. However, its overall remit was policy intervention and coordination.

While the EOC would focus on advocacy, monitoring and, where necessary, group grievances, a more direct effort to promote social diversity in the public and private sector was proposed by the expert group's report on the DI. This recommended the creation of a DI to oversee the encouragement of diversity in education, employment and housing societies (MoMA 2008c: 33). The DI would measure the 'diversity gap' in access to employment, education and housing provision of particular social groups—considered in terms of religion, caste, gender—in proportion to the population eligible for such benefits. The report suggested that significant under-representation of any category would be met through incentivisation in the allocation of state fund to institutions (for example universities in the public and private sectors), corporate social responsibility, backed with affirmative actions (public and private sector), and 'incentives to builders for housing complexes that have more "diverse" resident populations to promote "composite living spaces" for "socio-religious communities"' (ibid.: viii).

Overall, the recommendations represented a decisive shift in the framing of equality of opportunity in post-Independence India, especially for minorities. These were distinguished by a new 'out-of-the-box thinking that went beyond reservations in public employment and education' (Khaitan 2008: 8). Recognising religion as an important SRC around which deprivation can be clustered, the *SCR* challenged the post-Independence taboo about recognising religion in public policy. By proposing to include disadvantaged Christians and Muslims within the framework of reservations, the *RMCR* sought to create a level playing field, one in which caste was de-linked from religion. And the proposals to create an EOC and a DI attempted to move beyond a group-based system of protective equality, to establish a general equality framework aimed at combating discrimination and promoting diversity. The real challenge before the UPA was to translate policymaking into reality.

Decision-making: Understanding the UPA's Decisions and Non-decisions

Whereas the policymaking process was reasonably transparent, decision-making was rather opaque. As a coalition, the UPA needed to accommodate the interests of its partners and external supporters (for example the Left parties, the BSP and the SP)[7] who competed for different caste and religious constituencies. Moreover, within the administration itself, there was a clear division between those in government and some of their party members and leaders; additionally, within the UPA there was a two-fold division of authority: the Prime Minister, Manmohan Singh, and the President of the Congress, Sonia Gandhi (Baru 2014: 91–94).

Foremost among these institutional constraints was the BJP's ability to mobilise extensive institutional, political and social opposition to any change in the foundational settlement which appeared to 'appease' minorities. Although in opposition, the BJP and the forces of *Hindutva* could readily mobilise political opinion by playing on the emotional codes of Indian nationalism such as national unity and Partition that had become firmly embedded in the institutionalisation of state policies. The BJP and some sections within the Congress itself thus represented the 'permanent nationalist establishment' that could garner extensive sympathy within the civil service, both at the centre and in the states.

Equally important was the political opposition of SC, ST and OBC lobbies that resisted policy change in favour of religious minorities at their expense. As the main beneficiaries of the institutionalised reservations system, these lobbies objected strongly to any dilution of their existing quotas or change in the existing institutional arrangements that underpinned the regimes of 'competing equalities'. Sometime this institutional opposition was voiced directly by the lobbies' leadership and apex institutions; more often than not, it was articulated implicitly within the structures of governance that had emerged to oversee their interests and was recognised by the government in its policymaking process relating to these groups.

Finally, other institutional constraints were not inconsiderable. Since 1947, the civil service had been nurtured on the idea that religious demands, especially by minorities, were inadmissible. This secular outlook was also underpinned by the judiciary, which tended to interpret the foundational settlement in narrow and restrictive terms. While it has gradually relented in extending reservations, the inclusion of religious minorities within this framework continues to be a source of dispute. As we shall see, judicial activism was to play a significant role in limiting the executive's ability to develop and implement policy.

---

[7] Relations between the UPA government and outside parties were managed through the mechanism of a Coordination Committee.

Sachar Committee Report (SCR)

The *SCR* became embroiled in controversy even before it was published. When the Committee requested data from the armed forces on the proportion of Muslims in the army, it was accused in the press and Parliament of 'trying to "communalise" the army, with senior army officers particularly vocal in their protests' (Wilkinson 2012: 73).

Yet, before the report was tabled in Parliament on 30 November 2006,[8] the Prime Minister gave it his wholehearted support, affirming the need for 'fair and legitimate share for minorities in central and state government and private sector jobs' (Prime Minister's Office 2006b). Addressing at the National Development Council in December he said: 'We will have to devise innovative plans to ensure that minorities, particularly the Muslim minority, are empowered to share equitably the fruits of development. They must have the first claim on resources' (Prime Minister's Office 2006a) In a debate on the report in the Rajya Sabha, A. R. Antulay, the Minister of Minority Affairs, announced that the 'Sachar Committee's recommendations will be implemented'. However, he avoided direct comment on whether the recommendations would be debated in the Parliament, saying, 'I did not say that the SCR will be discussed in Parliament during the current session.'[9] Although a meeting was held at which minority Members of Parliament (MPs) from all parties attended, the minister confirmed it was not called to discuss the *SCR* but because there was no Parliamentary Standing Committee scrutinising the MoMA.[10] Subsequently, there were very limited references to the *SCR* in the Lok Sabha or Rajya Sabha,[11] but formally the government remained committed to fully implementing its recommendations.

One reason for this was the predictable response of the BJP which condemned the *SCR* as nothing but 'vote-bank politics' and 'minority appeasement' (BJP 2006). Pro-BJP media headlined the Prime Minister's earlier comments as 'Muslims must have first claim on resources'. Indeed, the BJP alleged the *SCR*'s findings had been manipulated because evidence from

---

[8] It is alleged that the copy of the report was tabled in Parliament and was given to MPs in both houses. However, it was not provided to Members of the Legislative Assemblies and Members of Legislative Councils (Mishra 2012).
[9] *Rajya Sabha Debate (RSD)*, 18 December 2006.
[10] Ibid.
[11] See *Lok Sabha Debate (LSD)*, 31 August 2008; *LSD*, 9 June 2009; *LSD*, 23 March 2011; and *LSD*, 18 December 2012.

the National Sample Survey Organisation report demonstrated that it was Christians not Muslims who suffered the highest unemployment rate (*Times of India* 2007). This position was also echoed by a senior BJP MP:

> We don't agree with [*SCR*'s] recommendations. We believe the SCR is divisive in nature, appeasing minorities, pro-Congress, and allows the Congress to consolidate the Muslim vote-bank.[12]

Rejecting the case for a more equitable representation of Muslims in state employment as a 'dangerous doctrine', the BJP spokesman said the party would fight the implementation of the *SCR* recommendations 'tooth and nail' (*Economic Times* 2006). In brief, the BJP's rhetoric of minority appeasement rekindled the spectre of the two-nation theory and religious separatism as the root of Partition and communal conflict (BJP 2004).

Ranganath Misra Commission Report (*RMCR*)

The BJP's vociferous opposition to the *SCR* report and institutional engagement with the *RMCR* ensured that the latter's recommendations would prove difficult to translate into policy. The report was completed on 10 May 2007 but not tabled in Parliament until after the 2009 Lok Sabha elections. By mid-2007, the UPA had begun to backtrack on its commitments to minorities. Among the explanations given for this turnabout are the BJP's opposition, the performance of the Congress party in mid-term elections and the growing difficulties of managing the coalition following the withdrawal of Communist support after the vote of confidence over the nuclear fuel deal with the US (Baru 2014: ch. 12). Equally relevant were the internal opposition within the Congress itself, and the increasing institutional and judicial opposition to the new proposals.

Despite the Prime Minister's support for the *RMCR*, by the end of 2007 the UPA had begun to distance itself from the report's recommendations. Although the contents of the report were widely leaked to the press, it was not immediately tabled in Parliament, nor circulated to India's premier policymaking body, the Planning Commission.[13] On 9 December 2009, Mulayam Singh Yadav (SP) in the Lok Sabha taunted the Prime Minister for not releasing the report:

---

[12]   Anonymised, interview, 14 March 2013, New Delhi.
[13]   Mahmood, interview, 20 February 2013, Noida.

RMCR was introduced in July 2007. The government is hiding it for two years and the report was not tabled in the Lok Sabha. Is it trivial? One day, two day, every day has been like that. Liberhan was also similar. Why no debate about this report has taken place for about two years? I want to ask this. Prime Minister is sitting here. Prime Minister, please tell us when this discussion session will take place.[14]

The report was kept under very restricted circulation. A member of the Commission recalls,

> On funny thing is that a couple of months after the report was tabled in Parliament, I received a phone call from the former deputy secretary of the Commission. He said he had been told that all copies of the report from all members and chairman must be submitted to the ministry. They were trying to suppress it. They didn't want the report to be circulated. Even after it was tabled, we were asked to return our copies. I refused and said that now the report is tabled in the Parliament, there is nothing confidential about it so I will release the report to the press. So I did that. That is how it became public. The government has not sent the report to any parliamentarian.[15]

Although the delay in making the report public might be considered a normal part of political calculations in weighing the costs and benefits, its potential implications for other groups—SCs, STs and OBCs—also needed to be taken into consideration. The government's referral of the report to the NCSC and NCBC elicited a reply from the former that 'Dalit Christians and Dalit Muslims cannot be included in the SC list as they do not "satisfactorily" fulfil the key criterion for being SC' (Z. Hasan 2009a: 213–214). Subsequently, this position was modified to one in which such inclusion of Dalit Christians and Dalit Muslims would be acceptable provided the share of reservation for 15 per cent of SCs were not encroached upon (NCSC 2011a). As late as 24 January 2011, the NCSC's position was that 'reservation should be extended to them but the share of 15 per cent of SCs should not be disturbed and the element of reservation for these communities (Dalit Christians and Dalit Muslims) should be determined by the Government keeping in view of their population. As per the direction of the Supreme Court, the overall reservation of 50 per cent has to be maintained' (ibid.). A month later, the NCSC added further

---

[14] *LSD*, 9 December 2009. Translated from Hindi.
[15] Mahmood, interview, 20 February 2013, Noida.

conditions that such an inclusion would have to demonstrate that after conversion Christian and Muslim Dalits were still following caste traditions and customs and were still suffering untouchability and discrimination (NCSC 2011b). This renewed emphasis on caste, and the need for a separate quota for religious minorities, reconfirmed the institutional position from the regimes of 'competing equalities'.

Equal Opportunity Commission (EOC) and the Diversity Index (DI)

Similar institutional factors appear to have impeded the UPA's decision-making process in its efforts to push through a new framework for managing equal opportunities and promoting diversity. When the expert group on the EOC submitted its report, along with the draft bill in February 2008, a Cabinet note was circulated to all ministries and departments.[16] Initially, the government supported the proposal, including it in the President's Address to Parliament on 4 June 2009; in a debate in the Rajya Sabha on 13 July 2009, Salman Khurshid (Minister of Minority Affairs) confirmed that the proposal for an EOC was under serious consideration by the government. The EOC Bill was listed for introduction in the winter session of Parliament in 2009, but because of its potential implications it was referred to the Group of Ministers, which included 11 Cabinet ministers. Reluctant to overturn the existing regimes of 'competing equalities', with their existing executive bodies and oversight, and facing bitter opposition within the ministries on whether the new body should be located in the MoMA or the MSJE, the Group of Ministers decided that the remit of EOC should be limited to 'minorities only'.[17]

---

[16] *LSD*, 17 December 2009.
[17] Key policy actors including Salman Khurshid, Justice Sachar, Abusaleh Shariff, Asaduddin Owaisi and, Wajahat Habibullah all objected strongly to the Group of Ministers' decision to limit the EOC's jurisdiction to minorities only. In similar vein, Zoya Hasan asserted, 'It does not make much sense to set up EOC while there are several commissions already. EOC makes sense when you don't have so many commissions. We have 15 commissions in India. However, if you have EOC it has to deal with all [the] marginalised groups. *But ministries and commissions which are opposed to EOC have said that EOC should be only for minorities. That doesn't make any sense at all. Consequently, it is going to end up ridiculously if it is decided to set up now to show that the government is doing something for minorities but it will be only for minorities. And there is already NCM. Government has set up two other minority-related commissions. So what is the point of setting up yet another commission*

Interestingly, as with the *RMCR*, the circulation of the DI report was also strictly controlled.[18] Soon after the report was submitted, it was criticised by the Central Statistical Office for being 'conceptually flawed', 'over-simplistic' and 'statistically challenging' (Manoj 2009a; 2009b). As a result, there were considerable inter-ministerial tensions over the report and its ownership. The Chairman of the expert group confided in an interview: 'Ministers have not done anything to promote this index. As far as DI is concerned, they received the report, made some copies, distributed a few, and forgot about it.'[19] Indeed, there was little in the DI to appeal to SCs, STs and OBCs because, with established national commissions and exclusive anti-discrimination legislation, the proposal either appeared to undermine the *status quo* or, at best, add another layer of unnecessary complexity. In fact, if the EOC and DI proposals had been implemented, alongside existing commissions, they would have produced a 'regulatory nightmare' (Khaitan 2008: 11). The idea of one single regulatory authority was clearly desirable but institutionally difficult within a framework of 'competing equalities' backed by powerful political lobbies. According to one senior analyst, the proposal for an EOC and a DI lacked a clear mandate for where they would be 'located at the heart of

---

for minorities? I think there is political opposition to it from other commissions and ministries. I think that is the reason for its failure' (Zoya Hasan, interview, 11 March 2013, New Delhi; emphasis added). A senior academic who was consulted by the expert group on EOC also criticised the decision of Group of Ministers on the EOC for not being 'conceptually clear' (anonymised, interview, 19 March 2013, New Delhi). Similar to the *SCR* and *RMCR*, the issues around the EOC Bill was not actively discussed in Parliament. 'Proposal is under consideration' was the most frequently repeated claims by the Ministry of Minority Affairs (*LSD*, 17 December 2009; *LSD*, 2 August 2010; *LSD*, 25 August 2011; *LSD*, 22 August 2013). In the quarterly review on the implementation of *SCR* recommendations, it was simply noted that the 'EOC submitted its report on 13 March 2008', without referring to further progress (*LSD*, 3 May 2010). Despite Salman Khurshid's announcement in 2012 to constitute an EOC during the Twelfth Plan, the EOC was still 'under consideration by the government' until the end of the UPA's tenure.

[18] 'We submitted the DI report to the government, but only 500 copies were made. It was not even distributed properly. The report did not reach all the relevant sections. The number of copy was much smaller compared to the SCR. SCR was uploaded online so at least it was available to people who could access to the internet. The DI report is now available online but it took a long time to get it online' (anonymised, interview, 10 February 2013, New Delhi).

[19] Anonymised, interview, 10 February 2013, New Delhi.

governance'. As a result, as generic measures and without community support, they were 'killed off by inter-ministerial in-fighting and the SC, ST, and OBC lobbies'.[20]

Implementation: Executive Action, Symbolism and Promotional Policies

As we have seen, the general view of UPA policies on minorities, particularly Muslims, is that they were framed by political calculations. It is argued that the decision to implement or not implement these policies was driven primarily by political calculations and the cost and benefits of political payoffs. But this is only a partial explanation. Institutional path dependence suggests that the UPA had to overcome three forms of opposition. First was the politically institutionalised opposition of the BJP and *Hindutva* forces, which articulated an anti-minorities construction of the foundational settlement. This opposition also had a significant constituency within the Congress itself. Second, the institutionalised path dependence of SC, ST and OBC interests, with increasingly powerful political lobbies, presented a formidable obstacle to the inclusion of minorities within India's framework of 'competing equalities'. At times, these interests were articulated as zero-sum conflicts of potential losses. Third, and perhaps most importantly, the institutionalised path dependent framework of dealing with minorities as communities of culture had become firmly embedded within the structures of the secular state so that provision of special programmes for minorities—of affirmative action or reservations—brought forth generally hostile responses.[21]

These 'assumptive worlds' or the 'mental models' with which the Indian state operated illustrate the embedded nature of resistance to policy change. These assumptions and understandings of minorities and the repertoire of everyday bureaucratic discourses were critical to shaping solutions and policy actions. Indeed, the problematic status of some minorities, and the associations of Muslims with the break-up of the country in the national imagination, suggests that the UPA policies needed a cultural transformation

---

[20] Surinder S. Jodhka, interview, 11 February 2013, New Delhi.
[21] 'It is not constitutional to have schemes just for Muslims. We cannot design schemes just for Muslims, or have budgetary allocations for Muslims, or call Muslims, Muslims. It is simply not constitutional. The Constitution makes special mention of SCs and STs for affirmative action, not of Muslims. We can only have intervention for all minorities' (Naqvi 2006).

to challenge embedded institutional opposition. In the absence of a political commitment and a capacity to overcome institutional cultures of resistance, policy implementation was reflected in 'executive action', 'symbolism' and 'promotionalism'.[22]

Executive Action

Executive action taken by the UPA government to implement its policy mix was of two types: symbolic and substantive. Symbolic measures included the launch of new commissions (National Commission for Minority Educational Institutions in 2004) and the reorganisation of existing administrative structures (the creation of MoMA in 2006). Carved out of existing functions within the Ministry of Human Resource Development and other departments, MoMA was launched as a nodal ministry with an overseeing role and a ministerial head with membership of the Council of Ministers.

However, from the outset the reorganisation of existing administrative structures into MoMA was resented by senior administrators as duplicating existing services. Figure 3.1 illustrates the location of MoMA among central ministries and commissions.[23] It does not represent the actual lines of authority. It is clear from the evidence and fieldwork data presented in subsequent chapters that MoMA was viewed as a coordinating ministry rather than an autonomous ministry. Lacking the authority of functional ministries, and severely under-resourced, it soon became a ministry for advocacy, constantly seeking feedback from and consultations with other ministries and relevant institutions within the administrative structure. Its ability to oversee programmes was severely limited (see Chapters 4 and 5). In fact, MoMA and its ministers struggled to fulfil the brief allotted to them, neglecting some essential parliamentary business. Eight years after its creation, by the end of UPA administration in 2014, MoMA was still struggling to establish an authoritative presence within India's central administration.

In contrast to these symbolic measures, executive authority was used to implement affirmative action short of reservation quotas. In January 2007, the Ministry of Personnel, Public Grievances and Pensions (MPPGP) issued an Office Memorandum which stated:

---

[22] For these modes of implementation, see Ball and Solomos (1990).
[23] Figure 3.1 excludes institutions that we do not cover in this research.

Figure 3.1 MoMA and organisational dependence: ministries and other structures

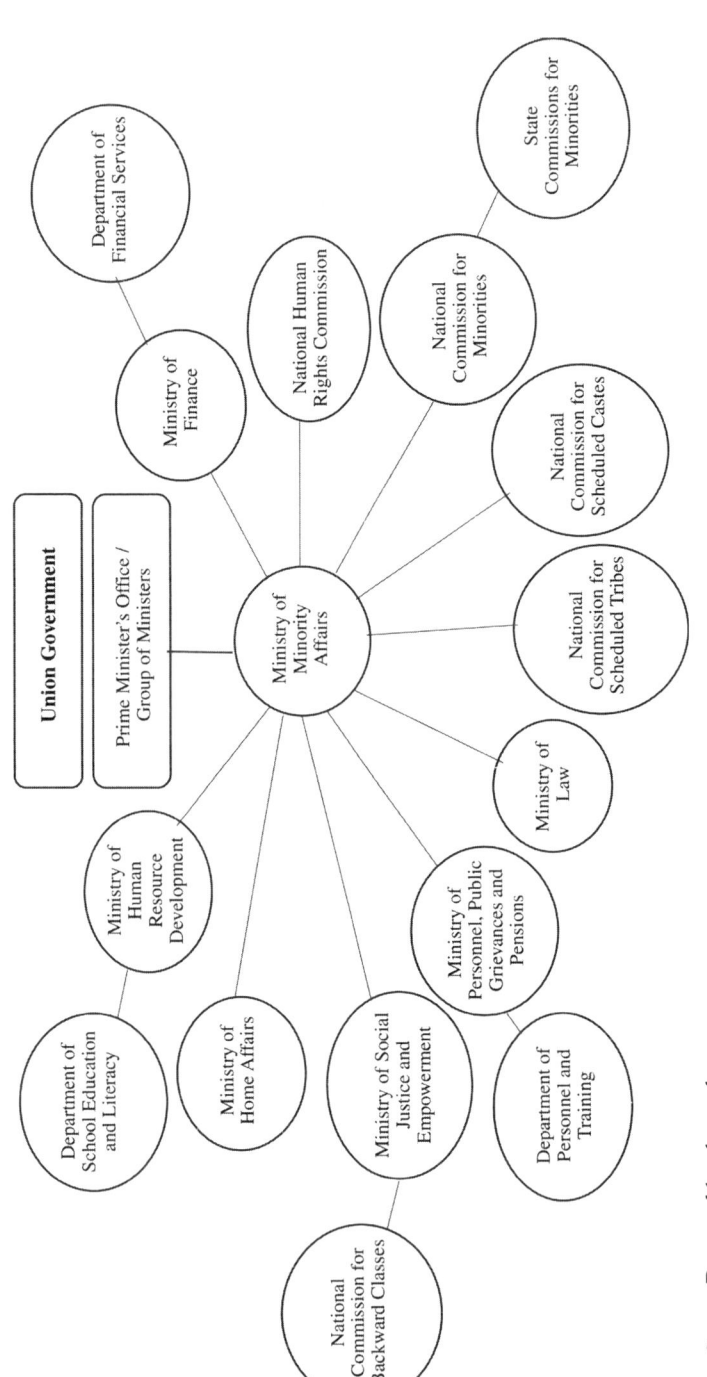

Source: Prepared by the author.

[A]vailable evidence indicates that the representation of minorities in Government service and public sector employment is not satisfactory ... Government is committed to ensuring fair representation to the minorities in Government employment, including public sector enterprises, public sector banks and financial institutions and the Railways. (Ministry of Personnel, Public Grievances and Pensions 2007)

As a result, all heads of department, public sector undertakings and para-government organisations were required to submit half yearly/annual reports to MoMA. The same approach was also used on 22 December 2011, when a new Office Memorandum was issued establishing a reservation of 4.5 per cent for minorities in the OBC quota. Although this action was probably more a matter of symbolic implementation, the use of an Office Memorandum was indicative of the government's intent to circumvent legal challenges.[24]

Substantive executive action was also evident in the case of affirmative action in service delivery. The 15-Point Programme, first launched by Indira Gandhi in 1983, aimed at areas of Muslim concentration, was revamped as the Prime Minister's new 15-Point Programme in January 2006, with a particular focus on four areas: education, employment, living conditions and the security of minorities. This initiative drew on existing programmes with the objective of earmarking 15 per cent of the total outlay for minorities. In 2007–2008, MoMA identified 90 MCDs, and the MSDP was launched in 2009 to overcome the '"development deficit" specially in education, employment, sanitation, housing, drinking water and electricity supply' (PIB 2008a). Significantly, the launch of this programme was accompanied by a range of affirmative action provisions that included targeting and monitoring of service delivery to ensure effective implementation. However, to what extent these instruments were actually utilised or were effective in delivering change to the targeted group (mostly Muslim communities) is something that is discussed at length in Chapter 5.

Symbolic Implementation

Alongside executive action many of the UPA policies on minorities amounted to 'symbolic implementation'—appearing to act on policies but failing to ensure that they are legislated for or implemented. This is

---

[24] However, as we shall see in Chapter 4, it was ostensibly rejected on technical grounds by the Supreme Court.

often viewed as 'tokenism', 'gesture' or 'performative politics' but can also be interpreted as framing policy within existing institutional constraints (Rai 2014).

The case of reservations for minorities in employment and education was firmly made by the *RMCR*. Yet the way the UPA attempted to implement these recommendations both in the first and second administration, in spite of the fact that the *RMCR* had declared that new legislation was unnecessary, was clearly more symbolic than indicative of an ability to successfully implement the measure. For most of its tenure, the government hesitated to move on the proposal because of the pending appeal to the Supreme Court by the Andhra Pradesh state government which had sought to institute 4 per cent reservations for Muslims in employment.[25] When the UPA did move, in late 2011, on the eve of elections in Uttar Pradesh, to institute a 4.5 per cent reservation for minorities in the existing OBC quota through an Office Memorandum, it was not only charged with opportunism but also accused of inadequate preparations to meet the potential legal challenges. Subsequently, the UPA's efforts and the Andhra Pradesh case became entwined: the Andhra Pradesh High Court's rationale was only too evident in the Supreme Court judgment rejecting the UPA's Office Memorandum (see Chapter 4).

Other policy measures that were part of symbolic implementation included the introduction of an anti-communal violence bill and a bill to give the NCM constitutional status. Both were high-profile measures designed to increase the threshold of penalties for those committing acts of communal violence and putting the NCM on a par with other 'protected minorities' commissions. Both, however, failed to reach the statute books. Whereas the institutional obstacles to the anti-communal violence bill remained considerable (see Chapter 6), the failure to secure constitutional status for the NCM needs to be understood against the backdrop of both institutional opposition from the key actors identified earlier and the shortage of parliamentary time in a congested time-table.[26]

---

[25] This case is further examined in Chapter 4.
[26] Despite moving the Constitution (103rd Amendment) Bill, 2004, to give constitutional status to the NCM, the bill was lost because of lengthy consultations with various ministries including the Ministry of Law and the dissolution of the Fourteenth Lok Sabha (MoMA 2013a: 44).

Promotional Policies

A large number of initiatives undertaken by the UPA can be interpreted as promotional, designed to improve the conditions of minority groups through 'low cost' options.[27] Wilkinson has commented that such 'underfunded and uncoordinated proposals' certainly helped the UPA to publicise the fact that it was 'doing something for minorities', but they were unlikely to challenge the underlying issues of economic and social development (2012: 76). Wilkinson's assertion that these measures were part of 'vote-bank' politics reconfirms the standard interpretation of the UPA's actions, but it overlooks how the administration was constrained from specific action or a more detailed assessment of this action itself. Certainly, the promotional policies—between executive action and symbolic implementation—enabled the UPA to directly appeal to the minorities, especially Muslims, but at the same time how these measures were framed and the resources allocated to them were also indicative of the institutional constraints within which the UPA was operating.

Overall, the process of implementation was far more complex than the electoral incentive model suggests: the broad range of policies resulted in a range of implementation strategies which were pursued with unequal vigour. Different approaches were used to address political, judicial and institutional constraints. While the UPA was clearly mindful of the political pay-off in these strategies, we should not overlook the real obstacles to policy formation and implementation in this highly contested policy sector.

Evaluation

Finally, the evaluations—political, administrative, and analytical and technical—undertaken by the UPA were partisan, but they give useful insights into the overall policy process and modes of opposition to the policies.

Politically, the UPA naturally sought to publicise its achievements. For instance, in the 2009 Lok Sabha elections, the Congress' manifesto highlighted the award of 400,000 scholarships to minorities, special programmes for

---

[27] They included: the vast majority of scholarship schemes targeted at minority students, better support for state Wakf boards (Muslim charitable endowments), more funding for the Maulana Azad Educational Foundation (catering for Muslim students), the Scheme of Leadership Development of Minority Women, the Scheme for Skills Development of Minorities, and the Free Coaching and Allied Schemes. See www.minorityaffairs.gov.in.

the 90 MCDs, and then went on to trumpet the fact that the Congress 'has pioneered reservations for minorities in Kerala, Karnataka and Andhra Pradesh in government employment and education on the basis of their social and economic backwardness. We are committed to adopt this policy at the level' (INC 2009: 14). At a conclave in Jaipur in January 2013, the Congress recommitted itself to 'the recommendations of the Sachar Committee' as a guide to the implementation of 'the PM's 15PP and other minority related programmes' (INC 2013: 5–6). It is indicative of how the Congress and the UPA have politically sought to assess their own achievements.

Such political self-evaluations have generally been dismissed by activists and NGOs working in the field. Several have produced highly critical assessments (see Chapter 1), questioning the very design and implementation of policies. According to press reports, the immediate trigger for the UPA to announce a new committee to evaluate the impact of the *SCR* recommendations was 'another well-publicised research paper by the chief scholar at the US–India Policy Institute, Abusaleh Shariff in which he argued that there was no perceptible improvement in the status of Muslims' (Ali 2013). Apparently this paper came on the back of several delegations by Muslim groups to the Prime Minister, Sonia Gandhi and Rahul Gandhi which made the point that 'minority welfare schemes [were] being ineffective' (ibid.). These persistent criticisms by policy networks and NGOs exerted some political effect. In February 2013, the Minister of Minority Affairs, K. Rahman Khan, announced the government decision to review and assess the implementation of the Sachar Committee's recommendations and the PM's 15PP (ibid.). The review committee was set up in August 2013 and instructed to submit its report within six months. However, after some extensions, the final report was submitted in September 2014 to the BJP-led NDA government (MoMA 2014).

Beyond the political and the incomplete administrative evaluations, the UPA policies on minorities were not comprehensively appraised until the end of its term. Technically, monitoring and evaluation, for example in the delivery of the 15-Point Programme, was built into the scheme. Monitoring data on employment of minorities should have been collected following the issue of the Office Memorandum in 2007. To what extent these data have been gathered, monitored and evaluated for better policy formation and implementation remains unclear.[28] Evidently, the use of policy instruments

---

[28] The Post-Sachar Evaluation Committee report briefly mentions poor monitoring of service delivery programmes but not in depth (MoMA 2014).

to collect such data to inform policy evaluation appears to have been highly inconsistent. Furthermore, there is very little evidence that such data have been made available to policy groups, activists, parliamentarians or generally placed within the public domain in a systematic form. The few case studies that have been undertaken portray weak policy design and implementation as well as gross misuse of targeted funds (Centre for Equity Studies 2012; Khan 2012; Shariff 2012).[29] Analytically, the use non-use, and denial of data on some of these policy areas by government officials and politicians raise further questions about the policy process that need to be addressed.

Conclusion

This chapter has attempted to provide an overview of the UPA policy process on minorities. It demonstrated that the policy process conformed to the 'policy cycle' outlined in Chapter 1 (see Figure 1.1) but the lines of demarcation between the stages, for instance, between decision-making and implementation, were sometimes unclear and often blurred. Between 2004 and 2007, there was a significant momentum behind policy change that suggested a wholesale revision of the foundational settlement through a new framework of equality of opportunity for minorities which included a mixture of affirmative action, reservations and new institutional innovations. Furthermore, these measures were designed to promote diversity and combat discrimination in the public sphere. Taken together, these proposals represented a new contestational juncture which held the promise of bringing religious minorities within the framework of protective equality and delivering substantive equality.

However, between 2007 and 2008, political and institutional factors appear to have undermined this momentum. The UPA, which was besieged on a number of fronts—and withstood a vote of confidence on the nuclear energy deal with the US—saw the desertion of some of its supporters, including the Left parties (Baru 2014: 11). At the same time, it began to encounter significant opposition to the proposals from the three main institutionalised forces: the BJP-led *Hindutva* brotherhood; the political lobby of SCs, STs and OBCs who viewed the proposals as a potential erosion of their protected equality framework; and sections within the state structure, principally the civil service and the judiciary. In the face of this determined opposition, the government

---

[29] The findings of these studies were confirmed by the Post-Sachar Evaluation Committee report (MoMA 2014).

resorted to three strategies: executive action, symbolic implementation and the use of promotional policies. Not unexpectedly, these approaches heavily diluted the prospects of major policy change while the administration attempted to maximise the political returns from its efforts. How this policy process worked in the sectors of employment, service delivery and security for minorities is examined in detail in the next three chapters.

4

UPA, Muslims and Public Sector Employment
Assessing the Record

Introduction

Equitable representation of racial, ethnic, religious and other minorities in public sector employment is recognised as a key outcome of substantive equal opportunity policies. Such policies increase the access of previously excluded or under-represented groups to public sector employment and can be transformative in challenging cultures of exclusion (Ball and Solomos 1990). In India, the Constitution specified the percentage of reservations in public sector employment for SCs and STs (15 per cent and 7.5 per cent respectively) since 1970;[1] they were extended nationally for OBCs in the 1990s. These measures are viewed as having contributed to significant improvement in the life chances of some of these groups. Recognising this fact and the gross under-representation of Muslims in public sector employment, the *SCR* called for 'equity and inclusiveness' in areas of 'education' and 'employment' (*SCR* 2006: 243), a recommendation supported by the *RMCR*.

This chapter presents a detailed case study of Muslim employment in central government during the UPA administration. Drawing on the framework of institutional policy analysis, it explores key decisions made by policy actors, the policy formulation process in Parliament and at the executive level, and the debate around reservations for minorities. It also assesses the utility and validity of employment monitoring data provided by the government. The policy process and the limited monitoring data available suggest that no appreciable inroads have been made into improving the availability and

---

[1] Reservations for SCs in government jobs have been in place since the pre-Independence period and those for STs have been provided through Resolution since 1950. The increased percentage (12.5 per cent and 5 per cent to 15 per cent and 7.5 per cent respectively) is the outcome of government efforts to provide reservation proportionate to their population based on the findings of 1961 Census (*RMCR* 2007: 115).

quality of employment of Muslims in the state sector. This outcome is not only the result of a lack of political will on the part of the UPA but also the product of entrenched institutional factors that have thwarted such change.

Agenda-setting

Both the *SCR* and *RMCR*—as well as previous surveys—acknowledge the gross under-representation of Muslims in public sector employment (ibid.: ch. 5; *RMCR* 2007: 152). This under-representation was found at all levels but was particularly striking in some of the large public sector undertakings. Nor was the picture noticeably different in the states: while the states in the south generally tended to have higher levels of representation than those in the north, nowhere (with the exception of Andhra Pradesh) did it match the actual Muslim share of the population in the state. The highest percentage of Muslims in government jobs was in Assam (11.2 per cent), but still significantly below the community's population in the state (30.9 per cent) (*SCR* 2006: 370). Data provided by the *SCR* also demonstrated that the Muslim OBCs who are included in reservation policies were also significantly under-represented, and performed poorly compared to Hindu OBCs or the Muslim general category.[2]

Conceptually, the *SCR* and *RMCR* proposed different policy approaches to this imbalance. Whereas the former was inclined towards positive action,[3] the latter recommended affirmative action, including reservations for poor Muslims in employment and education. The *SCR* acknowledged that there was a case for bringing very poor Muslims, who were 'cumulatively oppressed', within the Indian reservations system.[4] However, in general it 'did not believe

---

[2] 'The relative deprivation of Muslim OBCs', observes the *SCR*, 'is highest in the railways' (2006: 210).

[3] For the distinction between reservation, affirmative action and positive action see footnote 11 to the Introduction.

[4] 'Muslims in India', the *SCR* noted, 'in terms of their social structure, consist of three groups—ashrafs, ajlafs, and arzals. The three groups require different types of affirmative action. The second group, ajlafs/OBCs, need additional attention which could be similar to that of Hindu-OBCs. The third group, those with similar traditional occupation as that of the SCs, may be designated as Most Backward Classes as they need multifarious measures, including reservation, as they are "cumulatively oppressed"' (*SCR* 2006: 214).

in reservations', because they would 'benefit only a small number of people'.[5] Reservations, as one senior member of the Committee admitted in an interview, only contributed to 'individual gain, not public good'.[6] For him positive actions, which contributed to realising the principle of 'proportionality' and broad-based policies, were far more effective in getting 'Muslims into public sector jobs'.[7] Indeed, even Justice Rajinder Sachar appeared unsympathetic to the idea of reservations: when interviewed he avoided direct comments, declaring, 'I don't know about the legality part. We already have reservation for OBCs and others. Whether the Constitution permits this or not, that is a matter for the Supreme Court to give the final verdict.'[8] This mind-set, the terms and reference of *SCR*, and the fact that the *RMCR* was undertaking its work with specific reference to the question of reservations—all made the Committee reluctant to recommend reservations, for fear that in the absence of a constitutional amendment, reservations ran the risk of being challenged in the courts. Conversely, generic recommendations for *all* minorities would not attract any legal challenge.

As a result, the *SCR* recommendations were couched mainly within the framework of positive action: a more transparent system of recruitment by including minorities in selection committees; advertising posts in Urdu and vernacular newspapers, or including statements in job advertisements that 'women, minority, and backward class candidates are encouraged to apply'; strong emphasis on improving the educational attainment of Muslim students; and a raft of monitoring authorities, including the creation of a National Data Bank for data on SRCs, and the formation of an Assessment and Monitoring Authority that would monitor and review data on religious minorities, including employment data (*SCR* 2006: ch. 12). And, as we have seen in Chapter 3, these plans were also accompanied by a proposal to outlaw (in)direct discrimination through an EOC and a DI that would measure diversity in employment, public and private sectors, and housing.

Critics of the *SCR* found a serious disjunction between its analysis and its recommendations. While welcoming some of the recommendations, such as the creation of the EOC and DI, for Hasan neither of these proposals dealt

---

[5] Abusaleh Shariff, interview, 13 February 2013, New Delhi.
[6] Ibid.
[7] Ibid.
[8] Rajinder Sachar, interview, 14 February 2013, New Delhi. In a follow-up interview he clarified his view on reservation that 'only the better-off Muslims will get it. Not the poor Muslims' (14 April 2014, New Delhi).

'specifically with the problems of under-representation of Muslims [in public sector employment]' (Z. Hasan 2009c). Where radical and transformative measures were required, the Committee's recommendations were tentative and conservative.[9] Moreover, its proposals give further leeway to policymakers to use their discretion both in the interpretation of recommendations and the formulation of policy.[10] In brief, positive action was framed in terms of the needs of 'all minorities'.

In contrast, the recommendations of the *RMCR* on reservation for socially and economically disadvantaged Muslims in public sector employment were unambiguous. As the report concluded:

> Since the minorities—especially the Muslims—are very much under-represented, and sometime wholly unrepresented, in government employment, we recommend that they should be regarded as backward in this respect within the meaning of that term as used in Article 16 (4) of the Constitution—*notably without qualifying the word 'backward' with the words "socially and educationally"*—and that 15 per cent of posts in all cadres and grades under the Central and State governments should be earmarked for [minorities]. (*RMCR* 2007: 152–153, emphasis in original)

Of this 15 per cent, the Commission insisted, 10 per cent should be earmarked for Muslims, who constitute 73 per cent of all minorities, and 5 per cent for other minorities. According to the Commission, this recommendation was consistent with Article 16(4) of the Constitution which sanctioned reservations for SCs, STs and OBCs. Adding a rider, the Commission suggested that if this approach proved difficult, then within the 27 per cent OBC quota, 8.4 per

---

[9] Abusaleh Shariff confirmed that 'the Sachar committee was not constituted to give recommendation to government. It was a fact-finding committee, to investigate the socio-economic and educational status of Muslims. If you read the recommendations they are generic recommendations, not specific recommendations. The report was to highlight the condition of Muslims which has not been addressed by the previous governments. That was the main mandate. [It was a] status and diagnostic report. We have shown that Muslims are under-represented in government structure both in national and most of state governments. Let the government decide how to solve the problem. We entirely left it to government to solve it' (interview, telephone, 4 July 2013).

[10] Evidence of implementation of the *SCR*'s recommendations at the state level indicates that there were wide variations. See the sections on implementation and evaluation in this chapter and Chapter 5.

cent should be reserved for religious minorities, with 6 per cent earmarked for Muslims and 2.4 per cent for non-Muslims (ibid.: 153). In short, in a fundamental departure from the conventional understanding of the subject the *RMCR* insisted that reservations for 'backward' Muslims were not only within the remit of existing constitutional provisions but were also necessary and essential to establish a level playing field among all minorities and to end religious discrimination.

To summarise: the *SCR* and *RMCR* offered different policy alternatives for increasing Muslim employment in the public sector. Whereas the former was largely within the framework of positive action, consistent with the constitutional settlement that reservations for minorities *qua* minorities were unconstitutional, the latter held that the accepted understandings of the constitutional norms were 'discriminatory' and 'exclusionary'. This anomaly could be overcome by bringing Christians and Muslims within the existing regime of reservations. The UPA attempted to implement both of these approaches.

Policy Formulation

As noted previously, the stages in the policy process often overlapped. Whereas the *SCR*, despite political differences, was largely accepted by the government, and its implementation pursued through executive action, the *RMCR*, because of its recommendations, was less clearly identified with a distinctive policy process.

Sachar Committee Report (SCR)

Following its publication, the government gave the *SCR* full support.[11] Crucially, the initiatives taken centred primarily on executive action. The revamped PM's 15PP, for instance, required all ministries and departments to implement and monitor the schemes, including employment, and provide MoMA with monthly and quarterly reports.[12] The MPPGP further directed

---

[11] A. R. Antulay, the Minister of Minority Affairs, announced in the Rajya Sabha that the 'Sachar Committee's recommendations will be implemented' (*RSD*, 18 December 2006).

[12] A central level Committee of Secretaries was designated to monitor the progress of implementation every six months and report to the Union Cabinet. Moreover, this monitoring was to be further strengthened by a Review Committee, composed of key officers from all the ministries and departments concerned, at least once a quarter to review the progress and submit reports to the Union Cabinet (MoMA 2009: 3–4).

all heads of departments, public sector enterprises, public sector banks, financial institutions, quasi-government organisations and autonomous bodies, and all appointing authorities, to include at least one minority member in all selection committees/boards for recruitments to Group C and D posts. The guidelines also stated that for Group C and D posts information about the vacancies should be disseminated through schools or colleges in relevant areas. Furthermore, all ministries and government departments were required to submit half-yearly and annual reports to the MoMA on their recruitment of minorities. In committing itself firmly to substantive positive action, an Office Memorandum of January 2007 boldly declared that 'the Central and State Governments will give special consideration to minorities in appointments' (Ministry of Personnel, Public Grievances and Pensions 2007). These guidelines were followed up by the MoMA in drawing attention to the Department of Personnel and Training (DoPT) instructions that 'all Ministries/Departments and state governments ... [should ensure the] representation of minority community in selection committee/board for making recruitment to 10 or more vacancies in group "C" & "D" posts/services' (MoMA 2013b).

Ranganath Misra Commission Report (RMCR): the parliamentary and executive domains

Unlike the *SCR*, the *RMCR* and its recommendations on reservations in employment for minorities, particularly Muslims, became embroiled in political, parliamentary, executive and judicial quagmires. Initial opposition to the report, including within the Congress, led the Congress-dominated UPA to adopt an institutionally conservative position until the eve of elections in Uttar Pradesh in early 2012. In so doing, it reflected both the complex institutionalised opposition to the proposal within the policymaking subsystems and the party's desire to exploit the report for political advantage by partaking in 'symbolic implementation'. The Congress' efforts to push through the Andhra Pradesh model of reservations for Muslims in employment and education ultimately faltered on the rock of institutional opposition.

Parliamentary domain

We have seen how the Congress and the UPA backtracked from reservations for Muslims after the release of the *SCR*. Following the well-publicised leak of the *RMCR* (after it was finally submitted in May 2007 but before any official publication), the pressure on the government to distance itself from its recommendations further intensified. However, in December 2007 in the Lok Sabha, Devendra Prasad Yadav (Rashtriya Janata Dal [RJD]) urged an early implementation of the recommendations, lamenting the fact that despite the submission of the report, the Cabinet had not given a clear direction as to whether its recommendations would be incorporated into the Eleventh Five-Year Plan.[13] But there was no follow-up discussion, and the government studiously avoided further parliamentary discussion. Hence, when Mulayam Singh Yadav (SP) urged the government to lay the report before Parliament, he was frequently interrupted by the Speaker for not giving prior notice of the matter. Despite Basu Deb Acharia (CPI[M])'s support, the Speaker prevented Yadav from raising discussion of the subject.[14] Surprisingly, nor was the matter of the report raised in Parliament by Muslim MPs. The absence of a well-organised Muslim—or minority—MPs' caucus, as we shall see, was to prove important.[15]

Significantly, from May 2007 to May 2014, there was no notable debate in Parliament on policymaking on the subject, nor was the issue raised by Congress MPs. Historically, we have seen how Congress has followed a fine line between championing minorities while also nursing its Hindu majority constituency. These tensions surfaced as the government came 'under pressure from its own MPs and ministers ... not to concede the demand of inclusion of Dalit Christians and Dalit Muslims in the SC list'.[16] Allegedly, one of the reasons proffered for this resistance was the negative impact of such a proposal on Hindu SCs by lowering the cost of conversion to Islam or Christianity.[17] The UPA's ambivalence on policy discussion is captured in the words of Mahmood: 'The RMCR was never discussed in Parliament; it was discussed outside Parliament.'[18]

---

[13] *LSD*, 1 December 2007.
[14] *LSD*, 9 December 2009.
[15] The successful implementation of equal opportunity policies requires a committed lobby of politicians, administrators and civil society activists. The decline of Muslim representation in Parliament was noted by the *SCR*, and has been identified as a critical (missing) variable in explaining the failure of policy on minorities. See Z. Hasan (2009a: ch. 5).
[16] Ibid.: 215.
[17] Ibid.
[18] Tahir Mahmood, interview, 20 February 2013, Noida.

Executive domain

At the executive level, inner tensions between the various policy actors and subsystems can be seen in how they responded to the *RMCR*'s recommendations. On the eve of state elections in Uttar Pradesh in 2012, the government issued a special Office Memorandum providing a 4.5 per cent sub-quota for Muslims in the OBC's 27 per cent quota. The initiative for the Office Memorandum came not from the relevant ministries but the PMO. Given this, what was the role of the MoMA, the MSJE, and the DoPT in the MPPGP in policy formation (see Figure 3.1 for an organisational map of these ministries)?

In March 2010, the Minister of Human Resource Development, Arjun Singh, urged the government to act on the *RMCR*, saying 'we cannot just sleep over it' (*Outlook* 2010). Responding to Singh's remark, Abhishek Singhvi, a senior Congress MP, replied that 'it is this party and the government which had initiated the process. So there is no question of disowning [it]. There is no question of sleeping over (*Times of India* 2010a). Despite this statement, the MoMA remained silent on the matter until July 2010, when Salman Khurshid stated: 'We are actively looking at the reservation issue. We have a commitment in our manifesto. I am pushing for it all the time' (*Times of India* 2010b). He emphasised that the MoMA was in regular touch with the MSJE (ibid.). However, the nature of this cooperation remains unclear because as the guardian of SC, ST and OBC interests, the MSJE appeared reluctant to initiate inter-governmental consultations and seemed unenthusiastic about adoption of the *RMCR* because quotas for minorities posed a potential threat to SCs, STs and OBCs. Thus, it requested the NCSC to provide feedback on the recommendations of the *RMCR*.[19] In response, the NCSC agreed to extend reservation to Dalit Christians and Dalit Muslims, but without disturbing its share of 15 per cent of SCs and without breaching the overall reservation of 50 per cent (NCSC 2011a). The MSJE, allegedly, also consulted the NCBC to firm up this opposition.[20] The NCBC, perhaps because of the

---

[19] This referral can be perhaps explained by the historical opposition of the NCSC to inclusion of minorities within the SC list. For an interesting insight into the inter-organisational differences over the matter between the NCSC and the NCM, see Z. Hasan (2009a: 213–214).

[20] The NCBC is in charge of providing advice to MJSE in reference to castes, sub-castes and communities for inclusion in the central list of OBCs. The fact that MSJE requested feedback from NCBC was confirmed in the interview with Mahmood, 20 February 2013, Noida.

expected backlash from the OBCs for diluting their quota with Dalit Muslims and Dalit Christians, initially remained non-committal.[21] While these manoeuvres were undoubtedly part of the wider consultation process, they nonetheless highlighted the highly institutionalised resistance to change from among the state actors managing the administration of SC, ST and OBC provisions. Indeed, the MSJE, notwithstanding its considerable experience in policy formation in the subject, remained reluctant to lead on the matter.

Perhaps because of the sensitivities around the subject, or because of the reluctance to openly oppose the claims of poor religious minorities, the annual reports and official documents of the institutionalised caste lobbies—NCSC, NCST, NCBC—are largely devoid of any serious debate on the matter;[22] and the NCM's reports provide only fragmentary comments on the policy process.[23] However, the one exception to the rule is the NCBC annual report for 2010–2011: this report provides a damning critique of the *RMCR* and questions the Commission's competence to make the recommendations that it did (NCBC 2011: 65–80). It challenged the proposal that religious minorities, especially Muslims, be brought into the net of reservations as an effort to 'rewrite Article 16 (4) of the Constitution of India' (ibid.: 79). Reconfirming caste as the primary signifier of backwardness, the NCBC rejected the *RMCR*'s contention that backwardness be defined primarily with reference to a uniform criterion in which caste and religion are neutral. Indeed, in reconfirming the principles of the constitutional settlement, the NCBC asserted:

> Uniform criteria cannot be evolved for the reason that different considerations come into play in determining the social backwardness among SCs/STs and OBCs. SCs are those who suffered the indignity of 'untouchability'. Large sections of STs are far removed from civilisation. OBCs suffer from social backwardness. (Ibid.: 71)

---

[21] Ibid.

[22] There was no discussion of reservations for Dalit Christians and Dalit Muslims in these reports. The NCBC views on the provision of sub-quotas for poor Christians and Muslims, with the exception of 2010–2011 report, are largely silent.

[23] Remarkably, only the recommendation sections of annual reports are available online (see ncm.nic.in/NCM_Recommendations.html). In reference to the reservation issue, the annual report of 2008–2009 recommends that 'reservation for Dalit Christians and Dalit Muslims at par with SCs/STs should be given', but without any enforcing mechanism or detailed analysis of the policy process that had failed to produce such an outcome. (NCM 2009: 44). Other annual reports do not discuss reservations.

For the NCBC, the essential signifier of backwardness was the 'social inequality' arising from caste that has been established in last three millennia (ibid.: 67–68). In rejecting in total the *RMCR* recommendations, the NCBC annual report justified its response in drawing on the constitutional settlement, its affirmation in the *Indra Sawhney* case and, tellingly, the dissenting note of Asha Das to the *RMCR* which rejected the deletion of 'religion' from the Constitution (SC) Order of 1950 (ibid.: 80).

The NCBC statement is remarkable not only as a defence of an institutionalised caste lobby's interests but also because of its opposition to a contemporary concept of social justice for *all*. The idea of 'different considerations' underpinning 'competing equalities' which the NCBC supported was, in many ways, at the heart of the historical path dependence that had solidified around socio-economically disadvantaged castes. Indeed, the NCBC reacted with hostility to the *RMCR*'s suggestion that SCs, STs and OBCs had developed 'vested interests' in 'backwardness' in the ever-increasing list of these categories that were included in reservations. Such an observation, the NCBC pithily observed, was 'a sweeping criticism lacking in particulars and without any objectively verifiable data' (ibid.: 68).

The DoPT (in instructions through the MPPGP), another important actor in employment policy, was even less visible in this process. On 10 August 2011, the Minister of Personnel, Public Grievances and Pensions stated in the Lok Sabha that reservation for minorities in central and state governments was under consideration but that it was not possible to fix a time for taking a decision.[24] Yet, apart from this statement, the MPPGP deliberately remained in the background, not because it was unfamiliar with the policymaking process on the subject, but because their silence appeared to be directed at protecting the interests of SCs, STs and OBCs.[25] Until the DoPT circulated the Office Memorandum, the MPPGP avoided making official announcements or taking a lead on policy options.

---

[24] *LSD*, 10 August 2011.
[25] Interestingly, the Ministry of Personnel, Public Grievances and Pensions launched a special recruitment scheme to fill vacant reserved posts in government jobs for SCs, STs (2004) and OBCs (2008). Before the launch of this scheme, the Minister of Personnel, Public Grievances and Pensions made a careful review of the SC, ST and OBC employment data and directed the DoPT to provide ministries and departments with specific guidelines for implementation of this scheme (*Hindustan Times* 2011). This initiative is examined later in the chapter.

During this process the MoMA also avoided clearly stating its position on the matter. Only a few months before the Uttar Pradesh legislative assembly elections in 2012, the PMO asked the MoMA to draft a formal proposal for job quotas for Muslims within the OBC sub-quota for consideration by the Cabinet Committee on Political Affairs (*Financial Express* 2011). The MoMA's public position at the time was that it wanted 8.4 per cent of the OBC quota for minorities (*Indian Express* 2011), but it was reluctant to lead on the matter because of its cautious nature and because employment fell under the jurisdiction of the MPPGP. Furthermore, any such change required an amendment to the central OBC list, necessitating consultations with the MSJE. Given these powerful institutional players, the MoMA's ability to lead and coordinate was heavily compromised. Salman Khurshid had admitted that his ministry had evolved into a 'letter-writing ministry', constantly seeking feedback from and consultation with the other ministries and relevant institutions.[26] Khurshid's successor, K. Rahman Khan, also pointed out that the fractured system on minority issues hinders the MoMA from developing and implementing policy.[27]

Although these structural constraints certainly impacted the work of the MoMA, the ministers in charge failed to build a momentum for the policy. Meetings of the Consultative Committee on Minority Affairs in Parliament, for instance, were limited: there was no meeting in 2008–2009, a sole meeting in 2009–2010, a relative flurry of activity in 2010–2011 when the Committee convened on four occasions, a halving of the frequency of meetings in 2011–2012 and a final outburst of enthusiasm in 2012–2013, when four meetings took place.[28] Some of these meetings, for example in 2009–2010 and 2010–2011, were held in conjunction with the Ministry of Corporate Affairs. Employment was not on the agenda. Rather, they focused on the MSDP and scholarship schemes.[29] While it is possible that the Ministry of Parliamentary Affairs did attempt to allocate time to the MoMA, or that the minority issue was sidelined because of pressing parliamentary business, the MoMA itself

---

[26] Abusaleh Shariff confirmed Khurshid's remark in the interview, 13 February 2013, New Delhi.
[27] K. Rahman Khan, interview, 12 February 2013, New Delhi. See also Centre for Equity Studies (2012: xix) and Z. Hasan (2012: 172).
[28] See annual reports of the Ministry of Parliamentary Affairs (2009: 31–32, 2010: 86, 2011: 86, 2012: 90, 2013: 103).
[29] In any consultative committee meeting the issue of employment was never discussed.

expended little effort to increase the frequency of meetings of the Consultative Committee on Minority Affairs, or explore other options by holding cross-party forums in which MPs, ministers and senior government officers could discuss policy formulation and implementation. It appears in the absence of a strong lead from the MoMA, the government ultimately opted for a lower percentage of reservations for minorities at 4.5 per cent of the OBC quota.

The policymaking process in the final stages remains obscure. On 7 December 2011, it was noted in the Rajya Sabha that the percentage of quota for minorities was still 'in the domain of inter-ministerial consultations'.[30] However, the speed with which the policy was formulated, and without a parliamentary debate, indicates that whatever inter-ministerial policy consultation took place they were cursory. The decision was contrary to the MoMA's earlier proposal of 8.4 per cent, and allegedly more in line with the findings of the Mandal Commission than that of the *RMCR* (*Indian Express* 2012b). This drastic reduction was both a reflection of the serious political opposition to such a proposal and the UPA's desire to pursue 'symbolic implementation' in the face of powerful institutionalised resistance from SC, ST and OBC interests.

Decision-making

On 22 December 2011, the UPA government circulated an Office Memorandum to all ministries and departments stating that with effect from 1 January 2012 the existing 27 per cent quota for OBCs would have a sub-quota of 4.5 per cent for Socially and Educationally Backward Classes (SEBCs) belonging to minorities, as defined in Section 2(c) of the National Commission for Minorities Act, 1992 (Department of Personnel and Training 2011). Announced on the eve of the Uttar Pradesh assembly polls, the decision was universally derided. The BJP called it a 'dangerous political game', and the CPI(M) and SP condemned it as 'most inadequate' and 'tokenism' (*Times of India* 2011b). Since 35 Muslim groups in the OBC category were already entitled to reservations, amounting to 2–3 per cent under the 27 per cent OBC quota, the creation of a 4.5 per cent sub-quota for 'all minorities' replacing this existing entitlement potentially threatened to undermine the existing provision for Muslims because other SEBCs belonging to minorities, especially Christians and Sikhs, educationally outperformed Muslims. In its

---

[30] *RSD*, 7 December 2011.

haste to exploit the announcement for political advantage, the irony of this outcome was lost on the UPA.

The Muslim community itself was divided over the issue. While some activists supported the move, others, particularly those in states in the south, where Muslims have been included in OBC category since the pre-Mandal period, expressed exasperation at the centre's decision and held that the most privileged among the community, 'the creamy layer', would benefit (*Milli Gazette* 2011; *Times of India* 2011c). Asaduddin Owaisi, President of the All India Majlis-e-Ittehadul Muslimeen and MP from Hyderabad, maintained that the move was in the right direction towards more specific quotas for Muslims.[31] Similarly, Zoya Hasan, a leading academic and policymaker, argued that the institutional bias, institutional discrimination and institutional prejudice against Muslims in India made reservation necessary, and the government decision gave Muslims a better option, despite the very small percentage.[32] A leading member of the NCM, however, was more concerned about a more fundamental issue: he was in favour of de-linking SC status from a narrow definition of Hindu disadvantaged castes, so that poor Christians and Muslims could be brought under the category, but considered the UPA's effort too little to effectively address Muslim under-representation in government employment. While it was right to include poor Christians and Muslims in the definition of SCs and STs, he insisted, as caste discrimination was rooted in tradition, not religion, the real issue was the exclusion of a large number of backward Muslims from the OBC list. There was, in short, a need for a comprehensive and systematic restructuring of the Muslim OBC list.[33]

However, the government plan soon faced opposition from the Election Commission for violating its Code of Conduct. The Commission directed that the sub-quota should not be implemented in poll-bound states (Goa, Punjab, Uttarakhand, Uttar Pradesh and Manipur) until after the elections (*Times of India* 2012a). Subsequently, the Andhra Pradesh High Court struck down the reservation in government jobs on the grounds that it had been carved out in a 'casual manner', and that an Office Memorandum based on religious lines was not an 'intelligible consideration' (*NDTV* 2012). The Court held that the central government had violated articles 15(1) and 16(2) of the Constitution and failed to prove that religious minorities are homogeneous or

---

[31] Asaduddin Owaisi, interview, 6 March 2013, New Delhi.
[32] Zoya Hasan, interview, 11 March 2013, New Delhi.
[33] Wajahat Habibullah, interview, 12 February 2013, New Delhi.

more backward, hence deserving of 'special treatment' (ibid.). In response, the government filed an appeal to the Supreme Court, but this was rejected on three counts: that the Office Memorandum issued by the central government had no legal support; that the government had failed to produce data to back up its decision; *and that no policy consultation had been conducted with relevant statutory bodies such as the NCBC and NCM* (ibid.; *Indian Express* 2012b).

The Supreme Court requested the government to submit relevant supporting documents to explain how it had reached the figure of 4.5 per cent. These documents, including the *SCR*, extracts of the *RMCR*, and the *Mandal Commission Report*, were submitted in response. However, despite the Attorney General's assertion that the 4.5 per cent sub-quota was based on the calculations of the *Mandal Commission Report*, the Supreme Court refused to stay the Andhra Pradesh High Court's order. The wording in the Office Memorandum, '4.5 per cent sub-quota for socially and educationally backward communities belonging to religious minorities', was interpreted as violating the Constitution by making religion the basis of classification. In spite of Khurshid's argument that the sub-quota was based on the backwardness of a minority group, not on religion (Pandey 2013), and the Solicitor General's efforts to suggest that the sub-quota was not for all religious minorities but aimed at the lowest ranks of Christian or Muslim converts (*Indian Express* 2012c), the Supreme Court rejected that stand on the grounds that it was still difficult to prove *'this particular population is poorer than the rest of the OBCs'* (ibid., emphasis added).

In the interviews conducted during fieldwork, some leading office holders suggested that the government intentionally fielded inadequate counsel in its defence.[34] While this charge is difficult to prove, the post-verdict statements appeared to confirm the belief that the government was resigned to the outcome. Three months later, Khurshid was still expressing optimism that 'when the constitutional bench [of the Supreme Court] takes it [the case] over, I am very hopeful that we will get some relief' (*Zee News* 2012). In October 2012, following a Cabinet reshuffle, Khurshid was replaced by K. Rahman Khan at the MoMA. On taking office, the new Minister reaffirmed his commitment to the 4.5 per cent sub-quota, and referred to the Andhra Pradesh High Court's judgment as a 'misunderstanding'. He insisted, 'The court has not rejected the quota ... [it] has only said that the procedure adopted to ascertain backwardness is not satisfactory' (*Outlook* 2012b). Insisting that reservation

---

[34] Owaisi, interview, 6 March 2013, New Delhi.

is a 'constitutional right', he also affirmed support for the inclusion of Dalit Christians and Dalit Muslims in the SC category, but admitted that 'the government has left it to the court to decide ... So let us wait for the Supreme Court order' (ibid.).

Post-judicial intervention

Judicial intervention, both by the Supreme Court and the Andhra Pradesh High Court, confirmed the conventional view that the judiciary was inclined to take a conservative interpretation of any new proposal that challenged the constitutional settlement.[35] The UPA's efforts to apply the 'Andhra Pradesh model' were unable—both in Andhra Pradesh and nationally—to overcome institutionalised opposition to reservations for minorities.[36] At the same time, the commitment of the UPA to do so was, by this point, open to doubt. That the UPA government appeared to be engaged in 'symbolic implementation' is confirmed by a former senior member of the Ranganath Misra Commission who recalled:

> We submitted our report in May 2007, and nearly 6 years later, in fact 2 days ago [18 February 2013], I received a phone call from the former deputy secretary of the commission. He phoned me and said, 'Sir, we have met the Minister of Minority Affairs and he wants some clarification of our report.' Six years after, the new Minister of Minority Affairs [K. Rahman Khan] is seeking clarification about the report on what ground the recommendation of this report was made! I was very upset and furious. I said: "Where was the Minister of Minority Affairs sleeping all these days? Justice Ranganath Misra is dead, he is not available, Anil Wilson, who was an education member, is also dead. If he really wanted to seek the clarification, the minister could have called me or Mohinder Singh. Why should I reply to you?' Look what is happening. Six years after, they are asking me for clarification about the report. So they have no intention of taking any action on it. They are just beating about the bush.[37]

---

[35] For judicial resistance in the interpretation of minority rights, see Heredia (2012, esp. ch. 5).
[36] Interestingly, the efforts of the Andhra Pradesh Congress government to establish reservations for Muslims in employment and education were rejected by the Andhra Pradesh High Court on three occasions between 2004 and 2010.
[37] Mahmood, interview, 20 February 2013, Noida.

The UPA government showed a certain degree of passivity in allowing the Supreme Court verdict to block further movement on reservation for minorities. While the Supreme Court judgment clearly invalidated the *RMCR* suggestion that a constitutional amendment was unnecessary for such reservation, the UPA failed to build upon the creative proposals in the *RMCR* or create a climate in which a constitutional amendment, or the Supreme Court's reversal of its decisions, could have succeeded.

Minister K. Rahman Khan insisted that constitutional change was a necessary requirement for progress on reservation. As he stated in an interview:

> My opinion on the *RMCR* is that it is difficult to implement. In the present constitutional mechanism it is not possible. The report recommended 10 per cent for all and 5 per cent for particular backward people ... Now the Supreme Court verdict is that reservation should not be more than 50 per cent. How do you compromise this? We cannot implement this because of Constitution. We are not in the position to amend the Constitution because we don't have majority. What is recommended should happen but if government has to adopt it ... it is not necessary that all the recommendations should be implemented.[38]

This skillful blame displacement was also apparent in the Lok Sabha on 22 November 2012 in response to Shiv Sena and BJP interventions about the 4.5 per cent ruling.[39] Khan declined to comment directly, stating only that the 'Supreme Court observed that since similar issues were pending consideration before the Constitutional Bench, the matters concerning the 4.5 per cent reservation for minorities be tagged along with those matters. The matter is presently *sub-judice*'.[40] In March 2013, at a National Editors' Conference, Khan again sought to strike an optimistic note, referring to the Karnataka and Kerala quota systems and claiming that the government was 'trying to expedite the matter' (*Indian Express* 2013c). And in June 2013, at a conference in Jaipur on the *SCR*, both Khurshid and Khan expressed their desire to ensure the provision of the 4.5 per cent sub-quota for Muslims. Khan stated that the central government was willing to put it before the Supreme Court, while Khurshid added that '[the government] will try to convince the

---

[38] Khan, interview, 12 February 2013, New Delhi.
[39] *LSD*, Question No. 95 (22 November 2012), 27.
[40] Minister Khan's Answer to Question no. 95, 'Reservation for minorities', *Lok Sabha Q&A*, 22 November 2012.

Constitutional Bench of the Supreme Court that the sub-quota is not religion-based, but is on the basis of backwardness', and 'reservation is not granted to a particular caste, but if all people of that particular caste are backward, they can be granted reservation' (*Hindustan Times* 2013a; *Outlook* 2013a). The UPA government, before its demise in May 2014, failed to take any action either to pursue the matter in the Supreme Court or to explore alternative avenues to resolve the issue.

Implementation and Evaluation

This section discusses the issues related to public access to data on minorities, with particular reference to Muslim employment in the public sector. It then reviews the data provided by the MoMA on its websites to examine patterns of change in employment in central ministries and departments between 2006 and 2013. Finally, we reflect on the positive action taken by the Minister of Railways, Mamata Banerjee, in West Bengal between 2009 and 2011.

Data on Muslims in central government employment: public access and denial

Most of the affirmative action programmes launched in pursuit of *SCR*'s recommendations included monitoring mechanisms. Despite these publicly declared policy instruments, systematic collection, publication and use of monitoring data on employment have yet to become routine features of policy.[41] Furthermore, the MoMA, the DoPT and the Planning Commission (in its report of the steering committee on empowering minorities, Eleventh Five-Year Plan report and Twelfth Five-Year Plan report), have not clarified whether minority members have been included in selection committees, whether there has been any improvement in the proportion of minorities in Group C and D posts, in which ministries and departments the proportion has increased, decreased or remained the same, the reasons for such variations, or how the monitoring system has been used. As Khan acknowledged, monitoring of data on employment is yet to become a priority:

> The problem is that the monitoring is left to a certain committee which has no time to look into it. At the state level, the Chief Secretary is the chairman of monitoring committee. They have no time, they have no

---

[41] The paucity and unavailability of government data is also highlighted by Omar Khalidi (2006: 3–6; 2010: 42).

interest. They already have their own work. Monitoring is extra work. So they may monitor and they may not.[42]

Given this haphazard process of policy formation and implementation, therefore, these processes have yet to become routinised and in fact fully accepted within the civil service.

These shortcomings were also demonstrated during fieldwork. Most respondents were unaware of such data; some believed that the data might have been collected but was not generated into a computable form because of its potential political ramifications. In an interview with Minister Khan at his residence, it was disclosed that time-series data on employment of Muslims does exist, and that the proportion of Muslims in government employment has increased.[43] However, he failed to keep the subsequent appointment at which he had promised to provide these data.[44] Instead, his private secretary

---

[42] Khan, interview, 12 February 2013, New Delhi.
[43] 'Muslims get more employment. And we have year to year data that the level of Muslims is increasing. It is just 4–5 per cent, very small though,' Khan, interview.
[44] In parenthesis, it is worth recalling the Minister's response to my request for the data on Muslim employment. The Minister claimed to have specific data on 'Muslim' recruitment, and agreed to provide it if I visited his office the following day. We agreed on a definite time for the meeting, and the Minister assured me that he would inform his secretary about my visit. However, when I arrived at the Ministry reception the next day, at the appointed time, my name was not on the list of visitors. After some persuasion, the reception officer allowed me to make a call to the secretary of the MoMA, who checked the Minister's schedule for the day but found no record of the promised meeting. After waiting for half an hour outside the building, I managed to get into the MoMA office and once again had to explain to the secretary about my visit and what the Minister had promised the previous day. The secretary informed me that the Minister was in a meeting, but said that if I waited for about an hour until it finished, he would speak to the Minister to check what I had told him. After an hour, the secretary told me that the Minister had returned to his residence. As I was sitting on a sofa right next to the door of the Minister's office, it was impossible that he could have left without being noticed. The secretary introduced the private secretary to the Minister to discuss the data the Minister had promised. However, although I explained what data the Minister had claimed to have, the private secretary seemed very cautious and asked me to write down what specific data I needed. When I asked whether there is data on central government employment of Muslims, he insisted that it is on the website, and to my pointing out that the data reported there is not specific

directed me to the MoMA website which carries general—and not Muslim, or any other community specific—data on minorities in central government employment. In the absence of Muslim-specific data, we have focused our analysis on the MoMA website data. Such an exercise is clearly limited but, nonetheless, highlights how this data is distorted, misrepresented and, at times, deliberately concealed from the public. It also illustrates some general trends of the representation of minorities within ministries, departments and public sector undertakings.

Since most ministries and departments failed to submit figures on the employment status of minorities every year from 2006 to 2013, or even at regular intervals, the MoMA data is not sequential. This raises a number of questions: Does non-presentation of data in a particular year mean there was no recruitment that year? Does the information exist, but has not been generated into presentable format? Did recruitment take place, but because minorities were not employed the relevant ministries and departments withheld the data? And was the data submitted but the MoMA deliberately avoided including ministries and departments with low recruitment of minorities in the data sheet? While it was not possible to get further confirmation of these concerns from the Minister, or other key informants, the unsystematic way in which the information has been presented publicly suggests such considerations required further investigation.

More worryingly, however, the data provided by ministries and departments is frequently incomplete. Each year's data specifies the total number of persons recruited and the number of minorities employed. Clearly, the total number of persons employed should be greater than the number of minorities employed. However, in some cases, ministries and departments have submitted data which claims that the number of minorities employed exceeds the total. Furthermore, what ought to be simple calculations are often incorrect. Taking ministries at random and checking whether the sum of the total number of people employed in Groups A, B, C and D matches with the total number presented by the government reveals several inaccuracies. Such misrepresentation might have originated from the original figure submitted by

---

to Muslims but includes all minorities, he responded: 'It must be there. You missed it.' He said that someone would contact me when the data was collected. But by the time I left Delhi, there had still been no contact from the MoMA. The Post-Sachar Evaluation Committee report (MoMA 2014) also confirms that no separate data for each religious community was available for their analysis.

the ministry or department, or with the official who worked on generating the data sheet, but the failure to verify or cross-check these figures before placing them in the public domain appears surprising.[45]

These errors were also compounded by technical mistakes: in the data for 2007–2008, for instance, the first row of the first page of the data sheet is half missing, because the sheet was unskillfully uploaded onto the MoMA website. Fortunately, as the first row includes the names of ministries and departments, it is still recognisable. But this error is repeated in the final page of the 2007–2008 data sheet, where the last row is missing, so that it is not possible to see the number of minorities recruited. Had the ministries and departments monitored the aggregate data file to check whether their own employment data was correctly presented, these mistakes could have been easily corrected. If this is an indication of deliberate data distortion and evasion, then once again questions arise as to whether minorities were recruited in the ministries and departments included in this page, or whether other considerations came into play in not reporting the numbers. Remarkably, neither the Muslim NGOs active in this policy area nor the Muslim MPs have noticed these glaring errors—an indication of not only the weak monitoring regime but also the lack of development of an organised lobby campaigning for such change.

Finally, the MoMA's data sheet for 2006–2013 refers to 'minority persons employed during the year', without defining 'minority'—Buddhists, Christians, Jains, Muslims, Sikhs and Parsis, and whether or not they were recruited through the reservations. While the proportion of Christians and Muslims entitled to reservations is relatively small (via the OBC route), Buddhists and Sikhs, who are part of the SC category, could potentially distort the overall figures. If the Buddhists and Sikhs, who are already entitled to reservation, are nevertheless reflected in the figure provided by the MoMA, the real proportion of employment of minorities who are not entitled to reservation would be much lower. These intra-minority factors are not inconsequential: Muslim groups have long complained of being squeezed out of minority representation

---

[45] To name a few, in 2006–2007 data, the Ministry of Urban Development stated that out of 53 people recruited to Group D, 101 were members of minorities. In 2010–2011, the Ministry of Youth Affairs and Sports reported 19 minorities recruited out of a total recruitment of 12 for Group A, and 4 minorities were employed in Group D during a period when no recruitment took place in this group. Also in 2012–2013, in the Ministry of Coal while no person was recruited in Group A, 1 minority person was recruited.

in employment and other sectors by more educationally advanced minorities (Buddhists, Christians and Sikhs).

MoMA, minorities' employment data and monitoring

The data available on the MoMA website covers the period from 2006 to 2013. Of the 85 ministries and departments recorded, only 25 reported employment status in a regular sequence. These 25 were selected for detailed analysis, and ministries and departments that returned 'Nil' were excluded on the grounds that this could mean ambiguity, evasion or no recruitment. The proportion of minorities employed in each ministry was also calculated for the various grades (Groups A, B, C and D inclusive) to assess whether recruitment of minorities is still concentrated in lower grades.[46] The 25 ministries and departments were further divided into high (more than 10 per cent), medium (5 to 10 per cent) or low (below 5 per cent) recruiters of minorities. For detailed assessment, 4–5 ministries and departments were selected for each category.[47] A number of observations can be made from this data.

First, among the high recruiting departments (Table 4.1), in 3 of the 5 departments and ministries the average representation of minorities increased between 2006 and 2013. Recruitment in Agriculture and Cooperation was exceptionally high in 2006–2007 at 45 per cent. Conversely, in the Ministry of Coal no minority candidate was recruited in any group over the period. In general, recruitment of minorities was across the four grades, without noticeable concentration in the low grades (C and D). It is worth noting,

---

[46] The *SCR* had concluded that the employment of Muslims in ministries and departments was 'abysmally low at all levels' and 'the share of Muslims increases only marginally for lower level jobs but even in group D employment (which requires only a low level of education), the share is only about 5 per cent' (*SCR* 2006: 167).

[47] Under the Central Civil Services (Classification, Control and Appeal) Rules (1965) central civil posts are categorised into A, B, C and D according to pay scale. Group A carries 'a pay or a scale of pay with a maximum of not less than Rs. 13,500'. The range for Group B is not less than Rs. 9,000 but less than Rs. 13,500; for Group C, a pay with a maximum of over Rs. 4,000 but less than Rs. 9,000; and for Group D a pay with a maximum of which is Rs. 4,000 or less. In general, employment in Groups A and B requires a high level of education, while Group C and D posts are more manual and technical, with low educational requirements. See dopt.gov.in/ccs-cca-rules-1965.

however, that as these functional departments and ministries require a high level of educational attainment, and other things being equal, Muslims are likely to have been outnumbered by other minorities, especially Christians and Sikhs, though as we have seen previously, non-OBC Muslims do have representation within India's elite services such as the IAS and IPS. It is also noteworthy that all departments and ministries witnessed a decline in minority recruitment in 2009–2010, an election year. Overall, within the recruiting ministries and departments, the representation of minorities was still below the proportion of the minorities' share of the total population, with the highest figure being 14.79 per cent (Ministry of Commerce and Industry).

In the medium ranking ministries and departments (Table 4.2), the overall recruitment of minorities in all categories was insignificant. The two biggest recruiters, Post and the Railways, witnessed a significant shift, with the latter's average of minority employees increasing from 2.67 per cent in 2006 to 12.54 per cent in 2012. Numerically, most of this increase was in grades C and D, though the minority as a proportion of all higher grades also appear to have increased. As we shall see below, executive action by the Minister of Railways, Mamata Banerjee, seems to have contributed to the development. Some results, on the other hand, may be misleading or of little significance. For example, the Ministry of Parliamentary Affairs only recruited two minority candidates during the period which, due to low total recruitment, represents a large percentage increase in minority appointments.

In the low recruiting departments and ministries (Table 4.3) the average increase over the period was negligible. The data demonstrates that the Departments of Corporate Affairs and Biotechnology, and the Ministry of Overseas Indian Affairs are less likely to recruit minorities. In the Ministry of Housing and Urban Poverty Alleviation, apart from 2006–2007, when the employment of 16 minority candidates led to a large proportionate increase, the representation of minorities is very low: of 284 candidates recruited in 2011–2012, none were from the minorities. Given that most Muslims reside in urban areas, the lack of minority employment, particularly in Groups C and D, suggests that the 'special consideration' required by the Office Memorandum (2007) had not been put into practice. In the Department of Corporate Affairs, no minority individuals were employed in Groups C and D in 2006–2007, in Groups B and D in 2008–2009, in B, C and D in 2009–2010 and in B and C in 2010–2011. The Department of Biotechnology presents a similar picture: in 2008–2009, in a total recruitment of 35, no minority candidate was employed. Between 2006 and 2013, in the Ministry of Overseas Indian

Table 4.1 Central government and departments with high recruitment of minorities, 2006–2013

	2006–2007			2007–2008			2008–2009			2009–2010			2010–2011			2011–2012			2012–2013			A*
	Total number of persons employed	Total number of minorities employed	Proportion of minorities employed	Total number of persons employed	Total number of minorities employed	Proportion of minorities employed	Total number of persons employed	Total number of minorities employed	Proportion of minorities employed	Total number of persons employed	Total number of minorities employed	Proportion of minorities employed	Total number of persons employed	Total number of minorities employed	Proportion of minorities employed	Total number of persons employed	Total number of minorities employed	Proportion of minorities employed	Total number of persons employed	Total number of minorities employed	Proportion of minorities employed	
M/o Commerce and Industry, D/o Commerce			10.62			10.11			16.75			14.21			21.27			17.62			12.95	14.79
Group A	21	2	9.52	23	2	8.70	26	4	15.38	14	3	21.43	42	19	45.24	41	10	24.39	138	18	13.04	
B	32	4	12.50	65	10	15.38	74	14	18.92	54	5	9.26	86	18	20.93	58	10	17.24	103	14	13.59	
C	56	3	5.36	62	2	3.23	68	9	13.24	89	17	19.10	112	17	15.18	151	22	14.57	172	21	12.21	
D	51	8	15.69	28	4	14.29	23	5	21.74	40	3	7.50	28	3	10.71	5	1	20.00	4	1	25	
D/o Information Technology			7.33			32.78			11.07			9.09			12.03			11.74			9.38	13.35
Group A	192	13	6.77	260	73	28.08	179	21	11.73	40	3	7.50	82	13	15.85	133	11	8.27	57	5	8.77	
B	208	18	8.65	43	22	51.16	51	8	15.69	364	32	8.79	115	11	9.57	328	45	13.72	64	6	9.38	
C	49	2	4.08	55	21	37.50	66	4	6.06	20	2	10.00	65	8	12.31	84	8	9.52	39	4	10.26	
D	1	0	0	4	3	75.00	11	1	9.09	5	2	40.00	4	0	0	0	0	0	0	0	0	
M/o Coal			0			20			26.67			3.33			25			0			16.67	13.10
Group A	5	0	0	0	0	0	0	0	0	0	0	0	3	1	33.33	0	0	0	0	1	0	
B	17	0	0	0	0	0	0	0	0	0	0	0	0	0	0	0	0	0	0	0	0	
C	16	0	0	4	1	25.00	14	4	28.57	2	0	0	1	0	0	3	0	0	11	1	9.09	
D	3	0	0	1	0	0	0	0	0	28	1	3.57	0	0	0	1	0	0	13	2	15.38	

(Contd.)

(Contd.)

	2006–2007			2007–2008			2008–2009			2009–2010			2010–2011			2011–2012			2012–2013			A*
	Total number of persons employed	Total number of minorities employed	Proportion of minorities employed	Total number of persons employed	Total number of minorities employed	Proportion of minorities employed	Total number of persons employed	Total number of minorities employed	Proportion of minorities employed	Total number of persons employed	Total number of minorities employed	Proportion of minorities employed	Total number of persons employed	Total number of minorities employed	Proportion of minorities employed	Total number of persons employed	Total number of minorities employed	Proportion of minorities employed	Total number of persons employed	Total number of minorities employed	Proportion of minorities employed	
D/o Agriculture and Cooperation			45.00			13.57			7.02			6.98			5.64			6.55	No recruitment			12.11
Group A	13	12	92.31	28	7	25.00	5	0	0	26	2	7.69	46	4	8.70	33	2	6.06				
B	43	20	46.51	47	3	6.38	22	2	9.09	25	1	4.00	147	9	6.12	26	4	15.38				
C	26	12	46.15	62	9	14.52	22	5	22.73	27	1	3.70	63	2	3.17	101	4	3.96				
D	18	1	5.56	3	0	0	8	0	0	8	0	0	10	0	0	8	1	12.50				
D/o Space			14.66			16.24			13.21			10.95			9.92			10.56	No recruitment			10.79
Group A	245	24	9.80	323	44	13.62	391	52	13.30	470	49	10.43	381	35	9.19	364	23	6.32				
B	45	12	26.67	123	33	26.83	175	16	9.14	130	8	6.15	155	14	9.03	107	11	10.28				
C	194	33	17.01	170	22	12.94	322	48	14.91	228	34	14.91	210	25	11.90	381	56	14.70				
D	14	4	28.57	12	3	25.00	8	2	25.00	5	1	20.00	0	0	0	0	0	0				

Source: Ministry of Minority Affairs website, compiled by the author.

Notes: Unit: percentage. A*: Average.

Table 4.2 Central government and departments with medium recruitment of minorities, 2006–2013

	2006–2007			2007–2008			2008–2009			2009–2010			2010–2011			2011–2012			2012–2013			A*
	Total number of persons employed	Total number of minorities employed	Proportion of minorities employed	Total number of persons employed	Total number of minorities employed	Proportion of minorities employed	Total number of persons employed	Total number of minorities employed	Proportion of minorities employed	Total number of persons employed	Total number of minorities employed	Proportion of minorities employed	Total number of persons employed	Total number of minorities employed	Proportion of minorities employed	Total number of persons employed	Total number of minorities employed	Proportion of minorities employed	Total number of persons employed	Total number of minorities employed	Proportion of minorities employed	
M/o Women and Child Development			0			20			16.67			0			5			15.15	No recruitment			8.12
Group A	0	0	0	1	0	0	0	0	0	0	0	0	2	0	0	2	0	0				
B	3	0	0	0	0	0	0	0	0	1	0	0	7	1	14.29	10	1	10.00				
C	2	0	0	3	1	33.33	3	1	33.33	0	0	0	7	0	0	15	3	20.00				
D	2	0	0	1	0	0	3	0	0	0	0	0	4	0	0	6	1	16.67				
D/o Post			7.60			9.65			6.36			8.01			8.27			8.11			8.55	8.08
Group A	4	0	0	3	1	33.33	5	0	0	0	0	0	10	1	10.00	Not specified			20	1	5	
B	47	1	2.13	92	11	11.96	40	2	5.00	73	15	20.55	48	7	14.58				147	18	12.24	
C	4,382	348	7.94	4,682	425	9.08	2,419	157	6.49	7,473	589	7.88	14,840	1,175	7.92				2,642	222	8.40	
D	610	37	6.07	581	80	13.77	302	17	5.63	152	13	8.55	744	110	14.78				1,241	112	9.02	
D/o Expenditure			25.00			0			0			13.33			2.04			6.6	No recruitment			6.71
Group A	0	0	0	6	0	0	0	0	0	9	2	22.22	3	0	0	30	3	10.00				
B	0	0	0	2	0	0	4	0	0	0	0	0	34	1	2.94	49	2	4.08				
C	4	1	25.00	1	0	0	4	0	0	6	0	0	12	0	0	27	2	7.41				
D	0	0	0	1	0	0	0	0	0	0	0	0	0	0	0	0	0	0				

(*Contd.*)

(Contd.)

	2006–2007			2007–2008			2008–2009			2009–2010			2010–2011			2011–2012			2012–2013			A*
	Total number of persons employed	Total number of minorities employed	Proportion of minorities employed	Total number of persons employed	Total number of minorities employed	Proportion of minorities employed	Total number of persons employed	Total number of minorities employed	Proportion of minorities employed	Total number of persons employed	Total number of minorities employed	Proportion of minorities employed	Total number of persons employed	Total number of minorities employed	Proportion of minorities employed	Total number of persons employed	Total number of minorities employed	Proportion of minorities employed	Total number of persons employed	Total number of minorities employed	Proportion of minorities employed	
M/o Railways			2.67			6.31			8.32			6.55			8.72			12.54	Not specified			6.44
Group A	302	13	4.30	17	5	29.41	59	7	11.86	33	3	9.09	28	3	10.71	955	61	6.39				
B	0	0	0	450	49	10.89	472	90	19.07	421	35	8.31	422	41	9.72	434	59	13.59				
C	34,071	745	2.19	16,647	1,069	6.42	15,285	899	5.88	15,793	1,014	6.42	12,205	978	8.01	19,660	2,391	12.16				
D	20,111	698	3.47	19,239	1,172	6.09	20,397	2,016	9.88	9,374	653	6.97	5,596	569	10.17	7,036	1,010	14.35				
M/o Parliamentary Affairs																						
Group A	0	0	0	0	0	0	0	0	0	0	0	0	0	0	25	0	0	0	0	0	0	14.29
B	0	0	0	0	0	0	0	0	0	0	0	0	0	0	0	0	0	0	4	1	25	5.61
C	0	0	0	0	0	0	0	0	0	0	0	0	3	0	0	0	0	0	3	0	0	
D	0	0	0	0	0	0	0	0	0	0	0	0	1	1	100	0	0	0	0	0	0	

Source: Ministry of Minority Affairs website, compiled by the author.

Notes: Unit: percentage. A*: Average.

Table 4.3 Central government and departments with low recruitment of minorities, 2006–2013

	2006–2007			2007–2008			2008–2009			2009–2010			2010–2011			2011–2012			2012–2013			A*
	Total number of persons employed	Total number of minorities employed	Proportion of minorities employed	Total number of persons employed	Total number of minorities employed	Proportion of minorities employed	Total number of persons employed	Total number of minorities employed	Proportion of minorities employed	Total number of persons employed	Total number of minorities employed	Proportion of minorities employed	Total number of persons employed	Total number of minorities employed	Proportion of minorities employed	Total number of persons employed	Total number of minorities employed	Proportion of minorities employed	Total number of persons employed	Total number of minorities employed	Proportion of minorities employed	
M/o Housing and Urban Poverty Alleviation			25.40			8.33			0			0			0			0			0	4.82
Group A	29	2	6.90	12	1	8.33	1	0	0	2	0	0	2	0	0	2	1	0	1	0	0	
B	9	4	44.44	0	0	0	0	0	0	0	0	0	0	0	0	1	0	0	0	0	0	
C	9	8	88.89	0	0	0	0	0	0	0	0	0	0	0	0	147	0	0	0	0	0	
D	16	2	12.50	0	0	0	0	0	0	0	0	0	1	0	0	134	0	0	0	0	0	
D/o Corporate Affairs			4.82						0			6.45			1.96			14.07			5.71	4.72
Group A	39	1	2.56	0	0	0	0	0	0	29	4	13.79	69	2	2.90	21	1	4.76	44	3	6.82	
B	36	3	8.33	0	0	0	1	0	0	28	0	0	20	0	0	72	14	19.44	25	1	4	
C	4	0	0	0	0	0	0	0	0	1	0	0	13	0	0	82	11	13.41	1	0	0	
D	4	0	0	0	0	0	1	0	0	4	0	0	0	0	0	28	1	3.57	0	0	0	
D/o Biotechnology			5.26			2.44			0			10.53			1.38			5.62			5.36	4.37
Group A	15	1	6.67	22	0	0	19	0	0	11	0	0	88	10	11.36	52	3	5.77	34	4	11.76	
B	10	1	10.00	5	0	0	3	0	0	7	1	14.29	31	4	12.90	25	1	4.00	22	0	0	
C	14	0	0	14	1	7.14	9	0	0	20	3	15.00	37	6	16.22	12	1	8.33	10	1	10	
D	4	0	0	0	0	0	4	0	0	0	0	0	6	1	16.67	0	0	0	0	0	0	

(Contd.)

(Contd.)

	2006–2007			2007–2008			2008–2009			2009–2010			2010–2011			2011–2012			2012–2013			A*
	Total number of persons employed	Total number of minorities employed	Proportion of minorities employed	Total number of persons employed	Total number of minorities employed	Proportion of minorities employed	Total number of persons employed	Total number of minorities employed	Proportion of minorities employed	Total number of persons employed	Total number of minorities employed	Proportion of minorities employed	Total number of persons employed	Total number of minorities employed	Proportion of minorities employed	Total number of persons employed	Total number of minorities employed	Proportion of minorities employed	Total number of persons employed	Total number of minorities employed	Proportion of minorities employed	
M/o Overseas Indian Affairs																						
Group A	0	0	0	0	0	0	0	0	0	0	0	0	0	0	0	0	0	0	0	0	0	0
B	0	0	0	0	0	0	0	0	0	0	0	0	0	0	0	0	0	0	0	0	0	0
C	0	0	0	0	0	0	0	0	0	0	0	0	0	0	0	0	0	0	0	0	0	0
D	0	0	0	10	0	0	0	0	0	0	0	0	0	0	0	0	0	0	0	0	0	0

Source: Ministry of Minority Affairs website, compiled by the author.

Notes: Unit: percentage. A*: Average.

Affairs, over a period of seven years only 10 people were employed, none of whom belonged to minority groups. In brief, while the figures for recruitment to these departments and ministries were relatively low, the even lower or non-representation of minorities suggests positive action in recruitment to the central administration had made little impact.

Overall, the MoMA data does not support the assertion that the UPA's policies of positive action significantly improved the representation of minorities in public sector employment. Indeed, if overall minority representation did not increase, Muslim representation is also unlikely to have improved because even within this category Muslims have traditionally struggled to match the recruitment profile of other minorities. It would appear that in most cases 'special consideration' has been paid only in the constitution of selection committees (by including one minority member), but not in the actual recruitment of minorities itself.[48] Discriminatory recruitment practices continue at both central and state levels. For example, Maharashtra had one minority member on its selection boards but the level of Muslim representation has not increased. In the state, selection committees continue to insist that the Marathi language should be used in applications, thereby excluding local Muslims in Maharashtra who are mostly migrants from Uttar Pradesh and Bihar.[49] These cases prove that the inclusion of a minority member in selection boards is neither a necessary nor sufficient condition for improving the chances for employment of minority candidates. Rather, positive action has to be accompanied by a range of other measures—active monitoring, political support, institutional sympathy, a committed community/lobby behind the measure and, most importantly, a determination to address embedded cultures of resistance—if it is to be effective. Given the room for discretion in the use of positive action to promote better equal opportunities for minorities, it is perhaps unsurprising that these minorities seek reservations as the most effective way of improving their status.

Mamata Banerjee, the Railways and West Bengal: a successful model of positive action?

That the UPA policies on minorities, especially Muslims, could be turned into a potentially successful model of positive action is illustrated by the case of

---

[48] Habibullah, interview, 12 February 2013, New Delhi; see also the Post-Sachar Committee report (MoMA 2014: 122).
[49] Habibullah, interview, 12 February 2013, New Delhi.

Mamata Banerjee, the Minister of Railways (2009–2011), and later the Chief Minister of West Bengal. Minority employment in the Ministry of Railways witnessed a noticeable increase during her tenure. It is generally believed that Banerjee used executive discretion to push through measures aimed at the Muslim population in West Bengal, a state which had been governed by the Left Front—led by CPI(M) from 1977 to 2011 but one which the *SCR* found to have a particularly weak record in terms of minority public sector employment and service delivery. Accordingly, Banerjee, who was determined to build her constituency for the state elections in 2011, used the strength of her Trinamool Congress (TMC) 'in the national Parliament, the Lok Sabha, and [her] control of the Railway Ministry ... as platforms from which to display its commitment to addressing issues and grievances of concern to Muslim voters' (Nielsen 2011: 347). Measures used to increase employment of Muslims in the Ministry of Railways included advertising in Urdu newspapers; allowing candidates to take tests in Urdu; waiving 'the Railway Recruitment Board examination fee for applicants from minority backgrounds'; and increasing 'the frequency of trains in West Bengal to areas with high Muslim concentration' (ibid.: 361). There was a general anti-Left wave in the state, and the elections of 2011 brought Banerjee to power, in which the desertion of the Muslim vote from the CPI(M) played a pivotal role (ibid.).

It would be misleading, however, to interpret the Banerjee example as simply election-driven. She was not alone in promoting minority employment, on the eve of elections, as the Left Front also made extravagant promises to implement reservations for Muslims in the OBC quota, and took measures to effect this before the polls were scheduled (ibid.: 355–358). The institutionalised opposition to Banerjee's actions was somewhat blunted by decades of neglect of minorities' interest, the absence of a Dalit caste party in the state, *à la* BSP, and the fact that a large number of OBCs in the state were Muslims.[50] That the measures were taken at the level of the state, against a highly unpopular Marxist government, further undermined the institutionalised resistance against minorities. Hence, since the elections the TMC government has announced reservations for Muslims in employment

---

[50] OBCs are divided into two categories in West Bengal. OBC-A consists of more backward people, including 90 per cent of the state's Muslims, and OBC-B comprises backward Muslims and non-Muslims in the state who are better off than OBC-A. For a list of OBCs in the state, see wbxpress.com/list-other-backward-classes-west-bengal/.

and education but primarily by widening the inclusion of more Muslim groups within the OBC category rather than implementing the recommendations of the *RMCR*. In 2013, with the passing of the West Bengal State Higher Educational Institutions (Reservation in Admission) Act, more than 90 per cent of the state's Muslims are recognised as OBC, making them eligible for reservations in government jobs and higher education.[51]

Conclusion

This chapter has examined in detail the UPA's policy process aimed at increasing the Muslim presence in public sector employment. From the initial commitment of the government to support the recommendations of the *SCR*, to the later hesitancy and doubt over the recommendations of *RMCR*, the process was characterised by ambivalence, non-decisions and twin-tracking. From the limited evidence available in the public domain examined in this chapter, despite considerable efforts directed at positive action, the share of employment of Muslims in central government posts remains low, and is still considerably below the community's proportion of the population as a whole. This interpretation was supported by the government's own data which suggest an overall decline in minority recruitment to central government posts from 11.56 per cent in 2010–2011 to 6.89 per cent in 2012–2013.[52] Such an outcome is all the more surprising given that the positive action taken following the Office Memorandum (2007) was accompanied by a public announcement that 'special consideration' would be given to improve the under-representation of minorities in public sector employment. Evidently, the use of tried and tested policy instruments such as monitoring, targeting and regular reviews have yet to be firmly embedded and effectively utilised as tools of policy change.

It could be argued that this outcome was largely the result of the UPA's reluctance to implement the *SCR* and *RMCR* recommendations. In the face of strong opposition from the BJP and *Hindutva* forces against the recommendations of the *RMCR*—reservations for Muslims in the SC/OBC quotas—the government opted for 'symbolic implementation', or 'gesture

---

[51] Government of West Bengal, 'Circular' 2014. In 2012, the West Bengal state assembly passed a legislation, providing 17 per cent reservation for OBCs in state government jobs.

[52] Cited by Minister of State for Personnel, V. Narayanasamy, in reply to a Parliament question (*RSD*, 19 December 2013).

politics': appearing to pursue policies while recognising that they would be difficult if not impossible to implement. This approach was underpinned by political opposition to the measure within the Congress itself which feared it would undermine the foundational settlement by reducing the religious incentive to be a Hindu SC. But perhaps more importantly, the strongest opposition to the measure came from the Hindu SC/OBC institutionalised lobbies and their political and state interests. For example, the NCSC and NCBC viewed reservations for minorities as a zero-sum measure that struck at the heart of the foundational settlement closely identified with socially disadvantaged Hindu castes. Indeed, the judiciary's decision to reject reservations on the grounds of religion was the ultimate confirmation of the historically institutionalised approach to the subject.[53]

The UPA's policies on religious minorities can be further contrasted with its receptiveness to policy change on caste-based issues.[54] Analysts have

---

[53] Some studies attribute the low representation of Muslims in the civil service to the low level of participation of Muslim students in civil service examinations. In any case, such arguments merely push the issue back to deeper roots and constitute 'victim-blaming'. But this aspect is beyond the scope of this book (see Zaidi 2014: 23–25).

[54] In stark contrast, consistent efforts were made for SCs, STs and OBCs with similar policy instruments to monitor the employment status of these groups. For instance, the 'Brochure on Reservation for SC, ST, & Other Backward Classes in Services' provides detailed guidelines on how to fill reserved vacancies. It explains the recruitment process in detail, from advertising the post to reporting to the DoPT, with the number of vacancies reserved for SCs, STs and OBCs out of the total number of reserved seats. For example, it requires that whenever recruitment is to be made one single advertisement should be issued, specifying clearly the vacancies reserved for SCs, STs and OBCs. It also requires ministries and departments to send a requisition including the number of vacancies reserved for SCs, STs and OBCs out of the total number of vacancies. Hence, the ministries and departments must show that the number of vacancies reserved for SCs, STs and OBCs match the reservation quota fixed by government. If the number of SC/ST candidates is insufficient for the reserved posts, the DoPT requires the appointing authority to report the reserved vacancies to the Director of SC/ST Welfare in the states and Union Territories. The brochure also clearly states that 'where sufficient number of candidates belonging to SC/ST/OBC are not available to fill up the vacancies reserved for them in direct recruitment, the vacancies should not be filled by candidates not belonging to these communities'. Clearly, the de-reservation was systematically forbidden to ensure that benefit of

commented on how the government painstakingly sought to build a consensus on Mandal II—the imposition of reservations in higher education for OBCs (Z. Hasan 2009a: 110). As a result, the subsequent legal challenges were both limited and ineffectual. Similarly, the UPA was also favourably disposed to the BSP-sponsored Promotion Quota Bill (2012)—the Constitution (117th Amendment) Bill to provide quotas for SCs and STs in senior government promotions. This bill was brought in response to the High Court and Supreme Court decisions rejecting the Uttar Pradesh BSP government proposal to provide quotas for promotion for SCs and STs. In hindsight, though the bill lapsed and was not adopted by the Lok Sabha, the speed with which the government acted was not just the pay-off to the BSP for its support on the foreign direct investment vote, but an underlying demonstration of institutional consensus in favour of caste issues. Remarkably, while the 4.5 per cent sub-quota for minorities was still pending before the Supreme Court, the Congress continued to insist that '[the Promotion Quota Bill and *SCR*] are not contrary or contradictory' (*Outlook* 2012c).⁵⁵

---

reservation reaches the intended beneficiaries. The monitoring system is further confirmed by stating that every January appointing authorities are required to send SC/ST/OBC reports to ministries and departments, including the total number of employees and the number of SCs, STs and OBCs among them, and the representation of SCs, STs and OBCs in various levels. In addition, the guidelines specify the way in which the ministries and departments consolidate the reports received from appointing authorities and submit them to the DoPT by 31 March each year. The publication of such guidelines in a brochure provides a clear picture of who is responsible for collecting data, the date by which the data should be collected, how the data should be consolidated and the date for final submission. Hence, the DoPT has successfully provided directions for employment policy and practice with regard to SCs, STs and OBCs, and restricted as far as possible the potential for exercising discretionary power (Ministry of Personnel, Public Grievances and Pensions 2011a).

⁵⁵ The provision of promotion quotas for SCs and STs in high posts is in stark contrast to the state's approach to minorities. The SCs and STs have been entitled to reservation in promotion since 1954, and the quota was increased in the 1970s. The quota was to be discontinued after five years by the verdict of the Supreme Court in 1992, but the government amended the Constitution before the five year period ended, to continue to provide the quota, in 1995. In 2001, there was further amendment, using reservation to 'provide consequential seniority to SC and ST candidates promoted'. In 2006, the Supreme Court, in the case of *M. Nagaraj & Others vs Union of India & Others*, required the states to provide 'compelling

The uneven-handedness of the UPA's approach to the 'competing equalities', of caste and religious minorities, was further demonstrated during the debate on the Promotion Quota Bill. The Minister of Personnel, Public Grievances and Pensions asserted that there are no SCs among the 102 secretary-level officers in the central government. Of the 113 additional secretaries, only 5 were SCs, 1 ST and no OBCs. Furthermore, he claimed that the representation of SCs and STs in Groups A, B, and C was not equal to their proportion of the population, so that *'from our side we are convinced that [the SCs and STs] are backward per se'* (*Indian Express* 2012a). In addition, the MPPGP launched a special recruitment scheme to fill vacant reserved posts in government jobs for SCs, STs and OBCs, and even fixed a date for implementation by central ministries and departments (*Hindustan Times* 2011). Such efforts, as we have seen, were singularly absent for religious minorities, particularly Muslims. In short, the underlying principle of different approaches to different social categories (caste groups and minorities), dating from the critical juncture of Partition was the prime determinant of the UPA's path dependent policymaking and implementation.

Lastly, in assessing the UPA's policies on employment it would be mistaken not to acknowledge their effect in enabling change under appropriate conditions. The example of Mamata Banerjee in West Bengal illustrates that positive action on employment can deliver if appropriate conditions are in play. Yet, importantly, to avoid her initiatives being struck down by the judiciary, Banerjee exercised her initiatives within the existing framework of affirmative action (that is, widening the scope of the OBC category to include more Muslims). As we shall see in the next chapter, demands for improved service delivery for religious minorities would also have to operate within similar restrictive constraints.

---

reasons of backwardness, inadequacy of representation in a class of post(s)' prior to providing for reservation. The Uttar Pradesh government's proposal to give quotas for SCs and STs in promotion was rejected by the High Court in 2011 and the Supreme Court in 2012 precisely on the ground that the state government had failed to provide adequate evidence of the backwardness and under-representation of SCs and STs among its personnel (National Commission for Scheduled Castes 2013 [laid in Parliament on 23 December 2014]; *The Hindu* 2012).

5

UPA, Muslims and Service Delivery

Introduction

Equal access to services provided by the state is a necessary condition of effective equal opportunity policies. Historically, excluded ethnic, religious and linguistic minorities have often complained of the colour-blind practice of states in the provision of collective goods which produces discriminatory outcomes. With the development of affirmative action policies in the West, the principle of proportionality in resource allocation became an essential requirement of non-discriminatory service delivery (Ball and Solomos 1990; Ben-Tovim 1986). In India, with its regime of 'competing equalities', this principle was conceded for SCs and STs but not for religious minorities. In seeking to correct this imbalance, the UPA introduced a multitude of programmes for religious minorities, with a range of affirmative action provisions, including the targeting and monitoring of service delivery to ensure better implementation. However, despite these initiatives, efforts to improve service delivery for religious minorities, notably Muslims, encountered institutional barriers that remain to be overcome.

Given the vast range of the subject matter, we only review the policy process in key areas of service delivery. Accordingly, this chapter focuses on education (specifically the provision of scholarships for minority students), better provision of finance and a concentrated drive to improve socio-economic infrastructure in areas of Muslim concentration. These areas were selected because they provide a representative spectrum of the schemes under consideration: a recipient-led initiative (scholarships), a highly institutionalised and regulated sector drive (finance) and a broad area-based programme (MSDP). The different policy approaches reflect the constitutional and institutional constraints under which special programmes for religious minorities were developed. Finally, the chapter reflects on the policy process to assess modes of resistance to policy change.

Agenda-setting

Both the *SCR* and *RMCR* recognised the alienation of Muslims from, and their limited access to, state services. In education, the *SCR* found that limited availability of good government schools in Muslim localities resulted in pupils either attending private school or dropping out, particularly at primary, middle and higher secondary levels (*SCR* 2006: 60).[1] The literacy rate among Muslims (59.1 per cent) was below the national average (65.1 per cent) (ibid.: 52; *RMCR* 2007 16). Contrary to the popular myth, only 3 per cent of Muslim children of school age attend madrasas (*SCR* 2006: 77). The presence of Muslims in elite education institutions, such as Indian Institutes of Management (IIMs) and the Indian Institutes of Technology (IITs), was notably low: enrolment data for 2004–2005 and 2005–2006 indicates that Muslims accounted for a mere 1.3 per cent of students in all courses in all IIMs in India and 3.3 per cent in IITs (ibid.: 68–69). Muslims had the lowest proportion (3.6 per cent) of graduates among all the religious minorities (*RMCR* 2007: 17). Reflecting on this data, the *SCR* concluded that 'the changes in educational patterns across SRCs suggest that SCs and STs have reaped at least some advantages of targeted government and private action supporting their educational progress. *This reflects the importance of affirmative action*' (*SCR* 2006: 86, emphasis added). As a policy recommendation, the *SCR* called for a 'sharper focus on school education combined with more opportunities in higher education for Muslims' in addition to skill development initiatives for those who do not complete school education (ibid.).

In addition to education, easy access to credit is especially important for Muslims, a large proportion of whom are engaged in self-employment. However, data indicates that Muslims account for a smaller proportion of loans and amounts outstanding than other minorities (ibid.: 125–126; *RMCR* 2007: 103). Despite the RBI's effort to extend banking and credit facilities, the chief beneficiaries of these drives were other minorities (Reserve Bank of India 2001). The *SCR* pointed to an enduring difficulty because 'banks are ... able to direct credit to minorities, [but] they are not being able to do so specifically for Muslims' (*SCR* 2006: 128). Even more problematic was the fact that some banks had identified 'negative geographical zones' (large areas of Muslim settlement) with consequent poor provision of bank credit and other facilities (ibid.: 136). To address these discriminatory practices, the *SCR* recommended

---

[1] Only 17 per cent of Muslims above the age of 17 years have completed matriculation as compared to 26 per cent for all SRCs.

that 'steps should be introduced to specifically direct credit to Muslims, create awareness of various credit schemes ... [and] bring transparency in reporting of information about SRCs on provision of banking services' (ibid.: 137).

In addition to education or credit facilities, areas of high Muslim settlement were generally found to suffer an acute development deficit brought on by years of deliberate neglect, which often resulted in absence of basic infrastructure. The *SCR* found an inverse correlation existing between the proportion of the Muslim population and the number of schools in small villages (ibid.: 143). A similar pattern was also discernable in relation to medical facilities and post/telegraph offices. Simply put, the larger the proportion of Muslims in the population, the lower the provision of basic facilities was apparent. This trend was reported to increase as the size of the village increased (ibid.).[2] Although there is no indication that majority Muslim villages had fewer infrastructural facilities than non-Muslim ones, the picture in states such as Uttar Pradesh, Bihar, Assam and Jharkhand, with large Muslim populations, was bleak because it was here that the community's population was heavily concentrated (ibid.: 145). Underdevelopment and a high Muslim concentration produced a profile of a community suffering from cumulative disadvantage.

In short, underperformance in education, restricted access to finance and the lack of infrastructural development drew attention to discriminatory practices by the state in service delivery.[3] A wide range of interlinked factors, such as poverty, poor access to schools, low perceived return from school education, madrasa education, the usage of Urdu and the unwillingness of state governments to recognise minority educational institutions, had caused Muslims to feel discriminated against and led to the further deterioration of their educational condition (ibid.: 15–20). Similarly, perceptions of discrimination, by both public and private sector banks, in the provision of credit were widespread in most states. Officials denied any discrimination in the provision of services, but Muslims pointed to the poor civic amenities and infrastructure in the Muslim-concentrated areas (ibid.: 22–23).

---

[2] The *RMCR* also noted that 'among minorities, about one-third Muslims are living in kutcha houses, which lack basic facilities like drinking water, toilet etc. and likewise they live in rented houses' (2007: 30).

[3] 'The perception of being discriminated against is overpowering amongst a wide cross section of Muslims ... [the] sense of discrimination combined with issues of identity and insecurity has led to an acute sense of inferiority in the Community which comes in the way of its full participation in the public arena and results in collective alienation' (*SCR* 2006: 15).

Table 5.1 Some of the main recommendations of the *SCR* and *RMCR* on education, finance and infrastructure

Area	SCR	RMCR
Education	Initiation of evaluating the content of the school text book to prevent religious intolerance and caste bias	Enactment of comprehensive law detailing minorities' etducational rights
	Creation of local community study centre	Revision of Madrasa Modernisation Scheme
	Setting up of high quality government schools in Muslim concentration areas	Amendment of the National Minority Educational Institutions Commission to widen its functions and responsibilities
	Creation of mechanism to link madrasas with higher secondary school board to enable students to shift to mainstream education	Lower eligibility criteria for admission and lower rate of fees available to SCs and STs applicable to minorities
	Mapping of Urdu speaking population and provision of primary education in Urdu in areas where Urdu speaking population is concentrated.	Selection of at least one institution in states and Union Territories with substantial Muslim population to ensure it promotes education at all levels
	Technical and educational training for non-matriculates, skill development initiatives of Industrial Training Institutes (ITIs) in Muslim concentrated area, making madrasa-educated children eligible for such programmes	Earmarking 15 per cent seats in all non-minority educational institutions for minorities (10 per cent for Muslims, 5 per cent for other minorities). If difficult, 8.4 per cent (6 per cent for Muslims, 2.4 per cent for other minorities)
	University Grants Commission to evolve a system that allocation is linked to diversity in recruitment	Provide enhanced aid to Muslim-run schools and colleges
	Creation of alternative admission criteria to improve minority recruitment	
	Provision of hostels at reasonable cost to minority students	

(*Contd.*)

(*Contd.*)

Area	SCR	RMCR
	Teacher training programme for sensitisation of marginalised communities	
	Running Urdu medium schools	
	Setting up of exclusive schools for girls	
Finance	Policy formulation in the micro-credit schemes of National Bank for Agriculture and Rural Development to enhance participation of minorities	Revision of Central Wakf Council to focus on educational development of Muslims
	Provision of incentives to banks to open more branches in Muslim concentration area	Earmarking proportionate distribution of funds of Maulana Azad Educational Foundation
	RBI's priority sector advances (PSA) reports to include data on 'sanctions or disbursements to minorities' along with the 'amount outstanding'	
	Promotion of Muslims' access in PSA	
Infrastructure	Introduction of schemes with large outlays for welfare of minorities	Development of an effective mechanism for the development and modernisation of industries where minority groups are involved and for training of artisans and workmen
	Sensitisation of service staff regarding social exclusion	
	Facilitation of registration of trusts set up by the community	
	Provision of basic amenities	

Sources: SCR (2006: 237–254); RMCR (2007: 150–153).

These findings led the *SCR* and *RMCR* to adopt different policy approaches. While the recommendations of the *SCR* were centred on affirmative action, including positive action, for all minorities, the *RMCR* argued that in addition to providing general welfare measures, a certain proportion of reservations should be provided for socially and economically disadvantaged Muslims, in line with the provision of reservations for SCs, STs and OBCs. Despite these different policy approaches, as Table 5.1 shows, there was substantial agreement between their respective recommendations on proportionality and targeting.

Policy formulation

Although policy formulation was based on the recommendations of the *SCR* and *RMCR*, it also included a revamped PM's 15PP which had been running since 1983. Initially launched by Indira Gandhi, it was intended to 'tackle the situation arising out of communal riots', 'ensure adequate representation of the minority communities in employment under the central and state governments as well as public sector undertakings' and implement community development programmes (Planning Commission 2008: 122). As a part of the new policy approach to minority communities following the publication of the *SCR*, in June 2006 the UPA revised and relaunched the PM's 15PP as a flagship measure through executive action. Development projects in areas of AQ: minority concentration would now ensure that 15 per cent of the outlays under various schemes were earmarked for minorities. All central ministries, departments, state governments and Union Territory administrations were directed to implement the 15PP. Five central ministries—Human Resource Development, Labour and Employment, Housing and Poverty Alleviation, Rural Development, and Women and Child Development—were given specific responsibilities in relevant areas. Naturally, these initiatives led to a proliferation of complex and overlapping programmes under different ministries, while the newly created MoMA was given the role of overall coordination for the MSDP and the scholarship scheme for minority students (see Figure 3.1). Table 5.2 indicates the complex and diverse range of service delivery policies for minorities launched by the UPA government.

Viewed more broadly, the UPA's policymaking on service delivery was also shaped by the Eleventh Five-Year Plan (2007–2012). In a report by the Planning Commission's Working Group on Empowering Minorities, submitted in November 2006, the need to recognise developmental disadvantages of minorities, especially Muslims, was clearly acknowledged

Table 5.2 The multitude of schemes and initiatives for minorities under the UPA

Details of policy initiatives	Name of schemes / programmes	Lead ministry/department
Schemes considered amenable to earmarking of 15% for minorities under the PM's New 15 PP	Improving access to school education: Sarva Shiksha Abhiyan (SSA, universalisation of elementary education)	Ministry of Human Resource Development, (Department of School Education and Literacy)
	Integrated Child Development Services (ICDS)	Ministry of Women and Child Development
	Self-employment: Swarnajayanti Gram Swarozgar Yojana (SGSY, provision of sustainable income to the rural poor); Indira Awaas Yojana (IAY, provision of housing to the rural poor)	Ministry of Rural Development (Department of Rural Development)
	Industrial Training Institutes (ITIs)	Ministry of Labour and Employment
	Credit support under Public Sector Lending	Ministry of Finance (Department of Financial Services) / Reserve Bank of India
	Swarn Jayanti Shahari Rojgar Yojana (SJSRY, provision of employment to the urban unemployed and poor); Integrated Housing and Slum Development Programme (IHSDP); Basic Services to the Urban Poor (BSUP)	Ministry of Housing and Urban Poverty Alleviation
	National Rural Drinking Water Programme (NRDWP)	Ministry of Drinking Water and Sanitation
	Urban Infrastructure Development Scheme for Small and Medium Towns (UIDSSMT); Urban Infrastructure and Governance (UIG)	Ministry of Urban Development

(*Contd.*)

(*Contd.*)

Details of policy initiatives	Name of schemes / programmes	Lead ministry/department
	Recruitment to State and Central services	Ministry of Personnel, Public Grievances and Pensions (Department of Personnel and Training)
	Prevention of communal incidents; prosecution for communal incidents; rehabilitation of victims of communal riots	Ministry of Home Affairs
Schemes for minorities (100% budget provision for minorities) under the PM's New 15 PP	Schemes for Providing Quality Education in Madrasa; Schemes for Infrastructure Development of Minority Institutions (IDMI); Greater resources for teaching Urdu	Ministry of Human Resource Development (Department of School Education and Literacy)
	loan schemes of National Minorities Development and Finance Corporation (NMDFC)	Ministry of Minority Affairs
	Schemes of Maulana Azad Education Foundation for promotion of education	
	Maulana Azad National Fellowship for Minority Students scheme	
	Scholarships (pre-matric, post-matric, merit-cum-means)	
	Free Coaching and Allied Schemes	
	Equity to NMDFC (additional equity contribution to NMDFC for development of Wakfs has been merged with Grant-in-aid to NMDFC)	
	Scheme of grants-in-aid to Wakf for strengthening the infrastructure of Special Central Assistance of NMDFC	

(*Contd.*)

(*Contd.*)

Details of policy initiatives	Name of schemes / programmes	Lead ministry/department
	Computerisation of the records of State Wakf Boards Scheme	
	Nai Roshni (leadership development of minority women)	
	Seekho aur Kamao (skill development of minorities)	
	Research/studies, monitoring and evaluation of development scheme including publicity	
Area Development Programme for Minorities	Multi-Sectoral Development Programme (MSDP)	Ministry of Minority Affairs

Source: Ministry of Women and Child Development, Ministry of Human Resource Development, Ministry of Minority Affairs, Ministry of Rural Development, Ministry of Housing and Urban Poverty Alleviation, Ministry of Labour and Employment, Ministry of Finance, Ministry of Urban Development, and Ministry of Drinking Water and Sanitation websites.

(ibid.: 122–129). As a result, the Eleventh Five-Year Plan accorded the 'highest priority to the development of innovative programmes, expansion of existing schemes, implementation and monitoring of all initiatives for the minorities by making adequate budgetary allocation at every level of governance' (ibid.: 127). However, the proposal for a specific Minority Sub-Plan soon faced opposition in the Planning Commission. Zoya Hasan, who was chairperson of the Working Group on Empowering Minorities, recalls:

> There was a strong opposition within the Planning Commission. Some people were supporting it but most opposed it on the ground that this is unconstitutional. *You can have special programmes for SCs and STs, but not for minorities. It is unconstitutional.* That is what they said. That was the reason given. *But the real reason was that they just did not want to do it because they would have had to face the opposition from the SCs and STs, and within the Congress itself, and there were some communal elements.* But the official reason was that it is unconstitutional and the Ministry of Law said any special concern given to the minorities is against the secular basis of Constitution.[4]

This was in stark contrast to a Scheduled Caste Component Plan, which provided a policy framework to address the backwardness of caste groups, and came with clear directions for service delivery to these communities. Consequently, service delivery for minorities was not to be specifically defined by the Planning Commission's parameters but regulated by the norms and guidelines of the existing Centrally Sponsored Scheme, including the PM's 15PP. In hindsight, the reluctance to create a specific Minorities Sub-Plan within the institutionalised and heavily regulated framework of national and state planning gave considerable room for manoeuvre to state governments and administrations to determine the implementation of these programmes.

At the same time, the newly created MoMA was tasked with identifying 90 MCDs for an MSDP.[5] In policymaking on the MSDP, its Empowered Committee was given authority to approve the plans of blocks/towns/clusters from state level committees, to change the allocation of the blocks/

---

[4] Zoya Hasan, interview, 11 March 2013, New Delhi. Emphasis added.
[5] The proposal on identification of MCDs was first considered by the Committee of Secretaries and forwarded to the Cabinet for consideration. Finally, it was approved on 17 May 2007 (PIB 2014a).

towns to encourage and reward better performing blocks/towns/villages and to monitor implementation. In identifying the 90 MCDs, the Empowered Committee measured backwardness according to two criteria: religion-specific socio-economic and basic amenities indicators at the district level (MoMA 2012a).

To sum up: in formulating new policies to address the Muslim 'development deficit', policymakers came up against a strong institutionalised opposition to special programmes for religious minorities. As a result, they were inclined to support positive action but principally through executive action. At the same time, these policies suffered from a serious lack of executive ownership and clear coordination, producing contradictory and overlapping programmes without adequate monitoring, evaluation or sensitivity to the needs of the targeted recipients (Centre for Equity Studies 2012: xix, 45–48; Council for Social Development, Hasan and Hasan 2013, esp. contributions in Part II; Khan 2012: 11; Shariff 2012:10). It is against this backdrop that we examine the decision-making process and the policy tools used in the face of institutional resistance.

Decision-making

This section examines closely three policy areas—education, access to credit and the MSDP. It highlights how the UPA compensated for its constitutional and political inability to provide reservations for religious minorities in education and other state services by adopting new policy tools to enhance service delivery to the Muslim community.

Education: provision of scholarships to religious minorities

Soon after the creation of the MoMA, the Minister of Finance in the 2006–2007 Budget Session announced the distribution of 20,000 merit-cum-means-based scholarships to minority students (Ministry of Finance 2006). This was also underpinned by the Cabinet's approval of the revamped PM's 15PP in June 2006, and the tabling of the *SCR* in Parliament in November 2006. Anticipating opposition from political parties, particularly the BJP, and from state governments, the UPA used executive action to limit the need to bargain with other policy actors. As reservations in education for religious minorities were considered unconstitutional and carried the risk of being challenged, the provision of scholarships 'which have passed the constitutional test' was used to overcome institutional opposition—both political and administrative.⁶ The Cabinet Committee on Economic Affairs chaired by the Prime Minister gave approval to expand the provision of scholarships which had long been available to lower caste groups (in addition to reservation in educational institutions).⁷ Following this executive action the merit-cum-means scholarship scheme was approved for religious minorities in June 2007, the post-matric scheme in November 2007 and the pre-matric scheme in April 2008 (PIB 2007a, 2007b, 2008c). While all these scholarships were to be implemented from the financial year 2007–2008, the reasons behind this staged approval are somewhat unclear, though state assembly elections—in Goa, Gujarat, Himachal Pradesh, Manipur, Punjab, Uttarakhand and Uttar Pradesh (in February 2007)—might have influenced the timing. In any case, it appears that the use of scholarships as a policy tool was chosen because of its promotional value, low cost and high visibility as the number of scholarships was relatively small in relation to the total pupil population.⁸

---

6   The government's decision on scholarships for religious minorities was legally upheld following judgments of the Bombay, Gujarat and Delhi High Courts which rejected four petitions that questioned the constitutionality of the merit-cum-means scholarship provision for minority students. The Bombay High Court did not rule that scholarship schemes for minorities are constitutionally invalid or they discriminate against majority students. The decision appears to be based on Article 15(4) of the Constitution which provides that the state can make any special provisions for the advancement of any SEBCs of citizens. The decision of the Bombay High Court was supported by the judgment of the Gujarat High Court (Z. Hasan 2012: 175, 188).
7   According to Baru, the former media advisor to Prime Minister in UPA I, the biggest expansion of government-funded scholarship took place during Manmohan Singh's administration. The Prime Minister's effort was influenced by his own modest background which enabled him to complete his higher education in India and England with scholarships (Baru 2014: 153–154).
8   'Despite improved coverage 1 out of each 4.55 enrolled Muslim child in classes I–VII and 1 out of every 7.7 Muslim child in the entire age group obtained a scholarship. As importantly, the per capita allocation for awarded pre-matriculation scholarship (across all minority groups) was only Rs 1,009.25 a year for the 2010–2011 year. This is even less than each of the previous years in the 11th Plan: Rs 1,173.60 for 2009–2010 and Rs 1,213.48 for 2008–2009' (Centre for Equity Studies 2012: vii).

Finance: access to credit

In the light of the *SCR* recommendation to promote Muslim access to priority sector advances (PSA), the Eleventh Five-Year Plan report also acknowledged Muslims' poor access to bank credit, and suggested that all public sector banks should have targets for PSA to minorities, especially Muslims. As a result, measures were deemed necessary to 'create awareness about various credit schemes, organise entrepreneurial development programmes, and bring transparency in reporting on credit availability' (Planning Commission 2008: 128). Government recommendations included the opening of more branches, emphasis on transparency, promoting awareness of available schemes, an entrepreneurship development programme, micro-finance, enhanced authorised share capital of NMDFC, and priority sector lending (PSL). PSL specified that a portion of bank lending be made to a number of specific sectors, such as agriculture, micro-credit, education and housing. Therefore, in a broader context, PSL to minorities aimed at a more rounded development strategy for the whole economy rather than just improving the performance of the financial sector. This was particularly important for Muslims because large numbers are self-employed.

A circular issued by the RBI in June 2002 required that 'all banks are advised to initiate steps to enhance/augment flow of credit under Priority Sector to artisans and craftsmen as also to vegetable vendors, cart pullers, cobblers etc., and [those] belonging to the minority communities (Buddhists, Christians, Muslims, Sikhs, and Zoroastrians)' (RBI 2002). This was followed up, in April 2003, by a master circular detailing the reporting formats of the half yearly/quarterly statement showing the level of PSA granted to the members of the specified minority communities as a share of overall PSA, a list of the relevant MCDs,[9] and a recapitulation of the previous circulars consolidated by the master circular (RBI 2003a). In addition, this document suggested corrective measures to be taken by relevant banks. It highlighted the importance of each bank having a special cell to ensure smooth flow of credit to minority communities, and recommended that lead banks in MCDs should appoint an officer responsible exclusively for dealing with credit flow to minority communities; that monitoring data on credit assistance

---

9   MCDs were first prepared in 1987 using a single criterion of minority population of 20 per cent or more based on the 1971 Census, and in 2001 it was decided to identify districts on the basis of minority population as per the 2001 Census and backwardness parameters to ensure service delivery to the disadvantaged.

provided to members of minority communities should be submitted to the RBI, Ministry of Finance and Ministry of Welfare on a half-yearly basis; that progress should be monitored by District Consultative Committees and the State Level Bankers Committees; that bank staff should receive training on the various schemes for welfare of minorities, while sensitisation workshops should be organised for bank officials; and that banks should ensure good publicity about government anti-poverty programmes, particularly in the MCDs.[10] Furthermore, monitoring was to be strengthened by directing primary cooperative banks to submit half-yearly statements on the progress made in the deployment of credit to minority communities (RBI 2003b).

After the UPA came to power in 2004, there was no discernible change or new direction in the regulations and master circulars issued until 2007. In a 2005 master circular, a section was added to state that 'Lead Banks of the MCDs will have to exercise the pro-active role expected of them to ensure that the minority communities, particularly those who are poor and illiterate have access to bank credit for taking up productive activities' (RBI 2005). However, this section was inserted as a recommendation, without any enforcing mechanism. Following the approval of the revised PM's 15PP in June 2006, a circular was issued to commercial banks and urban cooperative banks to issue necessary instructions to their branch offices that sufficient care should be taken to ensure an equitable proportion of credit to minorities within the overall targets of priority sectors and the sub-targets of 10 per cent earmarked for weaker sections. Following the tabling of the *SCR* in November 2006, and in light of its findings, in January 2007, the central government circulated a proposal to banks to reserve a 6 per cent share of loans for minorities (Bhoir 2007a). The BJP inevitably condemned this proposal as being 'in contravention of prudent banking norms' and 'communalising a secular financial system', and suggested that it was motivated by concerns regarding the state assembly elections.[11] 'The Prime Minister's refrain of "first claim" of Muslims on India's development resources', a BJP spokesman claimed, 'is being systematically implemented in phases by communalising sector after sector' (Jaju 2007). The RBI and the Indian Banks' Association also expressed strong reservations on the ground that banks' lending practices are based on the borrower's creditworthiness and not on his/her caste or creed (Bhoir 2007b). Nevertheless, the Minister of

---

[10] These points are repeated in subsequent master circulars until the 2013 version.
[11] State assembly elections were scheduled throughout February 2007 in Goa, Gujarat, Himachal Pradesh, Manipur, Punjab, Uttarkhand and Uttar Pradesh.

Finance issued an executive order to the RBI to amend the priority sector norms to include minority communities under 'lending to weaker sections' (*Economic Times* 2007).[12] As a result of this executive order, religious minorities were included in the RBI list of weaker sections and, hence, entitled to secure loans from domestic banks—both government-owned and private—which were mandated to lend 10 per cent of their total loans to 'weaker sections'. The move was reflected in the master circular directing scheduled commercial banks to ensure 'minority communities receive a fair and equitable portion of the credit within the overall target of the priority sector' (RBI 2007). The centre pushed through further positive action by identifying additional MCDs, and almost immediately the RBI circulated this list to relevant banks to ensure equitable credit flow to minorities in the MCDs. In the following month, the RBI directed the scheduled commercial banks to issue necessary instructions to controlling offices and branch offices to monitor the credit flow to minorities in the final list of 121 MCDs.

Overall, the RBI was proactive in directing banks located in MCDs to ensure that credit flowed to minority communities. It issued at least four important regulations and master circulars in 2007—in contrast to one a year in 2001, 2004, 2005 and 2006, and two each in 2002 and 2003. This policy drive was further backed up with the Minister of Finance's executive order to widen the RBI's definition of 'weaker sections'.[13] Yet, while the provision of credit to religious minorities gained momentum, to what extent this facility was utilised by minorities, especially Muslims, will be assessed in the implementation cycle of the policy process.

MSDP

As one of the largest development initiatives since Independence, the MSDP was launched to address the chronic underdevelopment of MCDs. Following the findings of the *SCR* that a majority of the Muslim population

---

[12] The banking industry had been providing PSL to minorities, but clearly, minorities were not included in the 'lending to weaker sections' of the priority sector norms in the pre-UPA period.

[13] However, the master circulars issued from 2008 to 2013 are the same as the 2007 version, with a mere addition in the 2013 version that a sub-target of 10 per cent of adjusted net bank credit or credit equivalent amount of off-balance sheet exposures will be mandated for lending to weaker sections. For a list of master circulars, see Bibliography.

resides in states with poor infrastructure and amenities, and required focused government intervention in infrastructural development, the MSDP aimed to fill the gaps in the existing government schemes by providing additional resources, and encouraging take-up of new projects for the welfare of minorities (for example in education, skills development, health, sanitation, roads and drinking water). An inter-ministerial task force was constituted under the chairmanship of Bhalchandra Mungekar, a member of the Planning Commission, to devise an appropriate strategy and action plan for developing areas of minority concentration. As mentioned above, backward districts (in terms of socio-economic and basic amenities indicators) were selected with a 'substantial minority population' of at least 25 per cent of all five minorities, with no specific targets for Muslim concentration. However, by making the district the unit of programme implementation, 'funds could be spent anywhere and a project could be set up anywhere where Muslims are not present in substantial numbers, and yet it [would] meet the criteria regardless of its benefits going to the intended beneficiaries' (Hasan and Hasan 2013: 245). Despite the Secretary of the MoMA admitting that the unit of planning needed to be more tightly focused below the district level, and the Planning Commission's Eleventh Plan Working Group on Empowering Minorities recommending the unit be changed to the block,[14] the district was used as the unit of implementation. Following the submission of the *Implication of the Geographical Distribution of Minorities in India: Report, 2007* by an Inter-Ministerial Task Force (Planning Commission 2007) to the Prime Minister in November 2007, the MSDP was approved by the Cabinet Committee on Economic Affairs in March 2008 (PIB 2008b).[15] Thereafter, the Empowered Committee in the MoMA initiated the process by receiving proposals from states and approving proposed programmes and schemes in MCDs.

Implementation and Evaluation

Education: provision of scholarships targeted at religious minorities

In this section we analyse the state-wise take-up of the scholarship scheme. In a federal structure, the performance of the state government is the

---

[14] Hasan, interview, 11 March 2013, New Delhi.
[15] Every new scheme under MSDP has to be approved by the Cabinet Committee on Economic Affairs after consultation among the MoMA, the Ministry of Finance and the Planning Commission.

critical variable. As critics have argued, the scheme was accompanied by many problems which included low utilisation of funds, limited awareness among parents, complex and cumbersome procedures for applicants, poor institutional mechanisms, lack of administrative funds earmarked for implementing the scheme, and state governments' failure to prioritise the minority agenda (Centre for Equity Studies 2012; Hasan and Hasan 2013; Khan 2012). Moreover, despite the high take-up against the target set by the Eleventh Five-Year Plan, that target itself was very low in proportion to the numbers of Muslim students enrolled in educational institutions (Centre for Equity Studies 2012: 26–27). Yet, despite these shortcomings, the beneficiary-oriented scholarship scheme appeared to be one notable success in an affirmative action programme bedevilled by poor implementation and monitoring.[16] But did implementation vary according to the political party in power in the states?

The data covers the period from 2007 to 2014. The degree of implementation (in percentages) was calculated by comparing the numbers given for the 'target' and the 'implementation' achieved in government data. The result was further divided into high (more than 100 per cent), medium (50 to 99 per cent) and low (below 50 per cent).[17] The findings indicate significant variation across states in the take-up of pre-matric, post-matric and merit-cum-means scholarships. To see if implementation varied with the ideological outlook of the governing party, Table 5.3 identifies the ruling state parties.

---

[16] Weak monitoring of the government outlays on development programmes generally was highlighted by the Minister of Finance in a budget speech when he noted that 'robust economic growth has thrown up many new challenges, among them the need to put in place effective monitoring, evaluation and accounting system for the large sums of money that are disbursed by the Central Government to State Governments, districts level agencies and other implementing agencies. I think we do not pay enough attention to outcomes as we do to outlays; or to physical targets as we do to financial targets; or to quality as we do to quantity' (Ministry of Finance 2008).

[17] As the pre-matric scheme was approved in April 2008, the data for this scheme covers from 2008 to 2014, and the post-matric and merit-cum-means schemes from 2007 to 2014. The figure of 100%+ implementation would appear to suggest that in some states the targets were either deliberately exceeded or perhaps set too low for the financial year.

Table 5.3 States and political parties in distribution of scholarships (mid 2007–mid 2014)

Degree of implementation	Pre-matric	Political parties	Post-matric	Political parties	Merit-cum-Means	Political parties
High (100% +)	West Bengal	CPI(M)/TMC	Karnataka	BJP/BJP	Sikkim	SSP/SDF
	Kerala	CPI(M)/INC	West Bengal	CPI(M)/TMC	Kerala	CPI(M)/INC
	Tamil Nadu	DMK/AIADMK	Tamil Nadu	DMK/AIADMK	Tamil Nadu	DMK/AIADMK
	Karnataka	BJP/BJP	Kerala	CPI(M)/INC	Karnataka	BJP/BJP
	Mizoram	MNF/INC	Mizoram	MNF/INC	Jammu and Kashmir	PDP/National Conference
	Maharashtra	INC/INC	Uttar Pradesh	BSP/SP	Rajasthan	BJP/INC
	Rajasthan	BJP/INC	Andhra Pradesh	INC/INC	Bihar	JD(U)/JD(U)
	Andhra Pradesh	INC/INC	Gujarat	BJP/BJP	Uttar Pradesh	BSP/SP
	Uttar Pradesh	BSP/SP	Rajasthan	BJP/INC	West Bengal	CPI(M)/TMC
	Madhya Pradesh	BJP/BJP	Manipur	INC/INC	Manipur	INC/INC
	Punjab	INC/SAD			Gujarat	BJP/BJP
	Jammu and Kashmir	PDP/National Conference			Punjab	INC/SAD
	Odisha	BJD/BJD			Madhya Pradesh	BJP/BJP
	Delhi	INC				
Medium (50-99%)	Bihar	JD(U)/JD(U)	Maharashtra	INC/INC	Haryana	INC/INC
	Manipur	INC/INC	Madhya Pradesh	BJP/BJP	Mizoram	MNF/INC
	Meghalaya	INC/INC	Punjab	INC/SAD	Assam	INC/INC
	Chandigarh	INC	Bihar	JD(U)/JD(U)	Jharkhand	JMM/BJP
	Chhattisgarh	BJP/BJP	Jharkhand	JMM/BJP	Andhra Pradesh	INC/INC
	Daman and Diu	INC	Chhattisgarh	BJP/BJP	Delhi	INC
	Himachal Pradesh	BJP/INC	Jammu and Kashmir	PDP/National Conference	Puducherry	INC
	Sikkim	SSP/SDF	Sikkim	SSP/SDF	Maharashtra	INC/INC
	Assam	INC/INC	Himachal Pradesh	BJP/INC	Himachal Pradesh	BJP/INC

(Contd.)

(*Contd.*)

Degree of implementation	Pre-matric	Political parties	Post-matric	Political parties	Merit-cum-Means	Political parties
	Haryana	INC/INC	Puducherry	INC	Nagaland	NPF/NPF
	Jharkhand	JMM/BJP	Assam	INC/INC	Goa	INC/BJP
	Gujarat	BJP/BJP			Chhattisgarh	BJP/BJP
	Tripura	CPI(M)/CPI(M)			Odisha	BJD/BJD
					Uttarakhand	BJP/INC
					Chandigarh	INC
					Meghalaya	INC/INC
					Tripura	CPI(M)/CPI(M)
Low (50% -)	Puducherry	INC	Odisha	BJD/BJD	Daman and Diu	INC
	Dadra and Nagar Haveli	INC	Haryana	INC/INC	Andaman and Nicobar	INC
	Andaman and Nicobar	INC	Dadra and Nagar Haveli	INC	Arunachal Pradesh	INC/INC
	Nagaland	NPF/NPF	Tripura	CPI(M)/CPI(M)	Dadra and Nagar Haveli	INC
	Goa	INC/BJP	Delhi	INC	Lakshadweep	INC
	Uttarakhand	BJP/INC	Chandigarh	INC		
	Arunachal Pradesh	INC/INC	Daman and Diu	INC		
	Lakshadweep	INC	Goa	INC/BJP		
			Lakshadweep	INC		
			Uttarakhand	BJP/INC		
			Andaman and Nicobar	INC		
			Meghalaya	INC/INC		
			Nagaland	NPF/NPF		
			Arunachal Pradesh	INC/INC		

Source: For full names of political parties, see abbreviations. The data for this table was derived from MoMA website, compiled by the author.

Among the high implementation-level states, West Bengal ranked near the top in pre-matric and post-matric scholarships and also performed effectively in the merit-cum-means scheme. Kerala, Karnataka and Tamil Nadu also performed equally well. In Karnataka, notwithstanding the fact that the BJP was in power from 2008 to 2013 (except for the last year after Congress won the 2013 Legislative Assembly election), the take-up rate was also high. A similar pattern can be seen in Madhya Pradesh, ruled by the BJP, with a high-medium record in all three scholarship schemes. Uttar Pradesh was one of the high implementation states, unsurprisingly, given its large Muslim population. Interestingly, Bihar also achieved high-medium rates of implementation, scoring high in the merit-cum-means scholarship, and achieved a medium level of implementation for the pre-matric and post-matric scheme.

State capacity, 'the ability to monitor the progress of reform, coordinate the actions of different players, and mobilise administration for the achievement of goals' (Chand 2010: 29), perhaps explains the variations in policy performance. Under this definition, Gujarat clearly scored high on state capacity, but the take-up of schemes was lower than in states with much less effective administrations. Table 5.3 indicates that while Gujarat achieved high implementation in the post-matric and merit-cum-means schemes, the implementation rate was lower than the ones in West Bengal or Bihar. It should be noted that Gujarat appears to have achieved medium-level implementation in providing pre-matric scholarship. A close analysis of data, however, indicates that from 2008 to 2013 the level of pre-matric scholarships provided to minorities in Gujarat was zero. The Gujarat state government led by Narendra Modi refused to provide pre-matric scholarships to minorities on the ground that this would be discriminatory. However, the Gujarat High Court ruled that provision of scholarships to Muslim students is based on their educational backwardness resulting from their poverty and economically weak position, and hence justified. In reply, the Gujarat state government filed an affidavit in the Supreme Court arguing that the Sachar Committee was illegal and unconstitutional as it was set up by the UPA to investigate the socio-economic and educational status of Muslims only and ignored other religious minorities. The state government also argued that it had a similar state-sponsored programme for all students from backward communities, irrespective of their religion (Anand 2013). According to the State Government of Gujarat, the *SCR* had neither legal nor constitutional justification, and central government policies based on the recommendations of the *SCR*, including the provision of scholarships to religious minorities, were ultra vires (*NDTV* 2013).[18] Despite such arguments, the Gujarat state government tremendously expanded the provision of pre-matric scholarships in 2013–2014, over-achieving at 340 per cent. This last-minute change of heart qualified the government to be labelled as a medium-level implementer in pre-matric scheme. However, given the state's five years of resistance against funding minorities, the move was clearly inspired by the imminence of the 2014 general elections.

West Bengal, Bihar and Gujarat offer contrasting examples of state capacity, political will and institutional resistance in policy implementation. Despite the strong capacity of the Gujarat state government, political opposition to the scheme and institutionalised resistance against measures in favour of Muslims played a crucial role in poor implementation. Conversely, despite poor state capacity in Bihar and West Bengal, the take-up was impressive, perhaps aided by the fact, as we have seen in Chapter 4 in the case of West Bengal, that these schemes nurtured an important political constituency.

Finally, in assessing policy implementation, the historical background of the state is also relevant. Karnataka and Gujarat, for instance, were both ruled by the BJP, but showed a considerable divergence in performance. As noted in Chapter 2, states in the south, particularly Karnataka, had recognised Muslims as backward classes before the pre-Mandal period, and provided reservations to religious minorities in education and employment. Among the 16 backward castes recognised by the state government in 1977, Muslims were recognised broadly as a single category with a quota provided exclusively for them. In Gujarat, with no such tradition or history of interpretation of the OBC criteria, implementation remained weak.

The argument that policy implementation is more related to political commitment and determination than to the label of the political party in power is further supported by the Congress in Andhra Pradesh, and other Congress-led states, including the Union Territories. Andhra Pradesh showed a high rate of implementation in pre-matric and post-matric scholarships, with medium-level implementation in merit-cum-means schemes. However, the Maharashtra state government, also led by the Congress, over-achieved in terms of pre-matric provision, while reaching medium-level status

---

[18] Despite the affidavit filed by the Gujarat state government, the Supreme Court supported the Gujarat High Court's verdict that the scholarship scheme could not be equated with reservation for it was an 'affirmative action' of a non-discriminatory nature.

of implementation in the post-matric and merit-cum-means schemes. Surprisingly, the Union Territories, ruled directly by the centre, showed the weakest extent of implementation in all schemes. This can be partly attributed to the small number of minorities in some of the Union Territories or the lack of policy focus in these urban regions or, alternatively, the generally high rates of education and income found in these localities.[19]

Finance: access to credit

We have noted that the UPA pursued a proactive lending policy towards minorities, especially Muslims, but the actual take-up of these loans did not substantially increase. In the absence of a more systematic review of this data, and the shortcomings of monitoring and evaluation, here we focus on the debates which took place within the Rajya Sabha on the issue. The government was continuously questioned on whether positive action based on proportionality was actually legal and tantamount to quotas. Responding to a point made by an MP from Tamil Nadu, Minister of Finance P. Chidambaram played down the issue, declaring:

> There is no particular direction that loans should be given in some areas and loans should not be given in some areas. It is true that in areas where there is a large concentration of minority communities, banks have been advised that their lending must lean towards the minority communities which are concentrated in those areas. That does not mean that minority community borrowers in any other area will not get a loan.[20]

Throughout the debate, the Minister of Finance emphasised that the banks had been 'advised' to provide lending to minorities. But nowhere was there any mention of regulatory mechanisms to combat institutionalised resistance in the banking sector. In fact, in the Rajya Sabha debates from 2004 onwards on the subject, the responses of the Minister of Finance or other government members highlighted the directions to RBI on guidelines, or simply asserted that substantial allocations of loans to minorities had been made. Whenever a

---

[19] For instance, according to the 2011 Census, the literacy rate in Chandigarh was 86.05 per cent and the city's per capita income ranked third highest in the national ranking of 2011–2012 (*Financial Express* 2012; Planning Commission 2013).

[20] *RSD*, 19 December 2006.

specific question was raised about the exact figure, or by what percentage the provision of PSL had increased compared to the previous year, the government fell back on rhetoric such as the 'RBI has advised banks to ensure equitable flow of credit to minority communities'.[21] From 2004 onwards it is hard to find any debate that specified the percentage of PSL for each minority community. Sometimes the debates were deliberately interrupted.[22] For instance, on 19 December 2006, Brinda Karat (CPI[M], West Bengal) pointed out that while the amount of PSA had increased during the UPA administration, the percentage had decreased compared to that under the NDA government. She asserted that the decrease in percentage was a reflection of blatant discrimination against minorities, particularly Muslims. When she argued, on the basis of the *SCR*'s findings, that a large number of self-employed Muslims could not survive without bank credit, she was interrupted by the Chairman. The answer to her query from the Minister of Finance is noteworthy:

> P. Chidambaram: [as regard to 15PP], an appropriate percentage of PSL in all categories is targeted for minority communities. As I understand, it does not say 15 per cent of credit must go to the minorities. It is 15 per cent of outlays of scheme that must be targeted towards minorities and an appropriate percentage of credit must go to the minorities.
>
> Brinda Karat: What is that appropriate thing? Please quantify.
>
> P. Chidambaram: I cannot quantify. What it means is that they must step up sharply the lending to minorities and that is precisely what we are going to do.[23]

As the Minister continued to prevaricate, Karat criticised him by saying:

> What is this? Is this the way to answer a question? Sir, every time when the Finance Minister gets up he teaches us lessons, which we do not need to learn from him ... *we want to know what the percentage is.*[24]

Despite interruptions from the Chairman, and other MPs, after several further attempts Karat eventually managed to ask the Minister of Finance about the

---

[21] The data presented in the Rajya Sabha debate on 3 August 2010, provided by the Minister of State in the Ministry of Finance, included only information on amounts, not what percentage of the total those amounts represented.
[22] For instance, see *RSD*, 19 December 2006; *RSD*, 12 March 2007.
[23] *RSD*, 19 December 2006.
[24] Ibid., emphasis added.

15 per cent of credit earmarked for minorities. In response, the Minister of Finance confirmed the government's position by stating that '*we are not earmarking any percentage*' and the debate was abruptly ended by the Chairman. The RBI began providing figures for PSL from 2007–2008. Table 5.4 illustrates that as a result of the Finance Minister's executive order, the percentage of PSL provided to minority communities steadily increased, reaching 15 per cent by the end of the UPA II administration.

Table 5.4   Provision of PSL to minority communities

Year	2007–2008	2008–2009	2009–2010	2010–2011	2011–2012	2012–2013
Proportion (percentage)	10.6	12.24	13.01	14.16	14.55	14.59

Source: PIB (2014b).

However, the data was not classified according to religion, despite the RBI having issued a pro-forma instruction to submit a report on lending to religious minorities. The first religion-specific data reveal that for the year 2013–2014 up to September 2013, the proportions of PSL to minorities were as follows: Muslims (47.01 per cent), Christians (21.58 per cent), Sikhs (27.49 per cent), Buddhists (2.15 per cent) and Parsis (1.77 per cent) (PIB 2014b). However, Table 5.5 shows that most of the states with large Muslim populations, with the exception of West Bengal and Bihar in 2010–2011 and West Bengal again in 2013–2014, were medium-ranked in their achievement of PSL against targets to minorities. Interestingly, states where non-Muslims are the majority show high rates of implementation. For instance, Punjab was the only state that demonstrated high implementation throughout the period. States where Christians are the majority were also high-achievers (Arunachal Pradesh, Manipur, Mizoram and Nagaland). However, compared to the percentage of achievement in these states, the achievement rate in states with large Muslim populations is lower (Uttar Pradesh, West Bengal and Bihar). From this data and given the proportion of religious minorities in the total population, we can plausibly argue that non-Muslim minorities were able to corner the larger share of PSL.

Another important finding from this data is that Gujarat performed even worse than those medium-ranked states with a large number of Muslims scoring medium-low or very low. As we have seen in case of scholarship provision, the performance of banks in Gujarat in PSL provision shows the strong element of institutionalised resistance in service delivery towards Muslims.

Table 5.5 Degree of implementation in provision of PSL against targets to religious minorities (2007–2014) by state

Degree of implementation	2007–2008	2008–2009	2009–2010	2010–2011	2011–2012	2012–2013	2013–2014
High (100% +)	Odisha	Sikkim	Mizoram	Mizoram	Mizoram	Arunachal Pradesh	Pondicherry
	Chhattisgarh	Andaman and Nicobar Islands	Nagaland	Lakshadweep	Nagaland	Nagaland	Rajasthan
	Dadra and Nagar Haveli	Nagaland	Meghalaya	Andaman and Nicobar Islands	Meghalaya	Punjab	Uttaranchal
	Jammu and Kashmir	Arunachal Pradesh	Tripura	Meghalaya	Manipur	Kerala	Maharashtra
	Jharkhand	Meghalaya	Manipur	Nagaland	Tripura	Uttaranchal	Goa
	Mizoram	Punjab	Arunachal Pradesh	Sikkim	Lakshadweep		Chhattisgarh
	Uttaranchal	Mizoram	Andaman and Nicobar Islands	Tripura	Arunachal Pradesh		Tamil Nadu
	Chandigarh	Pondicherry	Lakshadweep	Manipur	Assam		Punjab
	Madhya Pradesh	Andhra Pradesh	Sikkim	Arunachal Pradesh	Andaman and Nicobar Islands		Chandigarh
	Tamil Nadu	Jammu and Kashmir	Jammu and Kashmir	Punjab	Goa		Lakshadweep
	Nagaland	Goa	Assam	Jammu and Kashmir	Punjab		Sikkim
	Delhi	Kerala	Kerala	Assam	Kerala		West Bengal
	Punjab	Karnataka	Punjab	Kerala	Sikkim		Manipur
	Pondicherry	Tripura	Himachal Pradesh	Bihar			
			Chandigarh	Uttaranchal			
			Pondicherry	Jharkhand			
				West Bengal			
				Goa			
Medium (50–99%)	Lakshadweep	Uttar Pradesh	Uttar Pradesh	Pondicherry	Uttar Pradesh	Meghalaya	Kerala
	Haryana	West Bengal	Jharkhand	Uttar Pradesh	Bihar	Mizoram	Andhra Pradesh
	Tripura	Tamil Nadu	Haryana	Odisha	Odisha	West Bengal	Karnataka
	Andhra Pradesh	Maharashtra	West Bengal	Karnataka	West Bengal	Andaman and Nicobar Islands	Assam
	Maharashtra	Himachal Pradesh	Uttaranchal	Tamil Nadu	Tamil Nadu	Sikkim	Dadra and Nagar Haveli
	Karnataka	Madhya Pradesh	Tamil Nadu	Haryana	Pondicherry	Goa	Jammu and Kashmir
	Gujarat	Chhattisgarh	Andhra Pradesh	Madhya Pradesh	Uttaranchal	Uttar Pradesh	Uttar Pradesh
	Goa	Rajasthan	Odisha	Chhattisgarh	Jharkhand	Tamil Nadu	Andaman and Nicobar Islands

(Contd.)

(Contd.)

Degree of implemen-tation	2007–2008	2008–2009	2009–2010	2010–2011	2011–2012	2012–2013	2013–2014
	Andaman and Nicobar Islands	Haryana	Bihar	Chandigarh	Karnataka	Jharkhand	Delhi
	Meghalaya	Odisha	Goa	Andhra Pradesh	Andhra Pradesh	Jammu and Kashmir	Madhya Pradesh
	Uttar Pradesh	Delhi	Karnataka	Daman and Diu	Rajasthan	Assam	Tripura
	Kerala	Jharkhand	Madhya Pradesh	Rajasthan	Jammu and Kashmir	Manipur	Bihar
	West Bengal	Daman and Diu	Rajasthan	Maharashtra	Chhattisgarh	Madhya Pradesh	Nagaland
	Sikkim	Lakshadweep	Delhi	Gujarat	Madhya Pradesh	Karnataka	Arunachal Pradesh
	Rajasthan	Assam	Chhattisgarh		Delhi	Odisha	Odisha
	Bihar	Bihar	Maharashtra		Haryana	Delhi	Haryana
		Chandigarh			Maharashtra	Rajasthan	Meghalaya
		Dadra and Nagar Haveli			Daman and Diu	Bihar	Gujarat
		Uttaranchal			Chandigarh	Chhattisgarh	Mizoram
		Manipur			Himachal Pradesh	Haryana	Jharkhand
		Gujarat			Gujarat	Andhra Pradesh	Himachal Pradesh
					Dadra and Nagar Haveli	Chandigarh	Daman and Diu
					Maharashtra		
					Himachal Pradesh		
					Gujarat		
Low (50%-)	Assam		Daman and Diu	Himachal Pradesh			Tripura
	Arunachal Pradesh		Gujarat	Delhi			Lakshadweep
	Daman and Diu		Dadra and Nagar Haveli	Dadra and Nagar Haveli			Dadra and Nagar Haveli
	Manipur						Pondicherry

Sources: The data for this table was derived from the MoMA website, compiled by the author. The data for Himachal Pradesh in 2007–2008 is unavailable.

It still remains difficult to estimate the real proportion of PSL provided to Muslims. In the absence of religion-specific distribution of PSL data, it is worth looking at the PSA in 121 MCDs by scheduled banks between 2008 and 2011. Figure 5.1 indicates that while the percentage of accounts for Muslims increased in 2007–2008 and 2008–2009, the share declined in 2009–2010 and 2010–2011, and hence the share decreased over the period as a whole. Since the figures are cumulative for each year, the declining share of the Muslim community is correlated to an increase for other communities. While these figures clearly have limitations, they do indicate that the share allocated to Muslims declined during that period (Shariff: 2012: 87).[25]

Although the percentage of PSL provided to minorities steadily increased, the situation for each religious community still remains unclear. The failure to generate data on religious minorities could be attributed to the political risks it might entail, but it also may have something to do with the gaps in the instruction provided by the RBI, which states that 'the [monitoring] data on assistance provided to members of minority communities should be furnished to RBI and to the Government of India, Ministry of Finance, and Ministry of Welfare, on a half yearly basis' by the relevant banks.[26] However, it is unclear who was to process this data into a consolidated data set. Interestingly, during the UPA's tenure little effort was invested in improving monitoring of these activities designed to enhance service delivery, and the problems that arose in employment data (see Chapter 4) also permeated financial statistics.[27]

---

[25] According to the field survey conducted in Barabanki in Uttar Pradesh, a state where 19 per cent of the total Muslim population of India reside, none of the 160 respondents had been provided credit through PSL for minorities or the 15PP (Khan and Parvati 2013: 259).

[26] This phrase was repeated in master circulars issued at least from 2003 to 2010 (see Bibliography).

[27] The Department of Financial Services in the Ministry of Finance, and the RBI, did not often specify the date a datasheet is generated, and it is common to find typos, misrepresentation, omissions and lack of data on implementation monitoring. With regard to access to credit, the direction of the Ministry of Finance to include minorities in the 'weaker section' of the RBI norm constituted substantive executive action to push through positive change, but it turned out to be ineffective in solving the core of the problem, since it failed to introduce any enforcing mechanism, or to combat discrimination in the banking structure. Overall, the failure centred on two problems: the weak monitoring mechanism of the RBI, and the reluctance of the relevant banks to submit data. First, to

Once again, the case of Gujarat demonstrates persistent institutional resistance in service delivery. Over the period 2009–2012, banks in Gujarat failed to achieve the target set for loans to minorities. In 2011–2012, they provided only 3.52 per cent of the total PSA to minorities (Dena Bank 2012: 15). Minorities have claimed that their applications for loans were rejected by the banks because they live in 'blacklisted areas of Ahmedabad'.[28] On the other hand, bankers argued that the failure to reach the target was due to the lack of demand from minority communities, while loan refusals were due

---

meet the objective of generating data on PSL provided to religious minorities, a reporting statement showing PSA granted to the members of the specified minority communities vis-à-vis overall PSA had been sent to relevant banks by the RBI since the pre-UPA period. The form was designed to collect the figures for Buddhists, Christians, Muslims, Sikhs and Zoroastrians, and carried the instruction that 'monitoring data on credit assistance provided to members of minority communities should be submitted to RBI, Ministry of Finance, and Ministry of Welfare on a half yearly basis'. In other words, data generation on religious lines was not a newly introduced measure by the UPA, and banks were already aware of the reporting system. However, there had been no enforcing mechanism to monitor the performance of relevant banks, and even after the UPA came to power, no noticeable changes were introduced. While the RBI was active in issuing circulars and instructions to relevant banks, neither the RBI nor the government made efforts to strengthen the monitoring system—the key measure to improve service delivery. While the government took a positive step in publicising data on the proportion of PSL given to religious minorities from 2012, the data generation process on the proportion of PSL provided to all religious minorities from 2007 onwards remains unclear. Second, although the RBI issued master circulars and guidelines every year to scheduled commercial banks in regard to credit facilities to minority communities, along with proforma instructions to submit an elaborate report on lending to minorities (on religious lines), in the absence of any monitoring mechanism the relevant banks continued to be inactive and reluctant to report and share data with RBI and central ministries on PSL for minorities. As a result, religion-specific data became available only from 2012, although it remains to be investigated whether the RBI did in fact collect religion-specific data from banks but was reluctant to make it public.

[28] 'The first question that banks ask is about the area in which an applicant lives and then, on the basis of the area of residence, they take a decision on the application for loan. There are certain areas such as Juhapura and Jamalpur which have been blacklisted' (Shah 2012).

Figure 5.1 PSA in 121 MCDs by scheduled banks

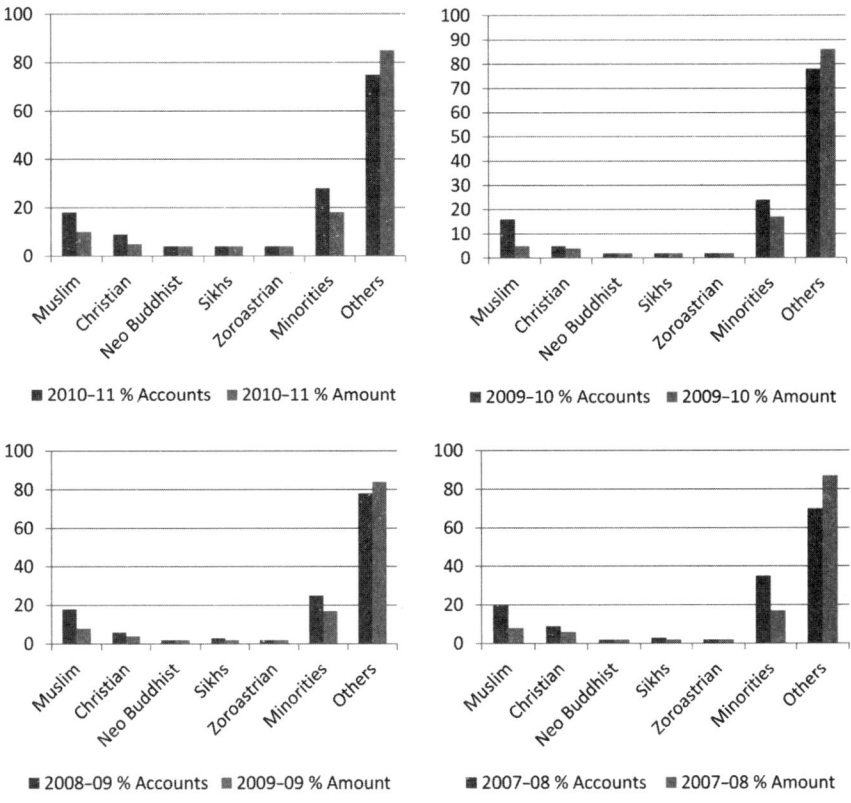

Source: Shariff (2012: 88).

to the absence of guarantors, proper documents and the capacity to repay. Despite the Finance Minister's executive order and guidelines and circulars, the practice noted in the *SCR*, whereby some banks had identified 'negative geographical zones', continued in Gujarat. As one Ahmedabad-based lawyer put it: 'He [an applicant] may have all the necessary documents but if he lives in a blacklisted area, he may find it difficult to get finance' (Shah 2012).

Our analysis of the limited data available in the public domain suggests that efforts to improve service delivery in the area of finance faced considerable institutional opposition. Executive action by the UPA government led to a steady increase in PSL provision to all minorities, but these efforts were insufficient to overcome institutional resistance. The absence of robust mechanisms for monitoring and constant evaluation of government and

RBI data resulted in ineffective use of such data for policy change. As a result, during the lifetime of the UPA administration, no disaggregated data on the percentage of PSL for each minority group had been made public.[29]

MSDP

The MSDP programme incorporated a wide range of programmes aimed at improving the conditions of minorities, especially Muslims. While it is important to examine the outcome of each scheme, our objectives here are to assess how MSDP policy was designed, presented and funded. Given that the MSDP was a flagship measure in the overall policy framework of the UPA, what does it tell us about the policy process and the modes of resistance to this policy?

According to the Eleventh Five-Year Plan, the MSDP was to 'adopt an area-based approach' (Planning Commission 2008: 128) with an emphasis on both infrastructure development and beneficiary-oriented programmes. This focus was confirmed by the minutes of Empowered Committee meetings which directed the state governments to implement schemes under the MSDP for area development rather than minority or community-specific development. From August 2008 to July 2011, in 39 out of 47 meetings, the MoMA repeatedly emphasised the need for implementation of the scheme to focus on *area development* rather than on *minorities*.[30] In the Eleventh Five-Year Plan, based on the 2001 Census, 90 districts were identified as

---

[29] Shariff also highlighted that 'neither RBI nor the Finance Ministry has reviewed or made public the reports on the access of development funds to the minorities although such data are collected as a matter of routine by RBI across India. The disaggregated information on the share of PSA for the minorities is in fact not being made accessible to the public at large' (Shariff 2013: 84).

[30] Out of 47 meetings, in the minutes of 8th–35th and 37th–47th meetings, it is stated that 'the fact that these districts were not just MCDs, having a substantial minority population, but also comprising of other communities who suffer from the same backwardness and deprivation, should not be lost sight of. It was important to keep in mind that the large presence of minorities may have resulted in the identification of such districts for appropriate developmental intervention, but the scheme, *while giving priority to villages/areas having a substantial minority population, was intended to benefit the district as a whole*' (for instance, see MoMA 2008b, emphasis added).

MCD using the criteria of 'backwardness',[31] gradually rising to 121 districts. Table 5.6 identifies these districts within the relevant states and, where available, the proportion of the minorities within the district. Muslims were the largest minority in 64 districts, Christians in 14, Buddhists in 9 and Sikhs in 1. Data for the remaining 33 is unavailable (MoMA 2011a).[32]

A number of points are worth noting about this data. First, though Muslims are in an overall majority in these districts, the MCDs cover only 47.66 per cent of the total Muslim community (Shariff 2013: 78). Second, due to the exclusion of urban areas from the MCDs and given the significant urban concentration of the Muslim population, many Muslim localities were excluded from the scheme. Third, the geographical dispersal of the Muslim community—in contrast to Christians, Sikhs and Buddhists who are more concentrated—makes the benefits of a district-based approach less effective than if the programme were targeted specifically at the community. Fourth, Table 5.7 indicates that as more MCDs were added the percentage of Muslims decreased. The government's effort to increase the number of MCDs using the above criteria resulted in a reduction in the Muslim share of the population benefitting from the scheme while increasing the coverage of other minorities (Christians, Sikhs and Buddhists). The criteria for the creation of MCDs and their subsequent expansion has led some critics to suggest that the area-based approach did not always seriously address the concerns of Muslim (and other minorities) underdevelopment because 'programme implementation can take place in such a way that the state religious groups are excluded from accessing the services' (ibid.: 79).

---

[31] This included, for the religion-specific socio-economic indicators at the district level, literacy rate, female literacy rate, work participation rate and female work participation rate; while the basic amenities indicators at district level comprised percentage of households with pucca walls, percentage with safe drinking water and percentage with electricity (Planning Commission 2008: 128).

[32] As the minutes of Empowered Committee meetings make clear, 'these districts have a substantial minority population, but also have other sections of the society who suffer from the same backwardness and deprivation, *as the identification of the district as backward have four parameters which are for the whole district.* The initiative is, therefore, a joint effort of the Centre and the States/Union Territories for inclusive growth/development, accelerating the development process and improving the quality of life of the people. MSDP aims at focused development programme for backward MCDs to help reduce imbalances and speed up development' (for instance, see MoMA 2011b, emphasis added).

Table 5.6 Proportion of minorities in 121 MCDs as per Census 2001

States	Districts	Muslims	Christians	Sikhs	Buddhists
Andamans	Nicobars		N/A		
	Andamans				
Andhra Pradesh	Hyderabad		N/A		
Arunachal Pradesh	Tawang	0.58	0.79	1.08	**74.72**
	East Kameng	0.67	**25.45**	0.08	1.23
	West Kameng	1.55	3.30	0.57	**44.38**
	Lower Subansiri	0.84	**24.51**	0.05	0.29
	Changlang	0.93	17.49	0.04	**34.08**
	Tirap	0.75	**50.04**	0.10	0.67
	Papum Pare	4.36	**29.98**	0.22	2.73
Assam	Kokrajhar	**20.36**	13.72	0.01	0.17
	Dhubri	**74.29**	0.76	0.01	0.02
	Goalpara	**53.71**	7.87	0.01	0.02
	Bongaigaon	**38.52**	2.07	0.06	0.04
	Barpeta	**59.37**	0.32	0.02	0.01
	Darrang	**35.54**	6.47	0.03	0.12
	Marigaon	**47.59**	0.10	0.01	0.01
	Nagaon	**50.99**	0.93	0.13	0.05
	Cachar	**36.13**	2.17	0.04	0.05
	Karimganj	**52.30**	0.87	0.01	0.03
	Hailakandi	**57.63**	1.00	0.00	0.11
	Kamrup	24.78	1.75	0.19	0.07
	North Cachar Hills	15.23	**54.57**	0.05	0.28
Bihar	Araria	**41.14**	0.06	0.02	0.05
	Kishanganj	**67.58**	0.22	0.04	0.03
	Purnia	**36.76**	0.17	0.05	0.00
	Katihar	**42.53**	0.21	0.09	0.00
	Sitamarhi	**21.21**	0.02	0.01	0.01
	Pashchim Champaran	**21.25**	0.20	0.02	0.05
	Darbhanga	**22.73**	0.02	0.01	0.00
Delhi	North east Delhi	**27.24**	0.43	1.05	0.27
	Central		N/A		
Goa	South Goa		N/A		
Haryana	Gurgaon		N/A		
	Sirsa	0.63	0.15	**27.13**	0.03
Himachal Pradesh	Lahul and Spiti		N/A		
	Kinnaur				
Jammu and Kashmir	Leh (Ladahk)	13.78	0.29	0.43	**77.30**
Jharkhand	Ranchi	**12.52**	9.10	0.27	0.05
	Gumla	4.44	**31.56**	0.04	0.02
	Sahibganj	**31.26**	6.33	0.03	0.00
	Pakaur	**32.36**	5.86	0.06	0.01

(*Contd.*)

(*Contd.*)

States	Districts	Muslims	Christians	Sikhs	Buddhists
Karnataka	Dakshina Kannada		N/A		
	Bidar	19.69	2.87	0.04	8.13
	Gulbarga	17.60	0.59	0.02	4.91
Kerala	Wayanad	26.87	22.48	0.00	0.01
	Malappuram				
	Ernakulam				
	Kottayam				
	Idukki				
	Pathanamthitta				
	Kozhikode				
	Kasaragod		N/A		
	Thrissur				
	Kannur				
	Kollam				
	Thiruvananthapuram				
	Palakkad				
	Alappuzha				
Madhya Pradesh	Bhopal	22.86	1.11	0.62	1.12
Maharashtra	Buldana	12.78	0.11	0.07	**13.73**
	Hingoli	10.45	0.05	0.05	**14.99**
	Parbhani	15.97	0.09	0.05	10.03
	Washim	10.96	0.12	0.05	**14.76**
	Akola				
	Mumbai				
	Aurangabad		N/A		
	Mumbai (Suburban)				
	Amravati				
Manipur	Senapati	0.41	**78.41**	0.10	0.82
	Tamenglong	1.28	**94.88**	0.06	0.01
	Churachandpur	1.13	**93.54**	0.05	0.02
	Ukhrul	0.63	**95.16**	0.07	0.06
	Chandel	1.96	**92.23**	0.11	0.05
	Thoubal	**23.85**	1.41	0.03	0.01
Meghalaya	West Garo Hills	15.23	**54.57**	0.05	0.28
Mizoram	Mamit	1.75	**80.53**	0.04	13.66
	Lawngtlai	0.31	44.66	0.10	**52.17**
Orissa	Gajapati	0.31	**33.47**	0	0.38
Pondicherry	Mahe		N/A		
Rajasthan	Ganganagar		N/A		
Sikkim	North Sikkim	0.95	3.96	0.36	**55.09**
	East				
	West		N/A		
	South				

(*Contd.*)

(*Contd.*)

States	Districts	Muslims	Christians	Sikhs	Buddhists
Tamil Nadu	Kanniyakumari		N/A		
Uttar Pradesh	Bulandshahar	21.07	0.13	0.16	0.07
	Budaun	21.33	0.11	0.09	0.16
	Barabanki	22.04	0.08	0.12	0.09
	Kheri	19.10	0.12	2.64	0.66
	Shahjahanpur	17.86	0.11	2.14	0.20
	Moradabad	45.54	0.23	0.23	0.06
	Rampur	49.14	0.38	3.21	0.12
	Jyotiba Phule Nagar	39.38	0.28	0.37	0.02
	Bareilly	33.89	0.26	0.80	0.20
	Pilibhit	23.75	0.11	4.59	0.11
	Bahraich	34.83	0.09	0.32	0.14
	Shrawasti	25.60	0.05	0.07	0.05
	Balrampur	36.72	0.08	0.08	0.18
	Siddharthnagar	29.43	0.06	0.06	0.39
	Bijnor	41.71	0.11	1.56	0.11
	Saharanpur	39.11	0.17	0.71	0.13
	Muzaffarnagar	38.09	0.09	0.54	0.07
	Meerut	32.55	0.25	0.88	0.09
	Baghpat	24.73	0.09	0.09	0.03
	Ghaziabad	23.79	0.27	0.64	0.10
	Lucknow	20.52	0.34	0.63	0.12
Uttaranchal	Hardwar	33.05	0.21	1.20	0.05
	Udham Singh Nagar	20.59	0.31	11.45	0.12
West Bengal	North 24 Parganas	24.22	0.23	0.12	0.07
	Kolkata	20.27	0.88	0.34	0.14
	Koch Bihar	24.24	0.09	0.01	0.02
	Uttar Dinajpur	47.36	0.54	0.01	0.01
	Dakshin Dinajpur	24.02	1.47	0.01	0.01
	Maldah	49.72	0.25	0.01	0.00
	Murshidabad	63.67	0.23	0.01	0.00
	Birbhum	35.08	0.24	0.01	0.01
	Barddhaman	19.78	0.23	0.32	0.02
	Nadia	25.41	0.64	0.02	0.01
	Howrah (Haorah)	24.44	0.15	0.09	0.03
	South 24 Parganas	33.24	0.76	0.02	0.03

Source: Ministry of Minority Affairs.

Table 5.7 Share of minority in total minority population in MCD

Minority districts	Total minority (millions)	Muslims (%)	Christians (%)	Sikhs (%)	Buddhists (%)	Zoroastrians (%)
India	189.5	72.92	12.71	10.14	4.20	0.04
121 MCDs	81.7	80.64	13.44	2.01	3.85	0.06
90 MCDs	58.2	89.96	5.67	1.87	2.50	0.00
41 MCDs	45.9	93.31	3.44	0.91	2.32	0.03

Source: Shariff (2013: 78).

Note: In the first and last rows, the sum of share of minorities is slightly more than 100 per cent due to reduction in the number of decimal places (rounding error).

The Post-Sachar Evaluation Committee in its review of the MSDP was highly critical of the performance of the scheme in targeting Muslim deprivation. It identified a number of concerns. These

> ranged from the fact that it is largely an area development scheme and does not focus on individual families ... and as the minorities are not uniformly concentrated in the districts, the schemes under the programme can be carried out without really benefitting the minorities. Only about 30 per cent of the Muslims ... can benefit from targeting 90 districts as implementation unit for MSDP; non-inclusion of a large section of Muslims in Below Poverty Line (BPL) list keeps them away from the benefits of many schemes. (MoMA 2014: 148)

The Committee's finding largely confirmed the evidence collected by NGOs and advocacy organisations that the MSDP had been in general badly designed as a means of addressing the needs of poor Muslims (ibid.).[33]

On the question of whether Muslims in MCDs were able to secure equitable access to various government programmes, much more rigorous analysis is required. As noted above, the government had decided to adopt the norms and guidelines of Centrally Sponsored Schemes in implementing the MSDP. Table 5.8 lists the schemes for minorities in MCDs, with the budget allocations during the Eleventh Five-Year Plan.

---

[33] Space precludes a more detailed assessment. The Committee's findings are reviewed in the Conclusion.

Table 5.8 Budget allocation by the Union government for minorities in the Eleventh Five-Year Plan

Schemes	Amount (Rs Crore)	Share (percentage)
BSUP	31,431.08	29.73
IHSDP	8,147.59	7.71
UIG	26,495.95	25.06
UIDSSMT	7,825.81	7.40
IAY	8,216.426	7.77
NRDWP	14,045.31	13.28
ITI	163	0.15
SJSRY	192	0.18
Madrasa Modernisation Programme	450	0.43

Source: Khan (2012: 12).

Four schemes—the Jawaharlal Nehru National Urban Renewal Mission (JNNURM), which was an umbrella scheme, and included BSUP, IHSDP, UIG and UIDSSMT—constituted 69.9 per cent of the total funds allocated for minorities. Launched in December 2005 as the largest initiative of the government for the planned development of cities, JNNURM aimed to improve urban infrastructure and provide services to the urban poor. As more Muslims reside in urban areas than in the countryside, and the poverty ratio among urban Muslims is high (*SCR* 2006: 158), this flagship city redevelopment programme should have disproportionately benefitted community development. However, upon closer examination, minorities, particularly Muslims, were almost non-existent in areas where the JNNURM was implemented.[34] Moreover, most of the allocations made under the JNNURM only reported the number and costs of projects sanctioned, not the beneficiaries or any data on minorities.[35]

---

[34] According to Jawed Alam Khan, 'MoMA provides the data on financial allocation made for minorities by JNNURM on its website but without any physical outcome. When I tried to probe it in states like Uttar Pradesh, West Bengal, Bihar and Haryana, the officials were unable to provide any data on Muslims/minorities' (interview, 11 April 2014, New Delhi). In the words of an official in Bihar: 'There is no exclusion of any section from these schemes, but no targeting of minorities too' (Centre for Equity Studies 2012: 34).

[35] It is in stark contrast to the budget statement for SCs and STs of the amount allocated under different ministries. In the guidelines of JNNURM there is neither provision for religious minorities nor a budget reporting mechanism.

Thus, the use of Centrally Sponsored Scheme guidelines in implementing the JNNURM was a major missed opportunity: it resulted in the failure to develop adequate policy tools to address the exclusion of Muslims in one of the largest development schemes sponsored by the central government.[36] In effect, the MSDP became a mechanism for increased funding for existing programmes rather than a qualitatively new departure from approaches pursued by previous governments.

With the exceptions of the JNNURM, IAY and SJSRY, other schemes in Table 5.8 were beneficiary-driven and aimed at poverty reduction. Yet, once again, large numbers of Muslims were excluded from these schemes because their names were omitted from the BPL list. Although the *SCR* had pointed out that many poor Muslims do not have BPL cards,[37] this shortcoming was not taken into account in policy design or execution, particularly in poverty reduction programmes, which were still being designed to benefit those in possession of the cards (Trivedi 2012: 239). But such failure in policy design and execution should be understood in a broader context: the last update of the BPL list was conducted by the government in 2002 although it should have taken place in 2007 and 2012.

[36] 'Most of the Centrally Sponsored Schemes that are part of the [15PP] have not been altered in any way (by way of bringing about changes in the scheme guidelines) to cater to the specific disadvantages and needs of the community. The state and district level implementing agencies do not have adequate clarity on the share of allocations available towards the programme given the lack of disaggregated data in most schemes' (Khan 2012: 19). Another example of rigidity adopted in using Centrally Sponsored Schemes in a government programme is the Mahatma Gandhi National Rural Employment Guarantee Scheme (MGNREGS)—the largest and most ambitious social security and public works programme in the world according to the Ministry of Rural Development. In MGNREGS only 13 per cent of Muslims were included while they constitute 36 per cent of the population and 45 per cent of the job card holders. But a field survey conducted in Mewat (74 per cent Muslim population) in Haryana revealed a worse scenario where people were unwilling to work through MGNREGS due to low wages and inordinate delays which contributed to the low take-up of the scheme (Centre for Equity Studies 2012: vii–viii; Khan and Parvati 2013: 260).

[37] 'Muslims are often not able to avail of the reservation benefits available to OBCs as the officials do not issue the requisite caste certificates ... many eligible Muslim OBCs were not included in the official list which results in denial of several benefits to the community' (*SCR* 2006: 24).

In the absence of the BPL census for 2007 and 2012, the government initiated a new census named the 'Socio Economic and Caste Census' in June 2011 (Ministry of Rural Development 2011).[38] However, the final results of this census were not published until 2015 by which the lifetime of the UPA administration had come to an end.

As well as poor policy design and execution, expenditure under SSA, SGSY and ICDS was badly publicised and ineffectively monitored. While many government schemes were aimed at area development, the few beneficiary-driven ones (IAY, SJSRY and SGSY) provided limited opportunity for Muslims (Khan 2012: 19). The absence of any fund allocation report for these schemes makes it difficult to assess whether Muslims have benefitted at all. Similarly, the NRDWP reports data by state but it is difficult to estimate the number of minorities who benefitted. The ITI also provides state data on targets and achievements but does not specify which minority communities benefit (ibid.: 5).[39] The funds for the Madrasa Modernisation Programme, the promotion of Urdu, and Haj subsidies combined were less than 1 per cent of the total allocation. Overall, the budget allocated to the MoMA for the various schemes merely combined existing allocations previously under different schemes and ministries. Yet even with this limited allocation, as Table 5.9 shows, the MoMA's funds remained poorly utilised.

---

[38] According to the Minister of Rural Development, this census was to generate a rank listing of rural households based on automatic inclusion criteria and deprivation indicators, and to be sent to state governments to determine the BPL households in states. The outcome of this census is particularly important for Muslims whose large population is excluded from the BPL list, itself largely based on caste considerations, and from the provision of BPL certificates. The result of this survey is also crucial because the government delayed its reply to the Supreme Court query in regard to provision of 4.5 per cent sub-quota in the existing OBC quota in employment and education to Muslims and Christians until the survey was complete. 'With the knowledge of proportion of SCs in the Muslim and Christian communities, the government wants to use the outcome as evidence in its reply to the Supreme Court' (Jawed Alam Khan, interview, 11 April 2014, New Delhi).

[39] 'If [ITIs] are to be built, there is no robust system to ensure that these will be located in Muslim localities' (Centre for Equity Studies 2012: viii).

Table 5.9 Fund utilisation by the Union government for minorities in the Eleventh Five-Year Plan

Year	BE (Rs crore)	RE (Rs crore)	Actual expenditure (Rs crore)	Utilisation (%)
2007–2008	500.00	350.00	196.65	39.33
2008–2009	1,000.00	650.00	619.02	61.90
2009–2010	1,740.00	1,740.00	1,709.425	98.24
2010–2011	2,600.00	2500.00	2,008.87	77.26
2011–2012	2,850.00	2,750.00	2,283.415	80.12
Total (2007–2012)	8,690	7,990	6,817.38	78.45

Source: Ministry of Minority Affairs, *Statement Indicating BE, RE and Actual Expenditure for the Years 2006–2007, 2007–2008, 2008–2009, 2009–2010, 2010–2011, 2011–2012, 2012–2013 and 2013–2014.*

Note: BE: Budget Estimate; RE: Revised Estimate. Utilisation has been calculated based on the BE.

During the Eleventh Plan, the Ministry spent only 6,817 crore rupees (78 per cent), and surrendered 1,872 crore rupees. The MoMA attributed this underspend to state governments:

> Unfortunately in the Eleventh Five-Year Plan, and the first year of the Twelfth Five-Year Plan, we could not spend the amount earmarked for MSDP, because states have to send the proposals, but they didn't send proposal in time. So we were not able to process them. The major responsibility is with the states. We had the money, we could have transferred it, but most of the states did not send the project. *They are not interested in these projects. State governments say it is central government projects, let them have it. They sometimes have their own state projects. States' bureaucracy was the source of [the] problem.*[40]

The same explanation is found in the report of the Steering Committee on Empowerment of Minorities of the Planning Commission which concluded that 'whole amount allocated could not be spent due to non-submission of complete and adequate proposals by the States/Union Territories, late

---

[40] K. Rahman Khan, interview, 12 February 2013, New Delhi, emphasis added. Low utilisation of funds was also discussed in the standing committee report on social justice and empowerment (MoMA 2012b: 29–33).

submission of utilisation certificates by the States/Union Territories, [and the] promulgation of code of conduct for elections in some States' (Planning Commission 2011: 14). The non-submission of proposals was also noted in Parliament: 'four states, viz. Arunachal Pradesh, Delhi, and Madhya Pradesh, Sikkim have not submitted their district plans'.[41]

Data, monitoring and evaluation

Many of the shortcomings in service delivery could have been anticipated by effective regular monitoring of data, constant evaluation and reassessment of targets. Yet throughout the fieldwork it was repeatedly stated by government officials and policymakers that it was against the spirit of the Constitution to generate data on religious lines. Even schemes designed for minorities, particularly those 'officially' sanctioned to earmark a certain portion of benefits to them, do not clarify the actual number of recipients among religious minorities. None of the monitoring data on schemes providing a flow of funds to MCDs[42] specifies the actual recipient.[43] Furthermore, the data by state on schemes under various ministries is incomplete as many states fail to file proper status/monitoring reports with the ministry.

In general, monitoring data on government schemes for minorities is inaccessible and poorly organised. The situation with the budget data is not an exception; rather, it can be convincingly argued that Indian government data is fragmented, sometimes deliberately misrepresented and incomplete. While the expenditure data are relatively well-structured and produced at regular intervals, they fail to show how the funds were utilised and whether they benefitted the intended recipients. The government's inactivity is well illustrated by an answer given in a Rajya Sabha debate by the Minister of State for the MoMA. Asked whether benefits from the schemes had reached the minorities, he responded that 'funds are released as per the norms'.[44] Parliamentary debates on monitoring are almost non-existent, and the remarks made by policymakers often give the impression that the government considers funds released and

---

[41] Se RSD, 7 December 2009; RSD, 14 December 2009.
[42] The schemes include BSUP, IHSDP, UIG, UIDSSMT and NRDWP.
[43] The weak monitoring system and improvement of monitoring mechanism was noted in the standing committee report on social justice and empowerment (Centre for Equity Studies 2012: xix; MoMA 2012b: 48; 50–51).
[44] RSD, 19 March 2012.

benefits to minorities as one and the same thing.[45] As a result of this inertia, of the various schemes under the PM's 15PP, not a single one reported the targets/outlays for minorities, or the religious status of the recipients.[46] On the other hand, data that does exist is very difficult to access, due to the absence or complexity of systematic reporting mechanisms on the various ministry websites, and because many different schemes are homed in different ministries with no consolidated or coordinated presentation of statistics. This is despite the fact that when the MSDP was launched, the Cabinet Committee on Economic Affairs announced that 'a suitable monitoring system would be put in place. An independent in-depth evaluation would be made after two years to assess the need for any mid-term correction' (PIB 2008b).[47] At the end of the Eleventh Five-Year Plan, the monitoring effort made by the government proved symbolic: it only generated data by state on financial and physical progress in the MSDP, without specifying the religious identity of the recipients (MoMA *MSDP for MCDs: Financial Progress Report*; *MSDP for MCDs: Physical Progress Report*).

However, as a result of these weaknesses, some policy changes have been made in the Twelfth Five-Year Plan. In July and October 2011, the MoMA

[45] The Minister of Minority Affairs, Salman Khurshid, stated in the Rajya Sabha debate that 'implementation of the scheme of MSDP for MCDs is reviewed regularly by the government with the state government/Union Territory administration concerned' (*RSD*, 7 December 2009). He further added that 'the implementation of MSDP is monitored at the district, State/Union Territory and centre at regular intervals to ensure that the budgeted funds are utilised fully' (*RSD*, 15 November 2010). It was confirmed by the former chairman of NCM that 'so far as the MSDP is concerned, the monitoring is confined to how much money is given and how much money is spent. Whether it really has gone to the minorities or not, it is not their concern' (Wajahat Habibullah, interview, 11 April 2014, New Delhi).
[46] Monitoring reports of SSA, SGSY, IAY, SJSRY, ITIs, operationalisation of Anganwadi centres under ICDS do not specify religious identity of beneficiaries.
[47] Despite poor monitoring, the monitoring mechanism of the PM's 15PP was also delineated in the Planning Commission's Eleventh Five-Year Plan report that 'the procedure for monitoring the outcomes of these multiple initiatives is clearly laid out. It will be done on a half-yearly basis by the Committee of Secretaries and the Cabinet' (Planning Commission 2008: 124). However, Zoya Hasan was adamant that as far as the MSDP is concerned, 'importantly, the government did not put in place a proper assessment and monitoring system other than a Planning Commission Steering Committee for this purpose' (2012: 174).

held consultations with experts, academicians and intellectuals from minority communities. Based on these consultations, and the recommendations of the Planning Commission's Working Group on Empowerment of Minorities, the MoMA formulated new proposals for the Planning Commission. In addition, the MoMA received recommendations from the National Advisory Council (NAC) on education and employment schemes, and made revisions to the MSDP guidelines. As a result, the Twelfth Five-Year Plan (2012–2017) demonstrates a more concentrated effort on proportionality. The Steering Committee of the Planning Commission recommended that for the Twelfth Five-Year Plan the government should adopt the 'block' as a unit of planning, allowing for better targeting of minorities, and the population criterion to identify MCDs should be reduced from 25 per cent to 15 per cent. A noticeable shift can be seen in the minutes of the Empowered Committee, with a new focus on proportionality. As the minutes of the Committee note:

> Secretary ... [of] Ministry of Minority Affairs emphasised that the benefits accrued by the implementation of MSDP should go to the Minority Community properly. Therefore, not only location of the assets in the areas having substantial minority population is important, but it is also equally important to see that the assets created are actually imparting benefits to the minorities. He requested the state governments to propose the locations accordingly.[48]

In the 25 meetings of the Empowered Committee that took place since September 2012, this focus on proportionality and targeted benefit has been mentioned in at least 24 occasions.[49]

Despite these official changes, institutionalised opposition to special treatment for Muslims remains strong. At the end of 2011, the Centre for Budget and Governance Accountability initiated a process to prepare a memorandum for the 2012 Budget Session on the Twelfth Five-Year Plan, with the aim of bringing government's attention to the need for specific planning

---

[48] This section is repeated in minutes of the 58th–83rd meetings. For instance, see MoMA (2011c).

[49] In the minutes of the 62nd meeting uploaded on the MoMA website, the scanned file of page 4, which might have contained the same paragraph, is missing. In the light of other meetings, it is assumed that focused effort on proportionality must also have been mentioned in the 62nd meeting.

intervention to address Muslim backwardness.[50] Following the endorsement of the memorandum by MPs, the Centre held a meeting with the Minister of Minority Affairs in May 2012. After the Minister's positive response, in July and August 2012, the Principal Secretary to the Prime Minister invited the line ministries, with responsibility for the implementation of the 15PP, to provide beneficiary data on religious minorities. But this request was refused.[51] In hindsight, most of the changes in the Twelfth Five-Year Plan were not transformed into reality.

Conclusion

This chapter has focused on limited case studies—scholarships, credit and the MSDP—aimed at improving service delivery for socio-economically disadvantaged Muslims. These policy initiatives were very different but encountered similar problems. In general, they were beset by poor design, ambiguous executive control, weak implementation,[52] chronic underfunding, bewildering complexity and overlap, and, above all, weak mechanisms of monitoring, evaluation and targeting of religious beneficiaries.[53] The absence

---

[50] Some of the key initiatives in this memorandum include focused effort on (*a*) strengthening the 15PP on the lines of the Scheduled Caste Sub-Plan and Tribal Sub-Plan along with reforms in the budgetary processes and institutions, (*b*) creating a separate budget statement on the 15PP along with earmarked budget heads in the detailed demands for grants like Scheduled Caste Sub-Plan and Tribal Sub-Plan, (*c*) annual reports of all ministries/departments should provide disaggregated religious group-wise data on Muslim beneficiaries in schemes, public employment and access to credit, (*d*) creating effective institutional mechanisms (Minority Welfare Department at district and state levels) and providing adequate staff for effective implementation at the state level and (*e*) expanding the coverage of the MSDP beyond the 90 MCDs to ensure service delivery to the community (Centre for Budget and Governance Accountability 2011).

[51] Jawed Alam Khan, interview, 11 April 2014, New Delhi.

[52] In Andhra Pradesh, not a single district was identified under the MSDP (*RSD*, 30 November 2009). In the case of Bihar, the strict selection criteria for MCDs failed to cover towns where there were sizeable populations of minorities (*RSD*, 17 August 2010).

[53] The guideline of the PM's 15PP stated that 'considering the complexity of the programme and its wide reach, wherever possible, Ministries/Departments concerned will earmark 15 per cent of the physical targets and financial outlays

of the latter was all the more surprising given that in policy announcements monitoring was regularly mentioned as an essential requirement of service delivery.[54] In large measure, these shortcomings stemmed from the UPA's reluctance to develop its policies for disadvantaged Muslims as a special programme *à la* SCs and STs. As any such special programme was equated by the UPA's opponents (and some of its own supporters)—political as well as administrative—with reservations and special treatment, the government was compelled to use executive discretion rather than primary legislation. As the UPA leadership struggled to explain satisfactorily the distinction between positive action and reservations, as we saw in the Minister of Finance Chidambaram's response to a parliamentary question, opposition to the schemes mounted nationally and within the states. While there have been some notable successes, for instance the take-up of the scholarship scheme, and the UPA's executive action also created an enabling environment in which pro-minority policy actors could mobilise and influence policy, such as the revisions for the Twelfth Five-Year Plan, the overall picture is one of determined political and institutional resistance. As the UPA's commitment to positive action for Muslims waned after 2007, the potential momentum for a new critical juncture to create a new paradigm of equality of opportunity for religious minorities had been lost. The familiar pattern of historical path dependence was all too evident in the symbolic implementation of, and the political distancing from, these policies long before May 2014.

---

for ministries'. However, in the explanation of how the scheme should be implemented, ambiguous terminology such as 'a certain percentage' gave leeway to administrators in interpretation and hence in implementation. Under the Eleventh Five-Year Plan, monitoring of all existing and new interventions was emphasised, and hence the MoMA had to ensure that other concerned ministries and departments monitored the implementation of the 15PP. The monitoring mechanism for implementation of the PM's 15PP appeared to be strengthened in 2009 through the government's approval that two members from the Lok Sabha, one from the Rajya Sabha, and two from the Legislative Assembly be nominated by the state government for inclusion in the State Level Committee. Despite these recommendations, the monitoring data for religious minorities has not been made public.

[54] In 2009, under pressure, the MoMA hurriedly assigned the task of monitoring the implementation of schemes for minorities to the National Productivity Council, an autonomous organisation under the Ministry of Commerce and Industry (PIB 2009).

6

UPA, Muslims and the Communal Violence Bill

Introduction

Equal protection under the law for racial, ethnic, religious and other minorities is considered a fundamental right, and in the 1980s and 1990s, Western democracies increasingly adopted legislation that outlawed specific forms of hate crime targeted at minorities (Addison 2007; Jacobs and Potter 1998). In India, special legislative provisions for vulnerable groups, such as the anti-discrimination measures in the Protection of Civil Rights Act (1955) and the Scheduled Castes and Scheduled Tribes (Prevention of Atrocities) Act (1989), have provided strong legal protection and security to caste groups in the wake of violence. In contrast, though religious minorities, especially Muslims, have been the target of violence during communal riots, they and other religious minorities lack equivalent protection. Hindu–Muslim riots and anti-Muslim pogroms have become the defining feature of post-1947 collective violence in India, and the regular recurrence of such events presents a serious challenge to the principles of secularism and religious tolerance. Recognising this fact, the UPA government promised to 'enact a model comprehensive law to deal with communal violence' (Government of India 2004).

In this chapter we undertake a detailed case study of the UPA's efforts to legislate for a model anti-communal violence bill by focusing on draft bills produced in 2005 and 2011 and the policy process thereafter. We highlight how the UPA's efforts to produce 'top-down' legislation were frustrated by the institutionalised opposition to such a measure—political, administrative and judicial—and how Muslim communities and civil society networks sought to build momentum for the bill. The goal of a new, normative legislation that could have significantly increased the penalties for committing communal violence, however, continued to elude the UPA. Faced with opposition within its own ranks, the Congress-led UPA eventually opted for symbolic implementation.

Agenda-setting

After 2004, the UPA government was determined to prevent Gujarat-type anti-minority massacres. Historically, in the aftermath of violence, state and central governments have usually taken action, some stronger than others, to deal with riots. State government and police have often been partisan in controlling violence, managing post-conflict situations, and providing relief and rehabilitation (Gonsalves 2002; Gupta 2011; Wilkinson 2004).[1] Discrimination against Muslims has been most visible in the use of force, preventive arrests and treatment of persons detained as well as in investigation, detection and prosecution of cases registered during riots.[2] Thus, the Gujarat riots resulted in the death of 2,000 Muslims and the displacement of 150,000 into relief camps, in significant part due to the ambiguous attitudes of the authorities and their failure to control the violence (Z. Hasan 2006: 201–202).[3]

Following the Gujarat riots, the United States Commission on International Religious Freedom expressed growing concerns about religious intolerance in the country.[4] The UPA had pledged to tackle anti-religious discrimination and to bring domestic legislation addressing increasingly active anti-religious discrimination following 9/11. The Congress-led UPA's NCMP promised

> ... to preserve, protect and promote social harmony and to enforce the law without fear or favour to deal with all obscurantist and fundamentalist elements who seek to disturb social amity and peace. (Government of India 2004)

Earlier, the Congress manifesto had promised to 'enact a model comprehensive law to deal with communal violence' (ibid.) by stating:

---

[1] Gupta (2011) notes that not only in the aftermath of the Gujarat riot, but also in other riots in the history of India, authorities have neglected to help riot victims.
[2] For the state's response to outbreak of communal riots, see Engineer (1994), Hansen (1999), Shani (2007), K. S. Subramanian (2007) and van der Veer (1996).
[3] It should be noted that the data on the death toll and the missing vary among sources. According to data provided by the Government of Gujarat, 254 Hindus and 790 Muslims were killed, 223 missing, 2548 injured, 919 were rendered widows, and 606 children orphaned during the riots. *RSD*, 11 May 2005.
[4] See Annual Reports of the United States Commission on International Religious Freedom, available at uscirf.gov/reports-briefs/annual-report.

The Congress will adopt all possible measures to promote and maintain communal peace and harmony, especially in sensitive areas. It will enact a comprehensive law on social violence in all its forms and manifestations, providing for investigations by a central agency, prosecution by Special Courts and payment of uniform compensation for loss of life, honour and property. (INC 2004)

The *SCR* focused on the socio-economic conditions of the Muslim community, and also expressed concerns about the lack of a sense of security among Muslims. This insecurity felt by the Muslim community, the *SCR* noted, was due to the lackadaisical attitude of governments in controlling outbreak of communal riots, inaction in punishing the guilty, particularly state officials, and the attitude of the police and the media in reporting the involvement of Muslims in violence. It also acknowledged that a bare minimum of compensation is awarded to the riot victims, and highlighted particular delay in payments when the victims are Muslims (*SCR* 2006: 13). The heightened fear of insecurity among Muslims has occasioned increasing ghettoisation. The *SCR* also attributed the bias within the police and law and order agencies to the lack of an adequate Muslim presence in the police force (ibid.: 14; see also Mander 2006). While the concern about fear for security of the Muslim community is rightly emphasised, the committee avoided making any specific recommendations on this matter.[5]

Policy formulation and decision-making

In terms of the policy cycle, while the agenda-setting stage was clearly identifiable, the process of policy formulation spanned both UPA I and UPA II. In fact, it

---

[5] While neither the *SCR* nor the *RMCR* provided recommendations in regard to protection of religious minorities (for it was not a part of their terms of reference), one member of the Ranganath Misra Commission, a jurist, confirmed his view on having a separate law to deal with communal violence because, according to him, the 'IPC is not enough, it is too old. It is based on the social situation at that time. The system of criminal procedure in the country which regulates the working of the IPC is very defective. The Code of Criminal Procedure was replaced with new version in 1973 but the new Code of Criminal Procedure is old wine in new bottle. It still regulates the working of IPC. And this regulatory law is more outdated, worse than the substantive law. IPC is not going to help check communal violence' (Tahir Mahmood, interview, 12 April 2014, New Delhi).

began properly with the introduction of legislation in Parliament.[6] There seem to have been limited consultations before the Communal Violence (Prevention, Control and Rehabilitation of Victims) Bill (2005) was introduced in the Rajya Sabha on 5 December 2005. In moving the bill, the Minister of Home Affairs claimed its aims were to

> empower the State Governments and the Central Government to take measures to provide for the prevention and control of communal violence which threatens the secular fabric, unity, integrity and internal security of the Nation and rehabilitation of victims of such violence and for matters connected therewith or incidental thereto. (Ministry of Home Affairs 2005b)

These aims were so broad that turning them into legislation would stoke the ire of opponents and supporters alike. The key challenge facing the government was not only to build effective political support for the measure among the states and national parties, but also to draft the legislation in a way which distinguished it from existing statutes. Thus, the bill created a new offence of communal violence, identified the target groups, enhanced the powers to control communally disturbed areas, increased the accountability of officials involved in the management of communal violence and provided for more effective rehabilitation and relief for the victims than done hitherto. Not unnaturally, these radical innovations faced significant challenges.

The bill sought to create a new framework for tackling communal violence. First, it redefined 'communal violence' as 'any act of omission or commission which constitutes a scheduled offence'.[7] Second, the target group was to include not only religious communities but 'any group, caste or community' (Ministry of Home Affairs 2005b: section 3[1]). Third, new powers were given to state governments to declare an area 'communally disturbed' when

---

[6] In India the mere introduction of a bill in Parliament is not the end point of the policy formulation process as far as the government is concerned, but often the beginning of long drawn-out policy formulation stage, with repeated resubmissions of bills following amendments and revisions by the government. As this bill extended over two Parliaments, we will consider the policy process under UPA I and UPA II.

[7] For a list of scheduled offences, see Ministry of Home Affairs (2005b: The Schedule).

criminal force or violence against any group, caste or community [is committed] resulting in death or destruction of property; [when] such use of criminal force or violence is committed with a view to create disharmony or feelings of enmity, hatred or ill-will between different group, caste or communities; [and] unless immediate steps are taken there will be danger to the secular fabric, integrity, unity or internal security of India. (Ibid.)

All three conditions had to be satisfied for an area to be declared communally disturbed. Fourth, new enhanced powers were also given to District Magistrates to empower them to prevent and control communal violence (ibid.: section 5[1]). Fifth, the powers of the centre to deal with states in situations of communal violence were further strengthened: the centre could 'draw the attention of the State Government to the prevailing situation in [violence afflicted] area' and 'direct the State Government to take all immediate measures to suppress such violence or the use of criminal force' (ibid.: section 55[1]). If the centre's voice were ignored, it could issue 'a notification declaring any area within a State as a "communally disturbed area"', and deploy armed forces 'on a request having been received from the State Government to do so' (ibid.: section 55[3]). Sixth, penalties to be imposed on public servants were enumerated. These included police officers and any public officer who failed to provide protection to victims, to record any information pertinent to the commission of any scheduled offence or to investigate or prosecute any scheduled offence (ibid.: section 17[1]). Finally, an elaborate institutional mechanism—at the district, state and national levels— was outlined for providing relief and rehabilitation to victims of communal violence (ibid.: sections 38–48).

Following its introduction in the Rajya Sabha, the draft bill was referred to the Standing Committee on Home Affairs.[8] While the Standing Committee sought comments from experts, state governments, political parties and civil society, there was strong opposition to the measure in Parliament. Almost all political parties, including the BJP, Biju Janata Dal (BJD), SP, BSP, CPI (M) and RJD, opposed the bill because it threatened states' rights, especially the

---

[8] The bill went through a number of reincarnations by December 2013. It was renamed as 'The Communal Violence (Prevention, Control and Rehabilitation of Victims) Bill (2009)', 'The Communal and Sectarian Violence Bill (2010)', 'The Prevention of Communal and Targeted Violence (Access to Justice and Reparations) Bill (2011)' and, finally, 'The Prevention of Communal and Targeted Violence (Access to Justice and Reparations) Bill (2013)'. Of the many drafts, only the 2005 and 2011 versions were made public.

right to control law and order. In the words of Devendra Prasad Yadav (RJD): 'We do not want the central government to encroach upon the rights of a state. Law and order is a State subject.'[9] Bhartruhari Mahtab (BJD) candidly admitted: 'No political party today wants police to become neutral. Nobody wants police to become independent in one way or other, each and every party is enjoying power either in some state or at the Centre.'[10]

Despite this opposition the UPA was determined to pass the measure. The Minister of Home Affairs, Shivraj Patil, insisted that the 'bill is before the Standing Committee and we are expecting [that] the bill should be passed immediately.'[11] He highlighted that 'everybody will be surprised that the bill is going to be very good for controlling the communal violence in the country', emphasising its key provisions, including the compensation for riot victims. Referring to the system of compensation as 'path-breaking', Patil noted it was the 'responsibility of the society to see that there is no communal violence and if anybody suffers in the communal violence, compensation should be given to him'. In response to the states' objection over the increased powers of the centre to intervene, he offered a consensual approach:

> We are not going to thrust this idea on the country without obtaining the cooperation of the State Government[s]. If you want that this should be done, we will do it. Otherwise, we will keep it aside, and try to persuade them ... It needs the concurrence of the State Governments. Our intention is not to impose this on the state governments without their concurrence. If there is concurrence, then something can be done ... Supposing something happens in a State that is not controllable, then the only remedy available with the Union Government is to remove that Government from its position and impose President's Rule to take action. This is the extreme step. If one area is disturbed in a particular State, then by taking this extreme step you are disturbing the entire state. Furthermore, if this extreme step is taken, then also objections are raised about it. This is the reason that it cannot be done very quickly.[12]

Even after the minister's request that the members consider his statement carefully, no follow-up discussion took place until the report of the Standing Committee of Home Affairs was laid before Parliament on 13 December

---

[9] *LSD*, 18 May 2006.
[10] Ibid.
[11] Ibid.
[12] Ibid.

2006. Chaired by Sushma Swaraj of the BJP, the Standing Committee made no substantive recommendations.[13] Although the Cabinet gave its approval for the enactment of legislation in March 2007, and notice was given several times (March 2007, December 2008 and February 2009) in the Rajya Sabha for consideration and passing of the bill, and for moving official amendments, it was not reintroduced. In fact, while the bill was pending there were several major incidents of communal violence: Mau (2005), Lucknow, Aligarh and Vadodara (2006), and Bangalore, Gorakhpur, Mewat-Parbhani and Indore (2007)[14] followed by debates in the Rajya Sabha.[15] But these debates took place without any substantive discussion on the Communal Violence (Prevention, Control and Rehabilitation of Victims) Bill (2005). Indeed, despite the UPA's declarations that the bill was part of its core agenda, there was no debate on its provisions until the end of the Fourteenth Lok Sabha.[16]

---

[13] The Standing Committee report did not raise objection to the main objective of the bill, to empower the government to prevent and control communal violence. It only recommended minor amendments to the definition, adding or deleting some phrases, and the inclusion of a woman member in the State Council (Department-Related Parliamentary Standing Committee on Home Affairs 2006).

[14] *RSD*, 23 November 2006; *RSD*, 14 March 2007.

[15] *RSD*, 4 May 2005 (Kerala riot); *RSD*, 11 May 2006 (communal violence in Goa, Uttar Pradesh and bomb blasts in Uttar Pradesh, Delhi, Jammu and Kashmir and other parts of the country); *RSD*, 16 May 2006 (communal violence in Gujarat); *RSD*, 14 March 2007 (major incidents of communal nature in Karnataka, Uttar Pradesh, Maharashtra, Madhya Pradesh); *RSD*, 21 March 2007 (data on statewise details of number of communal incidents and the casualties from 2006 to 2007 was presented); *RSD*, 11 December 2008 (a question on whether centre has sought reports from states on communal violence was raised); *RSD*, 1 December 2010 (state-wise details of the incidents of communal violence during the last three years). These debates were moved by politicians who belonged to CPI (M), CPI, JD(U), BJP and the Congress. On three occasions (11 May 2006, 16 May 2006, 11 December 2008), the debates were initiated by Congress members and the Minister of Home Affairs Shivraj Patil provided statistics on the communal situation on 16 May 2006.

[16] Although some debates did take place in the Lok Sabha during UPA I, none focused on the way in which the bill should be revised. The civil society network showed more engaged participation in discussion of the contents of the bill.

The bill, Muslim communities and civil society networks

From 2007 onwards, as we have seen in Chapter 3, the momentum in policy change was arrested by the broader political developments affecting the UPA; the bill was no longer perceived as a 'core' part of the UPA's agenda, and hence marginalised in parliamentary debates. In the absence of policy focus on the bill, Muslim communities and civil society networks were brought into the policy process.

The first national consultation of Act Now for Harmony and Democracy (ANHAD), an organisation set up after the 2002 Gujarat riots, was held on 16 June 2007. At this meeting, jurists, academics, activists and legal experts concluded that the bill was 'so flawed that it cannot be remedied by amending a few components' (*Milli Gazette* 2007). In this consultation, former Chief Justices and judges, including Justice Rajinder Sachar, criticised the UPA for failing to provide the promised 'comprehensive legislation' to fill the legal vacuum. The bill was characterised as 'entirely misplaced in its intent', as it empowered the centre and state governments, but not citizens or victims of communal violence.[17] Ironically, the contributors felt the enhanced powers could be misused to intimidate minorities rather than protect them. Second, it was suggested the bill inadequately defined the 'scheduled offence' because communal violence was often a targeted mass crime synonymous with genocide and, increasingly, aggravated acts of sexual violence directed at women of the targeted community. Genocide and sexual violence, therefore, were considered essential elements of communal violence in contemporary India. M. Ahmadi, a former Chief Justice of the Supreme Court, suggested that provisions related to genocide should be modelled on the Protection of Human Rights Act (1993). The proposed measure was also heavily criticised for affording limited protection to victims while continuing to provide significant loopholes for officials and administrators against acts of commission and omission. Among other groups, the NCM proposed that the language of the bill should be accessible to lower level state functionaries, the word 'communal' should be replaced with 'sectarian' and a uniform scale of compensation should be paid

---

[17] Harsh Mander raised a more fundamental issue, namely 'do the framers of the bill, or the members of the Union Cabinet who approved its submission to Parliament, genuinely believe that Narendra Modi in 2002, or indeed the administrations of Delhi, Nellie, Bhagalpur or Mumbai, when these also burnt in the past in raging communal fires, did not act because they did not have enough power to do so? Was the failure a result of disempowerment, or of criminally mala fide public authority in each of these cases?' (Mander 2005: 5527).

within 30 days of each incident (NCM, 'Suggestions'). Rejecting the bill in its entirety, the participants requested that the central government set up a Drafting Committee to formulate a new bill with the active participation of civil society (ibid.; *Milli Gazette* 2007).

It appears that despite these recommendations and pressures, the UPA government remained lukewarm in pushing forward with the legislation. There seems to have been little movement on the bill until early 2009. 'In UPA I', recalls a member of the NAC, 'there was no consultative process around the bill. The government just brought in its own poor draft in 2005. From 2005 to 2009 what we had was strong civil society opposition to that 2005 bill, which strengthened the State even more, instead of the citizen.'[18] In a context in which serious debates on the bill were missing from Parliament, the engagement of civil society groups in discussion and the submission of recommendations to government played a crucial role in the decision-making process. Such efforts seem to have been reflected in the 59 amendments cleared by the Cabinet in December 2009.

As we saw in Chapter 3, the nuclear deal with the US, the subsequent vote of confidence against the government and the loss of key coalition partners, as well as the loss of major state elections in 2007, are often cited as the reasons for this backtracking (Baru 2014: esp. chs 11 and 12). Yet these considerations and the exigencies of coalition politics proved less of a barrier for major constitutional initiatives on SCs, STs, OBCs and women.[19] The policy process around the 2009 amendments before and after the Lok Sabha elections remains obscure: it appears unclear whether the amendments were shared with relevant institutions, political parties and state governments; nor is the immediate reaction of the political parties public knowledge.[20] What is

---

[18] Farah Naqvi, interview, 16 April 2014, New Delhi. The annual reports of the Ministry of Home Affairs from 2004 to 2009 provide a few insights into the progress of the bill. In essence they emphasise five aspects: that the government decided to enact a model comprehensive bill; that the bill was referred to the parliamentary standing committee on Home Affairs; that three seminars were held to discuss the bill; that the government was in consultations; and the Union Home Minister's attempt to pass the bill in Parliament were unsuccessful. See annual reports of the Ministry of Home Affairs (2005a: 8, 129; 2006: 120; 2007: 5, 106; 2008: 105; 2009: 49–50).

[19] See Chapter 4 and Conclusion of this book.

[20] This interpretation appears justified given that several key informants interviewed were unable to shed any light on the hiatus.

clear, however, is that the UPA followed the familiar twin-track approach of announcing amendments to the 2005 draft barely a few months before the closing of the Fourteenth Lok Sabha. However, the problem was not simply that the provisions in the draft bill were weak and inappropriate; rather, the embedded culture of institutionalised resistance in the policy process, and political and institutional opposition, acted to frustrate the legislation.

Policy formulation: UPA II

In its 2009 election manifesto the Congress committed itself to 'ensuring the right to compensation and rehabilitation for all victims of communal, ethnic and caste violence on standards and levels that are binding on every government'. The 'Indian National Congress', the party's manifesto continued, 'will propose a law that empowers the National Human Rights Commission (NHRC) to monitor investigation and trial in all cases of communal and caste violence (INC 2009). While the 2004 manifesto had dealt with 'social violence', the 2009 manifesto delineated more precisely the target of the proposed bill as 'communal, ethnic and caste violence'. Now more emphasis was given to victims' right to compensation and rehabilitation, and the NHRC was to be responsible for monitoring investigations and trials.

Soon after the UPA won the 2009 general elections, Sabir Ali (Janata Dal [United], or JD[U], Bihar) asked about the status of the bill in the Rajya Sabha.[21] Questioned whether the government proposed to enact the bill, the Minister of State for Home Affairs simply pointed to the events following the introduction of the bill in 2005. Despite an attempt by Bihar MPs to raise the issue,[22] the Minister defended the position of the central government by responding that police and public order were states' jurisdiction, and guidelines to promote communal harmony had already been circulated to states and Union Territories in 2008. Concurrently, in the Lok Sabha the Congress MP P. C. Chacko confirmed the party's intent to adopt and implement the bill in full measure.[23]

Prior to the closing of the Fourteenth Lok Sabha, in early 2009, the UPA announced 59 amendments to the 2005 draft. The most notable amendment was that it gave the central government exclusive power to constitute a Unified Command following communal violence. The central government's obligation to constitute a Unified Command was substituted stating both 'the central or

---

[21] RSD, 15 July 2009.
[22] RSD, 2 December 2009.
[23] LSD, 5 June 2009.

state government *may* constitute' a Unified Command. The 2009 provisions was changed to ensure that 'the central government *shall* constitute' a Unified Command whenever central forces were deployed to control communal riots (Ministry of Home Affairs 2005b: section 55[4]; 2009c: section 55[4]). In addition, while the previous draft only allowed the central government to intervene and issue instructions to the state in the case of death or destruction of property, the 2009 amendments empowered it to intervene even where there has been no loss of life (Ministry of Home Affairs 2009c: section 55). Thus, the centre was empowered to deploy forces at sites where communal violence were likely to occur, or had occurred; it was also enabled to prevent further riots, even if state governments with anti-minority leanings were unwilling to act. If the central government were to play a partisan role, and choose not to deploy forces, the state governments would still be able to act independently. But despite these provisions, the 2009 amendments failed to make major revisions.[24]

After the Fifteenth Lok Sabha election, the Union Cabinet cleared the bill for introduction in Parliament in December 2009. The decision came a week after the government tabled the Action Taken Report on the Liberhan Commission Report on the 1992 demolition of the Babri Masjid on 24 November 2009. The Action Taken Report contained the promise that the government would bring in the bill at the earliest opportunity (Ministry of Home Affairs 2009b). By tabling the long-awaited report in Parliament and the action promised, the government appeared to have signalled its intent on the legislation. Vijay Bahuguna (Congress) welcomed the government's move by stating that the 2009 amendments to the bill

> would enable the centre to intervene in a situation of communal violence without waiting for orders from the Unified Command, district magistrate or state government. The state government will no longer have authority to set [up] Unified Command in situation of communal violence.[25]

The need to empower the central government was articulated by the Minister of Law, M. Veerappa Moily, who noted that during incidents, such as those in Gujarat and Odisha (2002 and 2007), 'the nation had to be a mute spectator. Sometimes, the party in power becomes [the] party in what is happening' (*Times of India* 2009).

---

[24] Most importantly, the amendments failed to protect victims and still maintained protection for perpetrators of violence.
[25] *LSD*, 8 December 2009.

Predictably, however, political parties, particularly the BJP, condemned the bill and the power it would give to the central government. A senior BJP leader, Arun Jaitley, claimed that the measure was a major encroachment on the federal structure of the country, and expressed 'serious doubts about the legislative competence of Parliament on a subject which deals with law and order' (*Outlook* 2009). Parties such as the SP, BSP and CPI chose not to take an official stance on the bill because they were unaware of the specific amendments. As noted earlier, it remains unclear whether the amendments were shared with these parties.

The bill, National Advisory Council and civil society networks: UPA II

After the clearance of the amendments by the Cabinet, ANHAD held a second round of national consultations with more than 200 participants across India to discuss possibilities and make recommendations. One outcome of this process was the formation of a core group for more engaged interaction with the government. These participants played crucial roles as policy actors at the regional level, organising public meetings across India to discuss the bill. The Delhi core group held consultations with the Minister of Law, ministry officials and the sub-group of the NAC to discuss amendments to the bill (*Counter Currents* 2010). Additional national consultations were also held, with seminars and conferences at the regional level. The engagement of the networks of civil rights activists, academics and jurists with the policy process was an important support for this bill.

Prompted by the suggestions made by civil society networks and incidents of communal violence, the NAC Working Group proceeded to draft a new bill (National Advisory Council 2010). A year later, the Prevention of Communal and Targeted Violence (Access to Justice and Reparations) Bill (2011) was published online to garner further public feedback. Among the provisions, several were noteworthy.

The bill commenced by addressing the nature of the offences covered. First, it made a crucial distinction between the dominant and non-dominant groups as targets of communal violence. Groups were identified by religion, language, or caste (SCs or STs), with the aim of providing equal treatment to non-dominant groups under the law (National Advisory Council 2011: section 3[e]).[26] This distinction was established to correct the institutional bias against

---

[26] The bill defined a 'group' as 'a religious or linguistic minority, in any State in the Union of India, or SCs and STs within the meaning of clauses (24) and (25) of Article 366 of the Constitution'.

groups considered particularly vulnerable at the state level. Second, it provided a more comprehensive definition of 'communal and targeted violence' as 'any act or series of acts, whether spontaneous or planned, resulting in injury or harm to the person and or property, knowingly directed against any person by virtue of his or her membership of any group' (ibid.: section 3[c]). Third, the range of offences in the new legislation included 'sexual assault' (ibid.: section 7).

The bill also focused on the accountability of public officials. First, to make officials and administrators more accountable for dereliction of duty, the bill proposed the punishment of public servants, with imprisonment for two years, extendable to five years, and liability to a fine (ibid.: section 117). In contrast to the 2005 draft, which provided legal immunity from prosecution to central or state governments and public servants if any action had been taken in 'good faith' or was 'intended to be done under the Act', the 2011 version significantly reduced the possibility for the exercise of discretion or institutional bias. Second, the bill introduced the idea of 'breach of command responsibility'—the exercise of superior command—to cover public servants, non-state actors and heads of associations (ibid.: sections 14, 15, 118, 119). Third, as in the previous legislative proposal, the new bill proposed to create new national and state authorities to give advice and recommendations, and to monitor the investigation, prosecution, trial of offences and provision of relief in order to ensure 'public functionaries act' in the wake of communal violence (ibid.: 20–54). Lastly, the Indian Penal Code (IPC) was superseded by not allowing the defence of 'sovereign immunity' (ibid.: section 73[2])—a defence which hindered questioning or prosecution of state officials.

In addition, the bill contained important provisions for victims. Relief and rehabilitation was to be awarded not only to religious and linguistic minorities, SCs and STs, but also to non-religious and linguistic minorities, non-SCs and non-STs affected by the communal violence. State Assessment Committees were to assess the extent of injury to life and property and all aspects of reparation and restitution, including the quantum of compensation and other measures to be taken in the wake of communal and targeted violence. Compensation was to be awarded within 30 days of the incident, and the amount of compensation for death and rape was specified. The failure of public servants to take all reasonable steps to ensure the provision of relief measures was defined as a dereliction of duty (ibid.: section 13[xi]).[27]

---

[27] There has been no law or guidance for people who are internally displaced due to acts of violence. Remedy and reparation for the victims have been left to state governments.

In the new NAC draft, dereliction of duty by public officials was placed at the heart of the bill. In the words of a member of the NAC Working Group:

> The bill not only held the public officials accountable but structurally gave them confidence and liberation from political control ... [it would empower] public officials to turn around to a political master and say 'No, you want me to do something, but I will not do it. Why? Because when it comes to facing prison sentence it is me, not you!' So the bill was to hold both of them accountable—hold the political executive accountable through the doctrine of command responsibility, and liberate police and public officials from political control, because it is political impulses that cause, manipulate, and allow communal violence to spread. This is why we need a law.[28]

Response to the draft bill

The draft bill was submitted to the Ministry of Home Affairs on 25 July 2011, along with the suggestions received. It was to be cleared before the Cabinet with a view to its introduction in Parliament, but the government avoided an official announcement on the measure.[29] Thus, when the draft was made public, some jurists opposed it on grounds that India already had more laws than anywhere else in the world.[30] In a similar vein, sociologist Dipankar Gupta criticised it as an unwelcome development:

---

[28] Naqvi, interview, 16 April 2014, New Delhi.
[29] 'NAC submitted a completely new draft (from the 2005 Bill). It was a recommendation to government. It is the government to ... [come up with] its own version as a law. We gave the recommendation but the government never came up with its own version of the bill in a robust manner' (ibid.)
[30] The former Chief Justice, and former Chairperson of the NHRC, J. S. Verma, who was proactive after the Gujarat riot, argued that no law can eradicate communalism, hence there is a 'need to identify the lacunae in the present laws, if any, and make amendments'. Justice B. N. Srikrishna, a former Supreme Court judge and Chair of the Mumbai riot inquiry report, said that 'there is no need for an elaborate separate Act for that. Large-scale communal riots like in Mumbai or Gujarat do not happen on the spur of the moment. These are the result of elaborate preparations. There should be an effective method of tagging known communal elements and for swooping down on them with preventive arrests in case of intelligence inputs ... What is needed is pre-facto not post-facto activism. The Bill suggests no such quick reactive machinery'. The Supreme Court advocate Harish Salve also pointed out that existing legislation is sufficient to deal with

The bill does not measure up. The basic point of the bill should be to hold accountable those under whose watch a riot has occurred. In particular, law enforcement officials must be held responsible for their laxity and inefficiency in this regard as it is their job to maintain civic peace. There is nothing wrong with our existing laws and we don't need a new bill. The main problem is not that we do not have a law, but it is with its implementation. Across the world, administrative inaction turns out to be an important correlate of collective violence. The Communal Violence Bill does not centralise this issue and is, therefore, of little use.[31]

The main criticisms from the BJP and other political parties were based on three grounds. First, most parties and state governments criticised the bill as a serious encroachment on the federal structure of India. Second, the BJP in particular argued that it was anti-majority, since it could be invoked only when minorities were attacked (Jaitley 2011). Finally, the BJP objected to the fact that the measure was drafted by the NAC, a body without constitutional or parliamentary status, and without consultation with state governments.[32]

Responding to these criticisms the Congress spokesperson, Manish Tewari, defended the party's position:

> Jaitley is giving the bill a communal twist and deliberately trying to spread misinformation. I am a Hindu from Punjab which makes me

---

communal violence, but emphasised good investigation and quick trial. In his words: 'Communities cannot be tried under criminal law. This law will only polarise the vote.' See Sahgal (2011) and Chishti (2011).

[31] Dipankar Gupta, interview, 12 March 2013, New Delhi.
[32] 'The NAC is an "advisory", not administrative, body that conducted a range of consultations with civil society on key social justice proposals which included the Right to Food Bill, the Mahatma Gandhi National Rural Employment Guarantee Act, far-reaching amendments to the SC & ST (Prevention of Atrocities) Act, and the Prevention of Communal and Targeted Violence (Access to Justice and Reparations) Bill, 2011, among others. It merely presented these to government. It was up to the government and the parliamentary process to discuss and debate these measures, have its own consultations, and give these proposals statutory status or not, as the case may be. In a significant sense, the NAC inaugurated a pre-legislative consultative process, which has been lacking in the way laws and schemes are drafted, passed and placed before people in a kind of fait accompli. Besides, every government has advisors. NAC was just that, no more. It gave advice. It did not make law' (Naqvi, interview, 27 February 2013, New Delhi).

a minority and a protected species under this bill ... If there is a riot instigated by a minority community in any state, then they will be dealt with in accordance with ordinary law. If instigated by the majority in any state, then this bill would apply in addition to IPC. (Sahgal 2011)

The Minister of Minority Affairs, Salman Khurshid, also confirmed that 'an attempt to emphasise protection for a minority ... is consistent with affirmative action under the Constitution. These are not departures from equality but the very effective implementation of equality' (ibid.).

Decision-making: UPA II

The UPA II's efforts to manage the policy formulation process soon ran into the ground. While the bill was embroiled in political, executive and judicial quagmires, the Prime Minister called a meeting of the National Integration Council (NIC)—a national platform for states, MPs, ministers and senior government officers. The agenda of the 2011 meeting included communalism, discrimination against minorities, civil disturbances and the radicalisation of youth (Ministry of Home Affairs 2011c), and despite requests from attendees to discuss the implications of the bomb blast in Delhi the previous week, the government placed the Prevention of Communal and Targeted Violence (Access to Justice and Reparations) Bill (2011) at the top of the agenda. Opening remarks of the Prime Minister confirmed the UPA's commitment to the new legislation:

> We ... need to recognise that members of minority communities often have a perception of being unfairly targeted by law enforcement agencies in the aftermath of unfortunate incidents. While law must take its own course, we need to ensure that our investigating agencies are free from bias and prejudice of any kind. (Ibid.: 6)

However, a close examination of the record of the proceedings reveals that discussion of the bill was hastily conducted, and the NIC meeting was used by the government to 'displace blame' onto other policy actors.

At the NIC the bill was opposed by the BJP-ruled states. Party leaders in the Rajya Sabha and Lok Sabha, Arun Jaitley and Sushma Swaraj, argued that it would 'encourage' rather than curb communal violence by increasing the divide between majority and minority communities (ibid.: 21–22; 25–27).[33]

---

[33] Pages 21–22 have been translated from Hindi.

West Bengal, ruled by the Congress' ally, TMC, failed to back the measure. It was also opposed by most political parties—BJP, SAD, JD(U), CPI(M), BJD, RJD and the All India Anna Dravida Munnetra Kazhagam (AIADMK)—and states because it made a distinction between victims on the basis of religion and language, and because it would erode the rights of the states in dealing with law and order. The CPI(M) explained its opposition on the grounds that 'the existing legal framework is adequate to deal with all kinds of law and order situations including the communal disturbances' (ibid.: 13). Naveen Patnaik (Odisha) pointed to 'many objectionable provisions, which impinge on the autonomy of the states' (ibid.: 8). Similar objections were expressed by the Chief Ministers of Madhya Pradesh, Punjab and most states in the North-east. The Chief Ministers from Gujarat (Narendra Modi), Bihar (Nitish Kumar), Uttar Pradesh (Mayawati), West Bengal (Mamata Banerjee), Tamil Nadu (J. Jayalalithaa), Punjab (Parkash Singh Badal), Rajasthan (Ashok Gehlot) and Kerala (Oommen Chandy) abstained from supporting the measure. Kumar expressed concern that the bill would create an impression that the majority community was 'always responsible for communal incidents' (*Times of India* 2011a), while Mayawati refused to make an official comment for she had not read the draft, criticising the centre for seeking the states' views without sending them the draft. The bill was supported by only four participants: John Dayal, a member of the NAC and NIC, and three social activists, including Asghar Ali Engineer (Dayal 2011). Perhaps most significantly, the absence of leading Chief Ministers from the NIC sent a clear message. As a result of this opposition, the Prime Minister had to give assurances in his concluding remarks that the UPA had no intention of disturbing the federal structure by enacting the legislation (Ministry of Home Affairs 2011c). The following day, Home Secretary R. K. Singh reconfirmed the government's commitment to keep the federal framework, and to engage in several rounds of consultation with states (*India Today* 2011).

It would appear that by placing the Prevention of Communal and Targeted Violence (Access to Justice and Reparations) Bill (2011) at the top of the NIC meeting agenda the government was signalling—as well as showcasing—its intent. However, the path taken by the UPA before that meeting was a clear indication of its ambivalence on minority issues.[34] As pointed out by Mayawati, the draft bill had not been circulated to political parties and state governments

---

[34] Asaduddin Owaisi, interview, 6 March 2013, New Delhi; see also *LSD*, 6 March 2013.

before the NIC meeting, and given the stiff opposition and criticism since its introduction in 2005, it was perhaps to be expected that the Congress would proceed cautiously.[35]

Following the NIC meeting, the government avoided any official announcement or parliamentary debate. It is unclear whether the draft bill was circulated to state governments and political parties. Meanwhile, the Rashtriya Swayamsevak Sangh (RSS) amplified the BJP's characterisation of the bill as anti-majority (*Economic Times* 2011). At a seminar held by the Advocates for Dharma, leading judiciary and police officers forcefully argued that such a measure was both undesirable and unacceptable. K. T. Thomas, a former judge of the Supreme Court, asserted that the bill would not stand the scrutiny of the Supreme Court because it contravened Article 21 of the Constitution.[36] Arguing that it would damage 'national unity and integrity [and] divide society and disrupt social harmony', he said it would lead to 'disintegration'.[37] Such powerful institutionalised resistance was also evident in the words of Joginder Singh, a former Director of the Central Bureau of

---

[35] The government's ambivalent approach on the bill during the NIC meeting was confirmed by key informants. 'The fact that the bill was not shared with political parties before the meeting gave me the feeling that the Home Ministry itself was interested in sabotage. The point of NIC meeting was to ensure that it is roundly criticised and never get consensus' (Habibullah, interview, 11 April 2014, New Delhi). Indeed, a second key informant noted: 'Nobody from the government defended the bill. The meeting was designed to kill the bill, not to create a consensus and move it forward' (Vrinda Grover, interview, 15 April 2014, New Delhi). A third interviewee commented: 'The opportunity was used to discredit rather than to defend and uphold the bill. There should have been discussions with all members of the NIC, explaining the provisions of the Bill, persuading them, adjusting the draft according to concerns expressed by NIC members. Simply placing it on the table was not constructive. Not owning its own bill, the government held the meeting, and just allowed the NAC draft to be critiqued by the political opposition. It was an act of bad faith' (Naqvi, interview, 16 April 2014, New Delhi). John Dayal, a member of NIC, substantiates this interpretation (Dayal 2011).

[36] Article 21 states that 'no person shall be deprived of his life or personal liberty except according to procedure established by law'.

[37] The remark of the former Judge K. T. Thomas should be distinguished from those of former Chief Justice J. S. Verma and Justice B. N. Srikrishna, in that while the former rejected the bill on the basis of principle and ideology, the latter emphasised increasing victims' access to justice by making amendments to existing laws.

Investigation. He termed the measure as 'absolutely stupid'. He insisted that India had never discriminated against minorities, and such a 'bill [was] more appropriate to Pakistan than to India' (*The Hindu* 2011).

Despite the launch of the third national consultation by ANHAD on 21 April 2012, and occasional campaigns by activists for the bill to be tabled, the government made no official move until August 2013, when communal violence erupted in Muzaffarnagar, leading to the displacement of over 50,000 Muslims.[38] The Minister of Minority Affairs urged the Prime Minister to take immediate action, and he vowed that perpetrators would be given the strictest punishment (Srivastava 2013; *Zee News* 2013). In the light of the Muzaffarnagar violence, the executive committee of the All-India Muslim Personal Law Board demanded the bill's early enactment (*Hindustan Times* 2013b). The 2013 annual meeting of the NIC was held on 23 September 2013 but the bill was not on the agenda.

Three months after Muzaffarnagar, the government finally tabled the bill in the Winter Session of Parliament in December 2013 (*India Today* 2013b). Before the session, the Home Secretary called for a meeting with the state Home Secretaries and Secretaries of central Ministries of Law, Social Justice, Minority Affairs, and DoPT (Jain 2013a). Not unexpectedly, the Home Secretaries from BJP-ruled states vehemently opposed the initiative. While the decision to convene the meeting may have seemed to indicate that the government was serious, one Home Ministry official candidly admitted that

> though the communal violence bill is being taken up on a priority basis, tabling it in Parliament is more a statement of intent by the ruling dispensation. The government wants to showcase its commitment to enacting a tough law against communal violence, whether or not it gets the support of other parties. (Ibid.)

This symbolic approach was further underpinned by the institutionalised opposition to the bill expressed in letters received from the Chief Ministers of Gujarat, Tamil Nadu, West Bengal and Odisha. Banerjee castigated the proposal as a 'political vendetta', denouncing it as 'totally anti-federal and unconstitutional' (*Outlook* 2013c). Similarly, Jayalalithaa warned that 'any hasty attempt to bring in such legislation without wide consultation amongst all political parties and stakeholders would be a completely undemocratic move'

---

[38] The riot resulted in 62 casualties and forced 51,000 people to flee their homes to temporary camps (*The Hindu* 2013).

(*Outlook* 2013b). Reiterating her objection to the 2011 draft, and her position in the 2011 NIC meeting, she argued that the changes were 'cosmetic at best' and that 'many of the serious issues with the earlier draft bill still remain[ed]'. On the day the Winter Session was scheduled to begin, 5 December 2013, Narendra Modi, the BJP's prime ministerial candidate in the forthcoming general elections, questioned the UPA's timing, terming the new proposal as 'ill-conceived, poorly drafted and a recipe for disaster' (Modi 2013).

Following Modi's letter, the Minister of Home Affairs, Sushil Kumar Shinde, declared: 'We will definitely pass the bill. The bill will be passed in this session. Modi is doing his work; we will do ours (*Business Standard* 2013). The Minister of Minority Affairs, K. Rahman Khan, also confirmed: 'It is our duty to pass the bill, as it will be of benefit to the people. Only certain states are opposing this bill. I think there is no basis to Modi's argument. His comments are unfortunate' (ibid.). Yet, despite these comments, media reports suggested that the bill underwent some dramatic modifications. Some of the major changes included:[39] the deletion of the distinction between minority and the majority groups; the rejection of the provision to create a new national authority; a reduction in the compensation for death caused by communal violence from 15 lakh rupees to 7 lakh rupees; reinstatement of the district magistrate and commissioner of police as the competent authority in a communally disturbed area; and limitation of the target group to 'religious or linguistic minorities' (*IBN* 2013; *Indian Express* 2013b; *Times of India* 2013c).[40] The government's response appears to have been shaped by what was politically feasible. As a senior official from the Ministry of Home Affairs observed, 'the reworked draft bill ensures that the centre does not override the states' powers, dispelling the so-called anti-federal concerns raised by BJP as well as parties like AIADMK, TMC and BJD' (Jain 2013b).

At the beginning of the Winter Session of Parliament, which opened on 5 December 2013, the UPA became preoccupied with passing the Lokpal and Lokayuktas Bill following reversals in the state elections in Delhi, Chhattisgarh, Madhya Pradesh and Rajasthan. It appeared that passage of the Lokpal and Lokayuktas Bill, and the determination of the BJP and dissidents within the Congress (over the creation of the new state of Telangana) to disrupt Parliament would crowd out the time for the bill. Fearing that it

---

[39] The revised version of the UPA's Communal Violence Bill was not made public.
[40] The exclusion of SCs and STs from the target group created uproar inside and outside Parliament.

might be lost, Muslim organisations tried to increase the pressure on the government. The Jamiat Ulama-i-Hind held a conference in Delhi to demand the bill's enactment, attended by thousands of Muslims and around 200 clerics from India and neighbouring countries (Chakrabarty 2013). Regionally, there were Muslim-led protests against victimisation and exclusion: victims of the Muzaffarnagar riots and lawyers from the Aligarh Muslim University Lawyers Forum demanded immediate clearance of the bill (*Firstpost* 2013). Unexpectedly, on 16 December the bill was cleared by the Cabinet—after further revisions, including a greater role for the NHRC to monitor the performance of civil servants in preventing and controlling riots. The Minister of Home Affairs announced that he would table the bill in Parliament the following day, despite uproar from the states and political parties.[41] Nitish Kumar, Bihar Chief Minister, welcomed the government's move, emphasising that the centre should be empowered to intervene in cases of communal riots (*Times of India* 2013a). On the increased role of the NHRC, however, the Chairman of that body, Justice K. G. Balakrishnan, lamented that it would place an added burden on the commission (*Economic Times* 2013). He later also noted that monitoring the work of civil servants during riots was outside the purview of the institution (Jain 2013c),[42] and that collecting information on the violence and issuing advice to the states were excluded by the Protection of Human Rights Act (ibid.). The NHRC's reluctance to take on the new role for which it was cast was perhaps due to legal limitations and lack of capacity: the institution had lobbied for the inclusion of SCs and STs as a target group under the bill (ibid.).

In the event, the final Winter Session of the Fifteenth Lok Sabha was unproductive. It transacted very little legislative business as a result of disruptions, walkouts and unparliamentary behaviour which included the use of pepper spray by one MP from Andhra Pradesh (*India Today* 2014b). In the turmoil which gripped Parliament and Indian politics in the run up to the 2014 Lok Sabha elections, the Prevention of Communal and Targeted

---

[41] It remains unclear whether the draft bill planned to be tabled was the same version as that announced in response to letters received from Chief Ministers. Media reports indicate that the new draft bill would empower the NHRC to monitor the performance of civil servants in preventing and controlling riots (*Indian Express* 2013a).

[42] The Chairman of NHRC argued, 'It would be impossible in practical terms for NHRC to do so. The Commission strongly urges that this section be deleted.'

Violence (Access to Justice and Reparations) Bill (2013) was its most high-profile casualty. The bill was again taken up for introduction in the resumed Winter Session in February 2014 but deferred due to the Opposition's stalling. In the words of a Supreme Court advocate, who was a former member of the drafting committee in the NAC:

> The government did not have the political will. The opposition, specifically the BJP, did not want this law. The process of drafting and advocacy for such a law should have factored the politically volatile nature of the Bill. Perhaps, the NAC was not suited to lead the advocacy for this Bill. The NAC made some strategic errors both in the rafting of fundamentals and in its advocacy. Leaders of the Congress party, who were part of the Central government, and the non-BJP party leaders publicly expressed reservations against the Bill. There were no takers for the Bill and the revised new Bill was never tabled before Parliament. On the political landscape the rise of the right wing BJP party with an avowed anti-minority agenda was clear in the run up to the general elections of 2014. A law that sought accountability of public servants and state machinery for targeted violence, could have been a game changer. I fear that we will be severely handicapped in the absence of such a law.[43]

Conclusion

The inability to control and manage effectively acts of collective communal violence is one of the major weaknesses of Indian democracy (Basu and Roy 2007; Nussbaum 2007). Following the election of the UPA in 2004, its commitment to enact model anti-communal violence legislation was a key component of its efforts to deliver a new framework of equality of opportunity for religious minorities. Such legislation, like the protective legislation for SCs and STs against caste violence, had the potential to create a new normative order by increasing the penalties for committing acts of communal violence.

However, as our detailed analysis of the bill's progress from 2005 onwards demonstrates, the UPA's commitment to the legislation was limited and half-hearted: it was characterised by ambivalence, non-decisions at crucial points, and efforts at symbolic implementation, particularly before the 2009 and 2014

---

[43] Grover, interview, 15 April 2014. Again, the annual reports of the Ministry of Home Affairs during the second UPA provide only cursory and factual commentary on the progress of the bill. See Ministry of Home Affairs (2010: 67, 2011: 93–94, 2012: 70, 2013: 70 and 2014: 93).

Lok Sabha elections. Thus, after the introduction of the bill in Parliament in 2005, the government referred it to the Standing Committee, and then made one feeble attempt by introducing 59 amendments before the general election in 2009. After 2009, its response to the bill was mainly reactive, until a new version was drafted by the NAC and discussed at the NIC meeting without adequate consultations with state governments or political parties. Displacing blame on to state governments and other political parties, the Congress itself was ambiguous in its support: the party's approach was high on political symbolism in pursuing a policy that was difficult if not impossible to implement. Symbolic implementation in the face of strong institutionalised resistance against religious minorities, especially Muslims, reasserted the familiar pattern of historical path dependence. It also reconfirmed that after mid-2007, when the UPA had to rebalance its political coalition, the momentum for converting the contestational juncture for the settlement of minorities' aspirations created by the election of the government into a critical juncture had been lost.

The UPA era ended with 'competing equalities' for SCs and STs, on the one hand, and religious minorities, on the other, largely in place. Despite the removal of SCs and STs as beneficiaries in the final draft of the bill, if the earlier versions had been enacted, they would have received additional protection as well as that afforded by the Scheduled Castes and Scheduled Tribes (Prevention of Atrocities) Act (1989). Throughout the policy process Dalit groups acquiesced to the bill, and only voiced their concerns when they were *excluded* as a target group—in stark contrast to their active engagement when the government wanted to open SC and ST reservations in employment to religious minorities (see Chapter 4). Today, SCs and STs thus have special legal protection, but such protection eludes religious minorities.[44]

One notable feature of the development of the bill was the engagement of Muslim communities and civil society networks around the proposed legislation. This activism, to some extent, led to a contestation of the 'top-down' policy approach and, ultimately, a significant input into the drafting of the UPA I and UPA II bills. It could be understood as the intensification of long-standing demands for more equal protection and security from the state against what Brass has called the 'institutionalised riot system' (Brass 2003: 15).

---

[44] The Scheduled Castes and Scheduled Tribes (Prevention of Atrocities) Amendment Act (2015) came into force providing tougher measures to protect SCs and STs in case of Dalit atrocities.

Ultimately what symbolised the UPA's inability to pass the bill was not its performance in Parliament but the Muzaffarnagar riots. As Zoya Hasan, a noted academic commented:

> Congress wants to do things for minorities, but only up to a point. Up to a point and no further. When it faces opposition, [it is] one step forward and two steps backward. That is the policy.[45]

In December 2013, while the debate on the bill was proceeding, Rahul Gandhi visited the Muzaffarnagar relief camps. When asked by a refugee whether a Muslim could be an Indian, he snapped, 'You are very much an Indian' (*Times of India* 2013b). But despite the subsequent request by Muslim leaders to pass the bill, neither Rahul nor Sonia Gandhi made any substantive comments on the proposal (Ghildiyal 2013).

---

[45] Zoya Hasan, interview, 11 March 2013, New Delhi.

Conclusion*

The May 2014 Lok Sabha elections mark a major turning point in Indian politics: the dramatic collapse in the Congress and UPA vote and representation in Parliament signals the end of the contestational juncture in policies on religious minorities which began in 2004. The transformational victory of the BJP, with 31 per cent of the popular vote and 282 MPs, is the first time that a single party has won an outright majority at the centre since 1984. The results seem to have arrested the long process of regionalisation of Indian politics that commenced in the 1980s, and though the BJP has formed a coalition with its NDA partners, the critical breakthrough in becoming the party of government, arguably, signifies the arrival of *Hindutva* as the governing ideology, albeit repackaged as development. The election of Narendra Modi, an OBC himself, who masterminded the campaign, and was the Chief Minister of Gujarat during the 2002 anti-Muslim riots, became the new symbol of the social and national transformation that had taken place in 'Manmohan's India' during the last decade.

The BJP in its election manifesto acknowledged that 'a large section of the minority, and especially Muslim community, continues to be stymied in poverty'. 'Modern India', it continued,

> must be a nation of equal opportunity. BJP is committed to ensure that all communities are equal partners in India's progress, as we believe India cannot progress if any segment of Indians is left behind. (BJP 2014)

The party's commitment to equal opportunities for minorities, especially Muslims, was devoid of any proposal for positive or affirmative action. In the event, the BJP's parliamentary party did not include a single minority MP: the party attracted the support of a mere 8 per cent of Muslim voters (Sardesai 2014). The BJP-led NDA's new approach to the minorities was articulated by Najma Heptullah, the Minister of Minority Affairs, who observed that

---

* Some parts of the Conclusion were previously published in Heewon Kim, 'Understanding Modi and Minorities: The BJP-led NDA Government in India and Religious Minorities', *India Review* 16, no. 4 (2017): 357–376.

'Muslims are not minorities. Parsis are' (*Times of India* 2014b). The minister alleged that the concerns of Muslims about security arise primarily out of a 'fear psychosis' that has gripped the community (Hebbar 2014), and claimed Muslims would not have voted for Modi if they were apprehensive (*IBN* 2014). She has also opposed reservations for Dalit Christians and Muslims on the grounds that they are unconstitutional, while criticising the Congress for supporting such policies. She further added that the implementation of all the *SCR* recommendations is 'not necessary' (*Firstpost* 2014). Similarly, Thawar Chand Gehlot, a Dalit and the Minister of Social Justice and Empowerment, has also come out strongly against any demands for religion-based reservations because, according to him, backward communities among all religious groups are covered under the OBC category (Ghildiyal 2014). Sanjay Paswan, secretary of the BJP's Scheduled Caste Cell, candidly professed that if poor Muslims and Christians who had converted from Hinduism to these faiths 'want [the] benefits of reservation, let them get converted back to Hinduism and accept *ghar wapsi* [literally "return home"]' (Singh 2016). To be precise, the rigid defence of the constitutional settlement, a religiously blind approach to affirmative action, and 'representation' rather than the 'politics of presence' seem to be the defining features of the BJP-led NDA's approach towards minorities.[1]

In contrast, the Congress' assessment of its policies on religious minorities, especially Muslims, before and after the general elections has been characterised by self-contradiction, ambiguity and political opportunism. The party's manifesto declared that the Congress had 'achieved [the 2009 mandate] in substantial measure' (INC 2014: 6), committing the party to working 'tirelessly to ensure that every single recommendation [of the *SCR*] is reviewed and efforts are made for their implementation' (ibid.: 27). In the same breath, it acknowledged the Congress-led UPA's effort to provide reservations for backward minorities in education and government employment. 'We will pursue this matter closely in Court', declared the manifesto, 'and ensure that the policy is implemented through proper legislation' (ibid.). Remarkably,

---

[1] The BJP appears oblivious to the need for minority representation in the party. Of its 482 candidates for the Lok Sabha only 7 were Muslims, all of whom were unsuccessful. Parliament has no Muslim MPs from Uttar Pradesh or Maharashtra; the only Muslim MPs are from West Bengal (8), Bihar (4), Jammu and Kashmir (4), Kerala (3), Assam (2), Andhra Pradesh (1), Tamil Nadu (1) and Lakshadweep (1). Of the 151 ministers in the 9 BJP-ruled states, only 1 is Muslim. Remarkably, this contrasts with 52 Muslim ministers in 13 non BJP-ruled states (*Times of India* 2014a).

despite the party's inability in office to enact the Prevention of Communal and Targeted Violence (Access to Justice and Reparations) Bill (2013) it dedicated itself to passing it 'as a matter of priority' (ibid.).

However, given the magnitude of the Congress' defeat and impending state elections, in June 2014, the beleaguered Congress–Nationalist Congress Party government in Maharashtra approved 5 per cent reservations for Muslims in education and government employment based on the criterion of social and economic backwardness used by the *SCR* and *RMCR*. If this measure is actually implemented, including the additional 16 per cent reservations for Marathas also announced, the overall reservations in the state will be 73 per cent—exceeding the 50 per cent limit imposed by the Supreme Court. Not unlike the Uttar Pradesh election in December 2011, the move was a form of gesture politics ahead of crucial state elections.[2] This measure, however, was in keeping with the party's approach to the subject which included its efforts to delay the publication of the Post-Sachar Evaluation Committee report until after the Lok Sabha elections. Paradoxically, the Congress had to contest the same ideological space as that occupied by the BJP and appeal to minorities to revive its electoral fortunes.

The assessment of the BJP-led NDA's policies on religious minorities and the actions of its associated organisations in the last three and a half years have not only raised concerns about intolerance and discrimination but also pushed the issue of substantive equality of opportunity for religious minorities off the political and governmental agenda for the foreseeable future. The 2014 Lok Sabha elections thus mark a return to the management of religious minorities with a strong ethnonationalist *Hindutva* bias. This has been further reinforced by the BJP's landslide victories in the state assembly elections in Uttar Pradesh in February–March 2017 and others. The victories significantly strengthen the BJP's ability to return to power in the national elections in 2019 as well as demonstrate the electoral appeal of *Hindutva*.

Some observers, on the other hand, have suggested that Indian democracy is now entering a new phase, one distinguished by post-Congress and post-*Hindutva* models of governance of minorities. According to Wright, the new government epitomises the dilemma for religious minorities in a multi-party, multi-ethnic democracy where one or more of the 'majority parties appear

---

[2] The 5 per cent reservations for Muslims in education was allowed by the Bombay High Court. But this measure was scrapped after the BJP's win in the state assembly elections of October 2014.

to be hostile to the interests or even the survival of the minority group' (Wright 2014: 1). He suggests that Modi and the BJP approach can be characterised by a new 'zone of consensus' which has been extended to 'incorporate the right wing, as left wing was incorporated much earlier in Kerala and West Bengal'. This change, moreover, has been accompanied 'without the Muslim minority having to pay a disastrous price' (ibid.: 6). For Baru, the ex-media advisor to Manmohan Singh, social and political change which underpinned the BJP's success is the precursor to India's second republic, one which is less hidebound by the legacy of colonialism and Partition.[3] However, the evidence that is emerging in the last three and half years (at the time of writing) suggests that the BJP-led NDA government's effort to establish a 'zone of consensus' or 'India's second republic' is being fashioned by the familiar tenets of *Hindutva*.

UPA, equality of opportunity and Muslims: reassessing the experience

The foregoing chapters have evaluated the Congress-led UPA's policies on religious minorities, particularly Muslims, to assess whether taken as a whole they amounted to a 'paradigm shift' in the definition of equality of opportunity by the Indian state. Conventional explanations of the UPA's policies, as we have seen in Chapter 1, emphasise electoral incentives, or ideology, without satisfactorily exploring the 'black box' of public policy formation and implementation. In taking our cue from policy studies, this book has sought to outline the elements of the policy process at the national level with special reference to government employment, aspects of service delivery and security for religious minorities. Again, as outlined in Chapter 1, these areas were selected because of the lack of evaluation of the UPA's policies and the importance of these dimensions in developing substantive equal opportunity policies as borne out by comparative experience. Although the range and nature of the UPA's policies on minorities was very broad (see Chapter 3), the detailed case studies were selected to focus on critical issues while exploiting the data sources available (at least at the time) in the public domain.

In addition to public policy analysis the book applies path dependent historical institutionalism to better understand the UPA's policy processes. The evolution of the different trajectories of 'competing equalities' between

---

[3] Sanjaya Baru, comments made at the launch of his volume *The Accidental Prime Minister* at the International Institute for Strategic Studies, London, 8 July 2014.

caste and religion, I have argued, can be better comprehended if we recognise the enduring significance of the settlement during the critical juncture of constitution-making which institutionalised this distinction, thereby creating lasting tensions but also providing increasing returns to lobbies and political formations centred on caste. Simultaneously, the political claims of religious minorities were progressively marginalised. Direct mobilisation by religious minorities in the 1980s, 1990s and early 2000s was one response to this marginalisation; UPA efforts after 2004 to address the claims of minorities, particularly after 9/11, was another.

In the event, the UPA was unable to deliver on its promise of 'full equality of opportunity' for religious minorities because its approach was shot through by pragmatism, symbolism and gesture politics. The root cause of this ambivalence, a willingness to do something for minorities but only 'up to a point', was not simply the result of electoral considerations, but is to be found in the institutional resistance to these policies from three core constituencies: the institutionalised SC, ST and OBC regimes and lobbies that view themselves as the guardians of these caste groups' interests, state structures (civil service and judiciary), and the BJP and the allied forces of *Hindutva*. The mode of path dependence created at the critical juncture of constitution-making has, as we noted above, provided increasing returns to caste-based lobbies: the distinction between caste and religion endures even with the emergence of the OBC category as a social and political force. As the substantive evidence presented in Chapters 4, 5 and 6 demonstrates, there is still a fundamental cleavage at the core of Indian nation-making between caste and religion. Today, this distinction is being used adroitly by the BJP in its construction of the nation. Or to put it differently, the divergent paths which Dalits and poor Christian and Muslim communities of the same social background since the 1950s have followed point to a major, ineradicable divide at the heart of the idea of modern Indian nationhood.

That the Indian state responds differently to policy demands from similar social classes if they are framed in terms of caste than religion was demonstrated in the UPA's approach to what has been termed Mandal II— the extension of a system of reservations in education for OBCs. The period witnessed the largest expansion of reservations since Mandal (Bajpai 2012; Deshpande 2006). Rhetorically and conceptually, this change was secured, as Bajpai has pointed out, by drawing on the discourse of social justice for socio-economically disadvantaged castes. Similarly, as we have demonstrated in Chapter 4, the state was also highly responsive to the BSP's demand for a

Promotion Quota Bill (to increase promotions for reserved groups) because it was framed in the language of social justice that provided further 'increasing returns' to institutionalised caste lobbies. But in contrast, the UPA struggled to articulate successfully—in terms of the 'common good'—the justification of special measures for religious minorities, especially Muslims. Whether such a discourse can be developed remains to be seen, though what is evident is that under the current BJP-led NDA government, the unevenness is further intensified in the Indian state's approach to demands from socio-economically disadvantaged castes—concerning reservations, security, or discrimination— and demands from socio-economically disadvantaged religious groups.

Sixty-eight years after they were crafted by the constitution-makers, 'competing equalities' are still largely intact. Despite the efforts of the UPA (I and II) to create a level playing field (see Chapter 3) that would end inequities and develop a new framework of equality of opportunity for a modern, socially inclusive and, increasingly, globalised society with multiple forms of discrimination and disadvantage, the institutionalised caste interests that have gained from the constitutional settlement played a crucial role in undermining such initiatives. The most telling illustration of this (see Chapter 3) was a recommendation by the OBC, SC and ST leaderships that the UPA's flagship measure, the Equal Opportunity Commission Bill, should apply to 'religious minorities only'.

Historical institutionalism and the associated concept of path dependence, as explained in Chapter 1, recognises that change is possible if groups or classes opposed to the original settlement are politically mobilised, thereby generating a 'contestational juncture' which, under appropriate conditions, can be transformed into another 'critical juncture'—an opportunity for redesigning the original settlement and establishing new institutions. Within the Indian political system, with different sub-national traditions, cultures and histories, the opportunities for change are significantly greater outside the Hindi belt. As we reviewed in Chapter 4, Mamata Banerjee's efforts to build a political base in West Bengal as the Minister of Railways produced a virtuous cycle for change which may or may not be sustained. In the south, states such as Kerala and Karnataka, with a long history of reservations for backward groups including religious minorities, the necessary and sufficient conditions for the delivery of substantive equality of opportunity are far more likely to occur (Thimmaiah 1997). In many ways, the irony of the UPA's experience in seeking to apply the lessons of the south to national politics was the failure to understand the distinctiveness of social and political conditions that had made these states' policies on religious minorities possible.

Post-Sachar evaluation: towards historical path dependence?

This book has been focused primarily on the forms of institutional and political opposition to UPA policies on religious minorities with special reference to Muslims. The review of literature in Chapter 1 emphasised that a systematic appraisal of these policies, and their actual impact on the ground for the intended recipients, was never seriously carried out, despite the efforts of advocacy organisations and NGOs. The UPA government during its tenure sedulously avoided such an evaluation. It eventually conceded this demand towards the end of its second term when the Minister of Minority Affairs appointed the Post-Sachar Evaluation Committee headed by Amitabh Kundu to make an assessment of the implementation of the *SCR* recommendations and the PM's 15 PP. Although the Committee was scheduled to report within six months, before the Lok Sabha elections in May 2014, it submitted its final report at the end of September 2014. Given the paucity of evaluative data, the difficult policy process on the subject, which included, as we saw in Chapter 3, efforts to suppress the release of the *RMCR*, and the need to provide further official evidence underpinning the argument in this book, a brief summary of the key empirical findings of the report is necessary.

Eight years after Sachar, the Post-Sachar Evaluation Committee found 'definite evidence that community-based discrimination and deprivation have not gone down in many of the social spheres in the country' (MoMA 2014: 11). In terms of employment of Muslims in the public sector, for instance, the report's data confirmed the analysis presented in Chapter 4 (see also Appendix). 'The relative employment situation of the Muslims as also other SRCs', the Committee noted, 'has not undergone much change since the adoption of the [Justice] SCR ... The share of minorities in government employment remains low—less than half of the share of their total population in the country— *despite all effort*' (ibid.: 35, emphasis added). Similarly, in assessing poverty levels across SRCs, the committee found no discernible change in the position of the Muslim community between 2004–2005 and 2011–2012 (ibid.: 43), and though educational attainment within the community improved slightly compared with 2004–2005, standards at all levels among all communities had risen during the period (ibid.: 89–91). The Committee's assessment of programmes and institutions designed to deliver the *SCR*'s recommendations was equally critical: the PM's 15 PP schemes were found to 'have too little funds and also tardy utilisation' (ibid.: 161); the MSDP had been 'implemented in non-minority concentrated blocks' (ibid.); within the states, there was 'lack of institutional mechanism and implementation staff at the state, districts [and] block levels' (ibid.); a large proportion of this staff lacked the 'motivation' to undertake these programmes (ibid.); non-Muslims and non-Buddhists were able to 'corner large share in PSL' (ibid.: 163); and the absence of monitoring of data at the local level in terms of SRC made it difficult to assess what share of resources had gone to any particular religious community (ibid.: 157–58). In short, the Committee concluded that '*the political promises and rhetoric for the minority development stands quite in contrast to the effective benefits to minorities from the schemes*' (ibid.: 161, emphasis added).

However, in spite of the above assessment, and the begrudging recognition by the Committee that the most deprived sections of the Muslim community be brought within the SC net of reservations (ibid.: 12), its main recommendations reaffirmed faith in the *SCR*: there was a need for a new approach to equality of opportunity that could 'result in transformation of the society' (ibid.); this approach required 'a paradigm shift in dealing with the problem of unequal access to socio-political spaces in the country' (ibid.); a cross-party political consensus had to be built for such change (ibid.); more information and data about religious minorities were necessary; and the state had to incentivise the promotion of diversity and empower citizens and civil society actors to effect such change (ibid.: 11).

In many ways the Post-Sachar Evaluation Committee and its recommendations are a product of two different masters: the UPA, which was reluctant to undertake an evaluation of its own policies, and the BJP-led NDA, which was implacably opposed to the politics of 'minorityism'. The recommendations of both the *SCR* and the Post-Sachar Evaluation Committee have been poorly, if at all, implemented under both governments. Overall, the government response to the Post-Sachar Evaluation Committee report falls into a well-trodden lineage of standardised institutional responses by the Indian state to the Muslim community dating from Nehru's time and the Gopal Singh Committee: as a formal response for policy failure and 'having done nothing for minorities' (Wilkinson 2012: 71–72).

Issues for further research

This book has drawn attention to some key areas in Indian politics that remain under-researched. Here we highlight three areas for further investigation.

The use of data on religious minorities

Foremost among these is to review (see Chapters 4 and 5) the collection and construction as well as the use and misuse of official data. In spite of official declarations, appropriate monitoring mechanisms for the regular assessment and progress of policies were poorly developed and operationalised. Frequently, data was misrepresented or inappropriately gathered and processed. In employment and service delivery there does not appear to have been a determined commitment to use data on religious minorities for effective affirmative action, either within the state structures or in making the data more transparent to political and civil society groups committed to improving the equality of opportunity for India's Muslims. In fact, notwithstanding the Sachar Committee's recommendation to establish a National Data Bank on the socio-economic condition of religious groups, the Post-Sachar Evaluation Committee found that there has been no 'concerted effort by the Government agencies to collect relevant data ... [and] only very limited amount of data are placed in the National Data Bank portal of the Ministry of Statistics and Programme Implementation which are mostly tabulated data from [the] Census and [the] National Sample Survey' (MoMA 2014: 173).[4]

Further developing institutional policy analysis

Analytically, the book combines policy analysis with historical institutionalism and path dependence, a hybrid-termed institutional policy analysis which better informs the policy process specific to a government and how it can be placed in an historical context. This approach was developed because of limited access to policy process (the lack of transparency in policy formulation, decision-making, implementation and evaluation) under the UPA—and most previous governments in India—and the need to historically

---

[4] In contrast to the relative 'perestroika' period of the UPA times, NDA authorities seem to have a less liberal attitude to data openness. For instance, the government no longer provides the data on recruitment of minorities in central government jobs since 2013. Also, the MoMA data on the number of primary schools constructed in 2015–2016 under the SSA scheme simply states 'state-wise details not available'. Data unavailability can (*a*) be politically misused to justify the policy 'inaction' of the government, (*b*) result in further delay or absence in policymaking for minorities which will exacerbate deprivation of minorities and (*c*) cause difficulty for researchers to verify data, produce the analysis and build on the findings for future research.

understand the path dependent nature of caste-based institutionalised politics and structures for SCs, STs and OBCs. Such a broad field, as explained in Chapter 1, necessarily required a focus on the formal structure of the policy process and its actors. As a result, limited key case studies were undertaken which could illuminate the 'black box' of public policy formation in key areas that had always been highly sensitive for the Indian state. In this respect, the book complements the growing field of public policy studies in India which is increasingly drawing on sophisticated tools of public policy analysis to understand issues such as regulatory reform or administrative change (Chand 2010).

Indeed, within policy studies, the book has highlighted its strengths and weaknesses of understanding research in a wide and contested policy sector. In the absence of established protocols for detailed policy research in this field in India, it was decided to focus on the formal policy process identified with the policy cycle (Figure 1.1). In two of the case studies (employment and service delivery), the policy process broadly corresponded with the 'cycle', though we have noted that sometimes the policy stages were merged. In the third (communal violence bill), policymaking spanned the UPA I and UPA II but terminated at the policymaking stage. The evidence and its analysis presented have thrown a new light on decision (and non-decision)-making, the considerations which influenced the actions (and non-actions), and the forms of implementation and evaluation (when undertaken) (Varshney 1994).[5] My work has also drawn attention on the interdepartmental rivalries that stifled the MoMA's autonomy (see Chapter 3, 4, 5 and 6). Institutional policy analysis, thus, has the potential to better illuminate the historical and institutional practices which produce—as well as reproduce—these outcomes, especially rivalries between functional and specialist departments. Political institutions themselves, notably the Parliament, also offer extremely invaluable insights into a re-examination of the role of key actors in policy formation. And as we noted above, institutional policy analysis has significant scope for operationalisation at the sub-national level in the states where size and historical traditions offer a more variegated experience of social and political policies on minorities.

---

[5] Other areas for application of institutional policy analysis include social and economic policy, with agrarian policy in particular providing rich insights into the endurance of patterns of politics around the agricultural lobby.

Civil society and political representation

Comparatively, the political and civil support from representatives of the target communities has been one of the key variables in developing substantive equal opportunity policies in developed polities. Hence, in the evolution of equal opportunity policies in local government in the United Kingdom in the early 1980s, for instance, the increasing representation of black and ethnic minority municipal leaders was accompanied by the rise of civic groups and black and ethnic minority workers within municipal government who were able to establish political coalitions for change (see Ball and Solomos 1990; Dancygier 2010; Solomos 2003). In contrast, the relative weakness in the national political representation of Muslims and Muslim civil society in India has limited opportunities for change.

Political commentators have noted the progressive decline of Muslim representation in Parliament since the 1980s. Beginning with 21 MPs in 1952, Muslim representation gradually increased, reaching a high point in 1980, but declined thereafter. This decline was most notable in the 1990s and 2000s. Precisely at a time when arguments for the 'politics of presence' and 'representation' have become mainstream for excluded groups such as Dalits and women, the representation of Muslims has been moving in the opposite direction, both at the national and state levels. The causes of this decline are many and complex, including the increasing assignment of Muslim majority constituencies as reserved constituencies for SCs (*SCR* 2006: 25). Yet, whatever the causes, the absence of a Muslim caucus in Parliament, as we noted in Chapter 4, militated against the more active promotion of the UPA's policies for the community and the formation of institutions within Parliament, *à la* OBCs, SCs and STs, that can better act as guardians of the community's interests. Without these institutions, and with the lowest representation of Muslims in Parliament since 1952, the 'politics of representation' without 'presence' is unlikely to advance the interests of religious minorities.

Similarly, the traditional weakness of Muslim civil society, a fact commented upon by the *SCR*, has also impeded better policy development (ibid.: 253). This may well be the outcome of the socio-economic underdevelopment of Muslim communities in India, but what this book has demonstrated is that under appropriate conditions, civil society networks can emerge to make a difference. The role of ANHAD, for example, in the debates about the Communal Violence (Prevention, Control and Rehabilitation of Victims) Bill (2005), is illustrative of how such advocacy groups can make an impact. Informal networks of policymakers and administrators for minority policies, as interview data has demonstrated, were catalytic in fostering a collective community interest around the UPA's policies. The emergence and activities, moreover, of advocacy organisations such as the Centre for Equity Studies, the Centre for Budget and Governance Accountability, and the US—India Policy Institute that engage with policymakers and key public institutions, such as the Planning Commission during the UPA period, represent new initiatives that are likely to promote both greater scrutiny and interest in policies directed at minorities. Some of these initiatives are reactive, that is, a response to the possible consequences of public policy. Others have been encouraged by the co-option and engagement of civil society networks in policy formation, for example, by the NAC. This interest in policymaking appeared to be further strengthened by the emergence of new Muslim political parties after the *SCR*, though they have yet to actively participate in the policy process.[6] Surprisingly, what has been absent from the Indian debate—in contrast to comparative experience of Western states following 9/11—is the active sponsorship of Muslim civil society networks by the state to counter-balance the historical underdevelopment of such associations within the community.[7]

Summing up: 'the verdict of history'

Reeling before the onslaught of the opposition parties, scandals and the lowest poll rankings of any Prime Minister in office, three months before the 2014 Lok Sabha elections, Manmohan Singh, defending his record in government at a press conference, invoked the judgement of history. 'I honestly believe', he declared,

> that history will be kinder to me than the contemporary media, or for that matter, the opposition parties in Parliament. I cannot divulge all things

---

[6] For instance, see Peace Party of India (2008, Uttar Pradesh), Welfare Party of India (2011, West Bengal), Awami Vikas Party (2012, Maharashtra), Popular Front of India (2006, started as a Kerala outfit but developed into a multi-state organisation by merging with other political groups) and Manithaneya Makkal Katchi (2009, Tamil Nadu).

[7] Post 9/11 the state in the United Kingdom has sponsored social and political organisations among religious minorities, especially Muslims. These initiatives have been justified as a part of 'capacity building' among communities that have traditionally lacked structures and organisation to interface with the state. See Biggs (2010).

that take place in the Cabinet system of government. I think, taking into account the circumstances, and the compulsions of a coalition polity, I have done as best as I could under the circumstances. (Quoted in Baru 2014: 276–277)

Although most analysts recognise that while the UPA II ended in a whirlwind of political vilification associated with a weak and ineffectual Prime Minister, yet its policy performances in some areas was creditable. Between 2003 and 2009, the economy grew at an average of 9 per cent per annum, enabling the government to fund extensive anti-poverty social programmes. There were also notable successes in foreign policy—the nuclear energy deal with the US, détente with China and a new dialogue with Pakistan (ibid.: chs 9, 10 and 11). Uniquely, among developing countries, according to James Manor, the UPA delivered 'inclusive growth' for a decade which witnessed rising incomes among rural Dalits, OBCs and Muslims. In so doing, the Congress-led UPA renewed its social democratic vision by skillfully balancing the management of a growing economy with the need for social welfare (Manor 2014).

However, these positive evaluations rarely if at all include any references to the UPA (I and II)'s policies on religious minorities. As the first minority community Prime Minister, and one to have won two successive general election victories, this silence was remarkable. In retrospect, the UPA I's first three years of policy formation on religious minorities, and Muslims in particular, probably represented the high watermark of India's 'liberal spring', that ephemeral moment when a range of out-of-the-box-thinking policy initiatives combined to create the potential for a new paradigm of equality of opportunity in twenty-first century India, as well as deliver the long-delayed promise of substantive equality for disadvantaged religious communities such as Muslims. The *SCR* and *RMCR* were the finest hours of this 'liberal spring'. But the new policy initiatives, as we have seen, were short-lived as the 'liberal spring' gave way to the intense heat of the Indian summer generated by the opposition to these proposals. When history judges the UPA (I and II), it will judge it not on scandals, political mismanagement or foreign policy, which are the normal failings of most Indian governments, but for missing a historic opportunity to provide substantive equality of opportunity to religious minorities. The reversion to the familiar pattern of historical path dependence suggests that it will be some time before such a public policy programme is again back on the political agenda.

Appendix

Recruitment of minorities in central government departments and public sector undertakings

Departments/ organisations	2006–2007 Minorities recruited (%)	2007–2008 Minorities recruited (%)	2008–2009 Minorities recruited (%)	2009–2010 Minorities recruited (%)	2010–2011 Minorities recruited (%)	2011–2012 Minorities recruited (%)
Government ministries/ department	5,485 (8.37%)	1,620 (8.71%)	2,593 (12.75%)	1,339 (8.22%)	22,349 (11.99%)	4,665 (4.10%)
Public sector banks and financial institutions	702 (6.93%)	1,615 (10.20%)	4,263 (8.87%)	2,930 (7.18%)	4,702 (7.36%)	4,245 (7.50%)
Paramilitary forces	2,700 (9.49%)	4,914 (9.90%)	3,068 (10.22%)	2,682 (8.16%)	4,539 (9.21%)	3,404 (5.60%)
Posts	386 (7.60%)	517 (9.65%)	176 (6.36%)	617 (8.01%)	1293 (8.29%)	768 (8.11%)
Railways	1,456 (2.67%)	2,295 (6.31%)	2,739 (7.56%)	1,705 (6.65%)	1,591 (8.72%)	3,521 (12.53%)
Public sector undertakings	1,453 (11.86%) (for 133 PSUs)	1,234 (5.52%) (for 126 PSUs)	2,107 (5.92%) (for 161 PSUs)	1,322 (5.92%)	1,218 (7.02%) (for 121 PSUs)	1,776 (6.91%) (for 157 PSUs)
Total minorities recruited and percentage	12,182 (6.93%)	12,195 (8.23%)	14,946 (9.90%)	10,595 (7.28%)	35,692 (10.18%)	18,379 (6.24%)

Source: Ministry of Minority Affairs (2014: 122).

Note: Figures in parentheses are the percentage to the total recruited employees in each organisation/department in the respective years.

Share (%) of persons from minority community recruited in 37 ministries/department of Government of India

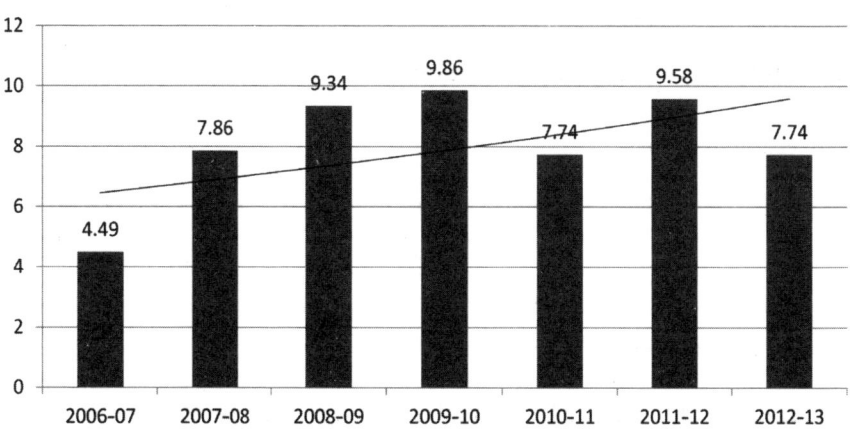

Source: Ministry of Minority Affairs (2014: 123).

Bibliography

Primary Sources

1. Official government publications

Government reports

Backward Classes Commission. 1991. *Reservations for Backward Classes: Mandal Commission Report of the Backward Classes Commission, 1980, along with [sic] Introduction.* New Delhi: Akalank Publications.

Department-Related Parliamentary Standing Committee on Home Affairs. 2006. *122nd Report on the Communal Violence (Prevention, Control and Rehabilitation of Victims) Bill, 2005.* New Delhi: Government of India.

Government of India. 2004. 'National Common Minimum Programme of the Government of India'. Available at nceuis.nic.in/NCMP.htm (accessed on 11 April 2012).

Government of West Bengal, 'Circular'. 2014. *Implementation of the West Bengal State Higher Educational Institutions (Reservation in Admission) Act, 2013 and the West Bengal State Higher Educational Institutions (Reservation in Admission) Rules, 2014.* 4 March. No. 267-Edn (U)/1U-89/13. Available at wbhed.gov.in/readwrite/uploads/1460111697.pdf (accessed on 2 August 2014).

———. n.d. *List of Other Backward Classes in West Bengal.* Available at wbxpress.com/list-other-backward-classes-west-bengal/ (accessed on 2 August 2014).

Ministry of Finance. 2006. *Budget 2006–2007: Speech of P. Chidambaram.* New Delhi: Government of India. Available at indiabudget.nic.in/ub2006-07/bs/speecha.htm (accessed on 31 January 2014).

———. 2008. *Budget 2008–2009: Speech of P. Chidambaram.* New Delhi: Government of India. Available at www.indiabudget.gov.in/ub2008-09/bs/speecha.htm (accessed on 6 December 2014).

Ministry of Home Affairs. 2001. *Census of India 2001.* New Delhi: Government of India.

———. 2005a. *Annual Report 2004–05.* New Delhi: Government of India.

———. 2005b. Bill 115, *The Communal Violence (Prevention, Control and Rehabilitation of Victims) Bill, 2005,* MGIPMRND-3981RS(S4). New Delhi: Government of India.

———. 2006. *Annual Report 2005–06.* New Delhi: Government of India.

———. 2007. *Annual Report 2006–07*. New Delhi: Government of India.
———. 2008. *Annual Report 2007–08*. New Delhi: Government of India.
———. 2009a. *Annual Report 2008–09*. New Delhi: Government of India.
———. 2009b. *Memorandum of Action Taken on the Report of the Liberhan Ayodhya Commission of Inquiry*. New Delhi: Government of India. Available at data.ndtv.com/downloads/atr.pdf (accessed on 24 December 2013).
———. 2009c. *The Communal Violence (Prevention, Control and Rehabilitation of Victims) Bill, 2009*. New Delhi: Government of India.
———. 2010. Annual Report 2009–10. New Delhi: Government of India.
———. 2011a. *Annual Report 2010–11*. New Delhi: Government of India.
———. 2011b. *Census of India 2011*. New Delhi: Government of India.
———. 2011c. *National Integration Council: Verbatim Record of the Proceedings*. New Delhi: Government of India.
———. 2012. *Annual Report 2011–12*. New Delhi: Government of India.
———. 2013. *Annual Report 2012–13*. New Delhi: Government of India.
———. 2014. *Annual Report 2013–14*. New Delhi: Government of India.
Ministry of Minority Affairs (MoMA). 2007. *Report of the National Commission for Religious and Linguistic Minorities*. New Delhi: Government of India.
———. 2008a. *Equal Opportunity Commission: What, Why and How?* New Delhi: Government of India. Available at www. minorityaffairs.gov.in/sites/default/files/eoc_wwh.pdf.
———. 2008b. *Minutes of the 8th Meeting of Empowered Committee*. 19 December. Available at www.minorityaffairs.gov.in/sites/upload_files/moma/files/pdfs/8thEC.pdf (accessed on 3 May 2014).
———. 2008c. *Report of the Expert Group on Diversity Index*. New Delhi: Government of India.
———. 2008d. *The Equal Opportunity Commission Act, 2008*. New Delhi: Government of India.
———. 2009. *Guidelines for Implementation of Prime Minister's New 15 Point Programme for the Welfare of Minorities*. New Delhi: Government of India.
———. 2011a. *India Map Showing Minority Concentration Districts*. 14 June. Available at www.minorityaffairs.gov.in/all_india_map (accessed on 15 January 2015).
———. 2011b. *Minutes of the 48th Meeting of Empowered Committee*. 2 September. Available at www.minorityaffairs.gov.in/sites/upload_files/moma/files/48thECmimutes.pdf (accessed on 3 May 2014).

———. 2011c. *Minutes of the 58th Meeting of Empowered Committee. 27 September*. Available at www.minorityaffairs.gov.in/sites/upload_files/moma/files/minutes_0.PDF (accessed on 3 May 2014).

———. 2012a. *Guidelines for Implementation of Multi-Sectoral Development Programme during Twelfth Five-Year Plan*. New Delhi: Government of India.

———. 2012b. *Standing Committee on Social Justice and Empowerment (2011-2012): The 27th Report*. New Delhi: Lok Sabha Secretariat.

———. 2013a. *Annual Report 2012-13*. New Delhi: Government of India.

———. 2013b. *Recommendation-wise Follow up Action on the Sachar Committee Report*. 11 July. Available at minorityaffairs.gov.in/sites/upload_files/moma/files/recommendationonsacharcommitteeinbrief.pdf (accessed on 30 July 2013).

———. 2014. *Post-Sachar Evaluation Committee Report*. New Delhi: Government of India. Available at iosworld.org/download/Post_Sachar_Evaluation_Committee.pdf (accessed on 2 January 2018).

———. n.d. *Multi-Sectoral Development Programme for Minority Concentration Districts—Approval for Eleventh Plan: Physical Progress Report for Period Ending 31/12/2013*. Available at www.minorityaffairs.gov.in/sites/upload_files/moma/files/Physical%2011th%20plan_0.pdf (accessed on 3 May 2014).

———. n.d. *Multi-Sectoral Development Programme for Minority Concentration Districts: Financial Progress Report as on 31/12/2013 for the Projects Approved during Eleventh Plan (Rs. in Lakh)*. Available at www.minorityaffairs.gov.in/11_plan (accessed on 3 May 2014).

———. n.d. *Prime Minister's New 15-Point Programme for the Welfare of Minorities*. Available at www.minorityaffairs.gov.in/sites/upload_files/moma/files/pdfs/amended_guidelines.pdf (accessed on 4 September 2013).

———. n.d. *Statement Indicating BE, RE and Actual Expenditure for the Year 2006–07, 2007–08, 2008–09, 2009–10, 2010–11, 2011–12, 2012–13 & 2013–14*. Available at www.minorityaffairs.gov.in/sites/upload_files/moma/files/BE_RE&Exp_2006-2012.pdf (accessed on 25 August 2014).

Ministry of Parliamentary Affairs. 2009. *Annual Report 2008–09*. New Delhi: Government of India.

———. 2010. *Annual Report 2009–10*. New Delhi: Government of India.

———. 2011. *Annual Report 2010–11*. New Delhi: Government of India.

———. 2012. *Annual Report 2011–12*. New Delhi: Government of India.

———. 2013. *Annual Report 2012–13*. New Delhi: Government of India.

Ministry of Personnel, Public Grievances and Pensions. 2007. 'Prime Minister's New 15-Point Programme for the Welfare of Minorities—Measures to Give Special Consideration to Minorities in Recruitment', Office Memorandum, 8 January. New Delhi: Government of India. Available at www.minorityaffairs.gov.in/sites/upload_files/moma/files/pdfs/DoPT_guidlines.pdf (accessed on 22 October 2011).

———. 2011a. *Brochure on Reservation for SC, ST & Other Backward Classes in Service*. New Delhi: Department of Personnel and Training, Government of India. Available at www.persmin.nic.in/DOPT_Brochure_Reservation_SCSTBackward_Index.asp (accessed on 24 May 2013).

———. 2011b. 'Reservation for Other Backward Classes in Civil Posts and Services under the Government of India—Sub-Quota for Minority Community', Office Memorandum, 22 December. New Delhi: Government of India. Available at ccis.nic.in/WriteReadData/CircularPortal/D2/D02adm/41018_2_2011_Estt_Res.pdf (accessed on 3 May 2013).

National Advisory Council. 2010. Press Release. 14 July. Available at nac.nic.in/press_releases/14_july_2010.pdf (accessed on 2 November 2013).

———. 2011. *Prevention of Communal and Targeted Violence (Access to Justice and Reparations) Bill, 2011*. New Delhi: Government of India.

National Commission for Backward Classes (NCBC). 2008. *Annual Report 2007–08*. New Delhi: Government of India.

———. 2009. *Annual Report 2008–09*. New Delhi: Government of India.

———. 2010. *Annual Report 2009–10*. New Delhi: Government of India.

———. 2011. *Annual Report 2010–11*. New Delhi: Government of India.

———. 2012. *Annual Report 2011–12*. New Delhi: Government of India.

National Commission for Minorities (NCM). 1999. *Annual Report 1998–99*. New Delhi: Government of India.

———. 2005. *Recommendation made in Annual Report 2004–05*. New Delhi: Government of India.

———. 2006. *Recommendation made in Annual Report 2005–06*. New Delhi: Government of India.

———. 2007. *Recommendation made in Annual Report 2006–07*. New Delhi: Government of India.

———. 2008. *Recommendation made in Annual Report 2007–08*. New Delhi: Government of India.

———. 2009. *Recommendation made in Annual Report 2008–09*. New Delhi: Government of India.

———. 2011. *Recommendation made in Annual Report 2010–11.* New Delhi: Government of India.

———. n.d. 'NCM Recommendations.' Available at ncm.nic.in/NCM_Recommendations.html (accessed on 8 January 2015).

———. n.d. 'Suggestions of NCM on Communal Violence Bill 2005.' Available at www.ncm.nic.in/ncm_hindi/Suggestions-of-NCM-on-Communal-Violence-Bill-2005.html (accessed on 4 December 2013).

National Commission for Scheduled Castes. Various years. *Annual Reports of the NCSC.* Available at www.ncsc.nic.in/pages/display/47 (accessed on 8 January 2015).

———. 2011a. *Minutes of the 7th Meeting of the NCSC.* New Delhi: 24 January. Government of India. Available at ncsc.nic.in/files/ncsc/144.pdf (accessed on 14 May 2013).

———. 2011b. *Minutes of the 9th Meeting of the NCSC.* 14 February. New Delhi: Government of India. Available at ncsc.nic.in/files/ncsc/148.pdf (accessed on 14 May 2013).

———. 2013. *Special Report on Reservation in Promotion submitted to the President of India.* 21 February (laid in Parliament on 23 December 2014). Available at ncsc.nic.in/files/Reservation%20in%20Promotion.pdf (accessed on 2 February 2018).

National Commission for Scheduled Tribes. n.d. *NCST Reports.* Available at ncst.nic.in/content/commission-reports (accessed on 8 January 2015).

Planning Commission. 2007. *Implication of the Geographical Distribution of Minorities in India: Report, 2007.* Report by the Inter-Ministerial Task Force. New Delhi: Government of India.

———. 2008. *Eleventh Five-Year Plan 2007–2012, Vol 1. Inclusive Growth.* New Delhi: Government of India.

———. 2011. *Report of the Steering Committee on 'Empowering of Minorities' for the Twelfth Five-Year Plan.* Available at planningcommission.nic.in/aboutus/committee/strgrp12/sc_emp_minorties.pdf (accessed on 4 February 2014).

———. 2013. *Final Population Total (PCA)—India: Data-Sheet Based on Census 2011.* Available at planningcommission.gov.in/data/datatable/1203/table_308.pdf (accessed on 1 May 2014).

Prime Minister's High Level Committee. 2006. *Social, Economic and Educational Status of the Muslim Community of India: A Report (Sachar Committee Report [SCR]).* New Delhi: Government of India.

Prime Minister's Office. 2006a. *Clarifications on Prime Minister's Reference to 'First Claim on Resources'*. 10 December. Available at pmindia.nic.in/press-details.php?nodeid=516 (accessed on 2 June 2013).
———. 2006b. *Prime Minister Inaugurates National Conference of State Minorities Commissions*. 2 November. Available at pmindia.nic.in/content_print.php?nodeid=458&nodetype=2 (accessed on 10 May 2012).

Press Information Bureau notes

Press Information Bureau (PIB). 2007a. 'Scheme of Merit-Cum-Means Based Scholarship to Students Belonging to Minority Communities'. 21 June. New Delhi: Cabinet Committee on Economic Affairs.
———. 2007b. 'Scheme of Post-Matric Scholarship for Students Belonging to Minority Communities'. 30 November. New Delhi: Cabinet Committee on Economic Affairs.
———. 2008a. 'Initiatives Taken by the Ministry of Minority Affairs'. 19 December. New Delhi: Ministry of Minority Affairs.
———. 2008b. 'Multi-Sectoral Development Programme for Minority Concentration Districts'. 27 March. New Delhi: Cabinet Committee on Economic Affairs.
———. 2008c. 'Scheme of Pre-Matric Scholarship to Students Belonging to Minority Communities'. 30 January. New Delhi: Cabinet Committee on Economic Affairs.
———. 2009. 'Ministry of Minority Affairs Launches National Monitoring Schemes'. 4 December. New Delhi: Ministry of Minority Affairs.
———. 2011. 'Socio-Economic and Caste Census, 2011 Is Not a BPL Survey, Says Rural Development Minister'. 8 August. New Delhi: Ministry of Rural Development.
———. 2014a. 'Minority Community Welfare Efforts Got a Boost during the Year'. 21 February. New Delhi: Ministry of Minority Affairs.
———. 2014b. 'Implementation of Recommendations of Sachar Committee'. 21 February. New Delhi: Ministry of Minority Affairs.

Constituent Assembly Debates (Proceedings)

Volume VIII (26 May 1949).

Parliamentary debates

Lok Sabha Debates

18 May 2006; 1 December 2007; 31 August 2008; 5 June 2009; 9 June 2009; 8 December 2009; 9 December 2009; 17 December 2009; 3 May 2010; 2 August 2010, 23 March 2011; 10 August 2011; 25 August 2011; 22 November 2012; 18 December 2012; 6 March 2013; 22 August 2013.

Rajya Sabha Debates

4 May 2005; 11 May 2005; 11 May 2006; 16 May 2006; 23 November 2006; 18 December 2006; 19 December 2006; 12 March 2007; 14 March 2007; 21 March 2007; 11 December 2008; 15 July 2009; 30 November 2009; 2 December 2009; 7 December 2009; 14 December 2009; 17 August 2010; 15 November 2010; 1 December 2010; 7 December 2011; 19 March 2012; 19 December 2013.

Supreme Court judgments

Indra Sawhney Etc. Etc. vs Union of India and others, Etc. on 16 November 1992.
M. Nagaraj & Others vs Union of India & Others on 19 October 2006.
Mrs. S. Yasmine vs The Secretary on 13 June 2013.
P. A. Inamdar & Ors vs State of Maharashtra & Ors on 12 August 2005.

2. Bank and Reserve Bank of India Reports

Dena Bank. 2012. *Minutes of 133rd State Level Review Meeting for Gujarat State for the Year Ended March 2012*. Ahmedabad: State Level Bankers Committee. Available at slbcgujarat.com/newdata/133-slrmmnts.pdf (accessed on 4 March 2014).

Reserve Bank of India. 2001. *Credit Facilities to Minority Communities—Evaluation Study*. RPCD No. SP.BC. 13/09.10.01/2001-02. 13 August.

———. 2002. Reg. Priority Sector Advances—Credit Flow to Minority Communities, UBD.POT.PCB.No. 51/09.09.01/2001-02. 20 June.

———. 2003a. Master Circular, Priority Sector Lending—Credit Flow to Minority Communities, RPCD No. SP.BC. 87/09.10.01/2002-03. 23 April.

———. 2003b. Priority Sector Advances—Credit Flow to Minority Communities, UBD.CO. BPD./ 52/09.09.01/2002-03. 13 June.
———. 2004. Master Circular, Priority Sector Lending—Credit Flow to Minority Communities, RPCD No. SP.BC. 37/09.10.01/2004-05. 29 September.
———. 2005. Master Circular, Priority Sector Lending—Credit Flow to Minority Communities, RPCD No. SP.BC. 07/09.10.01/2005-06. 1 July.
———. 2006. Master Circular, Priority Sector Lending—Credit Flow to Minority Communities, RPCD No. SP.BC. 09/09.10.01/2006-07. 5 July.
———. 2007. Master Circular, Priority Sector Lending—Credit Flow to Minority Communities, RPCD No. SP.BC. 12/09.10.01/2007-08. 5 July.
———. 2008. Master Circular, Priority Sector Lending—Credit Flow to Minority Communities, RPCD No. SP.BC. 6/09.10.01/2008-09. 1 July.
———. 2009. Master Circular, Priority Sector Lending—Credit Flow to Minority Communities, RPCD No. SP.BC. 5/09.10.01/2009-10. 1 July.
———. 2010. Master Circular, Priority Sector Lending—Credit Flow to Minority Communities, RPCD No. SP.BC. 4/09.10.01/2010-11. 1 July.
———. 2011. Master Circular, Priority Sector Lending—Credit Flow to Minority Communities, RPCD No. GSSD.BC. 1/09.10.01/2011-12. 1 July.
———. 2012. Master Circular, Priority Sector Lending—Credit Flow to Minority Communities, RPCD No. GSSD.BC. 2/09.10.01/2012-13. 2 July.
———. 2013. Master Circular, Credit Facilities to Minority Communities, RPCD No. GSSD.BC. 2/09.10.01/2013-14. 1 July.

3. Political parties

Bharatiya Janata Party (BJP). 2004. 'Why We Are Opposed to Communal Reservations: L. K. Advani'. Press Release. 14 August. Available at www.bjp.org/en/media-resources/press-releases/why-we-are-opposed-to-communal-reservations-l-k-advani (accessed on 9 March2013).
———. 2006. 'Presidential Speech by Shri Rajnath Singh at the National Council Meeting, Lucknow (Uttar Pradesh)'. 23 December. Available at www.bjp.org/index.php?option=com_content&view=article&id=6294:presidential-speech-by-sh-rajnath-singh-in-national-council-meeting-lucknow-uttar-pradesh&catid=69:speeches&Itemid=495 (accessed on 19 February 2013).

———. *Ek Bharat, Shreshtha Bharat. Sabka Saath, Sabka Vikas: Election Manifesto.* Available at www.bjp.org/images/pdf_2014/full_manifesto_ english_07.04.2014.pdf (accessed on 30 March 2014).

Indian National Congress (INC). 2004. *Manifesto 2004.* Available at www.indian-elections.com/partymanifestoes/party-manifestoes04/congress.html (accessed on 12 April 2012).

———. 2013. *Jaipur Declaration.* Available at aicc.org.in/pdf/Jaipur%20 Declaration%20-%20Final.pdf (accessed on 14 February 2013).

———. 2009. *Lok Sabha Elections 2009 Manifesto.* Available at aicc.org.in/pdf/manifesto09-eng.pdf (accessed on 2 December 2013).

———. 2014. *Your Voice, Our Pledge. Lok Sabha Election 2014 Manifesto.* Available at www.inc.in/en/in-focus/inc-manifesto-2014 (accessed on 1 April 2014).

Jaitley, Arun. 2011. 'An Analysis of the Communal Violence Bill as Drafted by NAC'. 26 May. Available at www.bjp.org/index.php?option=com_content&view=article&id=6859:an-analysis-of-the-communal-violence-bill-as-drafted-by-nac&catid=111:interview-a-articles&Itemid=1067 (accessed on 2 December 2013).

Jaju, Shyam. 2007. BJP Press Statement. 17 January. Available at www.bjp.org/index.php?option=com_content&view=article&id=5302&catid=68:press-releases&Itemid=494 (accessed on 16 February 2014).

Modi, Narendra. 2013. 'Letter: Shri Narendra Modi to PM on Revised Prevention of Communal Violence Bill, 2013'. 5 December. Available at www.bjp.org/index.php?option=com_content&view=article&id=9241:letter-shri-narendra-modi-to-pm-on-revised-prevention-of-communal-violence-bill-2013&catid=68:press-releases&Itemid=494 (accessed on 8 December 2013).

Secondary sources

1. Books

Abdelhalim, Julten. 2016. *Indian Muslims and Citizenship: Spaces for Jihād in Everyday Life.* Milton Park, Abingdon, Oxon: Routledge.

Acemoglu, Daron and James A. Robinson. 2012. *Why Nations Fail: The Origins of Power, Prosperity and Poverty.* London: Profile.

Addison, Neil. 2007. *Religious Discrimination and Hatred Law.* London: Routledge-Cavendish.

Afzal, Muhammad M. 2014. *Bharatiya Janata Party and the Indian Muslims.* Karachi: Oxford University Press.
Anderson, James E. 2006. *Public Policy-Making: An Introduction.* Boston: Houghton Mifflin.
Anderson, Perry. 2013. *The Indian Ideology.* London: Verso Books.
Ansari, Iqbal A. 2006. *Political Representation of Muslims in India: 1952-2004.* New Delhi: Manak Publications.
Austin, Granville. 1966. *The Indian Constitution: Cornerstone of a Nation.* Oxford: Clarendon Press.
———. 1999. *Working a Democratic Constitution: The Indian Experience.* Oxford: Oxford University Press.
Aziz, Mazhar. 2007. *Military Control in Pakistan: The Parallel State.* London: Routledge.
Ball, Wendy and John Solomos, eds. 1990. *Race and Local Politics.* London: Palgrave Macmillan.
Bajpai, Rochana. 2011. *Debating Difference: Group Rights and Liberal Democracy in India.* New Delhi: Oxford University Press.
Bardhan, Pranab K. 1984. *The Political Economy of Development in India.* Oxford: Blackwell.
———. 1988. 'Dominant Proprietary Classes and India's Democracy'. In *India's Democracy: An Analysis of Changing State-Society Relations*, edited by Atul Kohli, 214–224. Princeton: Princeton University Press.
Baru, Sanjaya. 2014. *The Accidental Prime Minister: The Making and Unmaking of Manmohan Singh.* New Delhi: Penguin.
Baruah, Sanjib, ed. 2010. *Ethnonationalism in India: A Reader.* New Delhi: Oxford University Press.
Basu, Amrita and Srirupa Roy, eds. 2007. *Violence and Democracy in India.* Calcutta: Seagull Books.
Ben-Tovim, Gideon. 1986. *The Local Politics of Race.* London: Macmillan.
Bhambri, C. P. 2006. *Sonia in Power: UPA government, 2004–2006.* New Delhi: Shipra.
Bhargava, Rajeev. 2002. 'India's Secular Constitution'. In *India's Living Constitution: Ideas, Practices and Controversies*, edited by Zoya Hasan, E. Sridharan, and R. Sudarshan, 105–133. New Delhi: Permanent Black.
———. 2010. *The Promise of India's Secular Democracy.* New Delhi: Oxford University Press.
Boin, Arjen and Sanneke Kuipers. 2013. 'Institutional Theory and the Public Policy Field: A Promising Perspective for Perennial Problems'. In *Debating*

Institutionalism, edited by John Pierre, B. Guy Peters, and Gerry Stoker, 42–65. Manchester: Manchester University Press.
Bose, Sumantra. 2003. *Kashmir: Roots of Conflict, Paths to Peace*. Cambridge, MA: Harvard University Press.
Brass, Paul. 2003. *The Production of Hindu-Muslim Violence in Contemporary India*. Seattle: University of Washington Press.
Chand, Vikram K., ed. 2006. *Reinventing Public Service Delivery in India: Selected Case Studies*. New Delhi: Sage.
———, ed. 2010a. *Public Service Delivery in India: Understanding the Reform Process*. Oxford: Oxford University Press.
———. 2010b. 'Context, Complexity, and Contingency: Understanding the Process of Reforming Public Service Delivery in India'. In *Public Service Delivery in India: Understanding the Reform Process*, edited by Vikram K. Chand, 1–35. Oxford: Oxford University Press.
Chandra, Kanchan. 2004. *Why Ethnic Parties Succeed: Patronage and Ethnic Headcounts in India*. Cambridge: Cambridge University Press.
Corbridge, Stuart and John Harriss. 2000. *Reinventing India: Liberalisation, Hindu Nationalism and Popular Democracy*. Cambridge: Polity Press.
Council for Social Development, Zoya Hasan and Mushirul Hasan, eds. 2013. *India—Social Development Report 2012: Minorities at the Margins*. New Delhi: Oxford University Press.
Dancygier, Rafaela M. 2010. *Immigration and Conflict in Europe*. Cambridge: Cambridge University Press.
Dhavan, Rajeev. 2008. *Reserved! How Parliament Debated Reservations 1995-2007*. New Delhi: Rupa and Company.
Dumont, Louis. 1972. *Homo Hierarchicus: The Caste System and its Implications*. London: Paladin.
Dye, Thomas R. 2008. *Understanding Public Policy*. New Jersey: Pearson Prentice Hall.
Engineer, Asghar Ali, ed. 1995. *Problems of Muslim Women in India*. Mumbai: Orient Longman.
———. 2010. 'Identity and Social Exclusion in India: A Muslim Perspective'. In *The Politics of Social Exclusion in India: Democracy at the Crossroads*, edited by Harihar Bhattacharyya, Partha Sarkar and Angshuman Kar, 76–85. London: Routledge.
Fazal, Tanweer. 2010. 'Between Identity and Equity: An Agenda for Affirmative Action for Muslims'. In *Religion, Communities and Development: Changing Contours of Politics and Policy in India*, edited by Gurpreet Mahajan and Surinder S. Jodhka, 228–247. London: Routledge.

———. 2014. *Nation-state Minority Rights in India: Comparative Perspectives on Muslim and Sikh Identities*. London: Routledge.
Franke, Marcus. 2011. *War and Nationalism in South Asia: The Indian State and the Nagas*. London: Routledge.
Galanter, Marc. 1984. *Competing Equalities: Law and the Backward Classes in India*. Berkeley: University of California Press.
Ganguly, Sumit. 1997. *The Crisis in Kashmir: Portents of War, Hopes of Peace*. Cambridge: Cambridge University Press.
Gaur, Sanjay. 2012. *The UPA Government: Achievements, Failures and Challenges*. Jaipur: Yking Books.
Gayer, Laurent and Christophe Jaffrelot, eds. 2012. *Muslims in Indian Cities: Trajectories of Marginalisation*. London: Hurst.
Glazer, Nathan. 2007. 'Minorities and India's Democracy'. In *Democracy and Diversity: India and the American Experience*, edited by K. Shankar Bajpai, 144–191. New Delhi: Oxford University Press.
Guha, Ramachandra. 2007. *India after Gandhi: The History of the World's Largest Democracy*. London: Macmillan.
Guha Thakurta, Paranjoy and Shankar Raghuraman. 2007. *Divided We Stand: India in a Time of Coalitions*. Thousand Oaks: Sage Publications.
Gupta, Dipankar. 2011. *Justice before Reconciliation: Negotiating a 'New Normal' in Post-Riot Mumbai and Ahmedabad*. New Delhi: Routledge.
Hansen, Thomas Blom. 1999. *The Saffron Wave: Democracy and Hindu Nationalism in Modern India*. Princeton: Princeton University Press.
Hardgrave, Robert L. 1965. *The Dravidian Movement*. Bombay: Popular Prakashan.
Hasan, Mushirul. 1997. *Legacy of a Divided Nation: India's Muslims since Independence*. London: Hurst.
Hasan, Zoya. 2006. 'Mass Violence and Wheels of Indian [In]justice'. In *Violence and Democracy in India*, edited by Amrita Basu and Srirupa Roy, 198–222. Oxford: Seagull Books.
———. 2009a. *Politics of Inclusion: Castes, Minorities, and Affirmative Action*. New Delhi: Oxford University Press.
———. 2012. *Congress after Indira: Policy, Power, Political Change (1984–2009)*. New Delhi: Oxford University Press.
Hasan, Zoya and Mushirul Hasan. 2013. 'Assessing UPA Government's Response to Muslim Deprivation.' In Council for Social Development's *India—Social Development Report 2012: Minorities at the Margins*, edited by Zoya Hasan and Mushirul Hasan, 242–249. New Delhi: Oxford University Press.

Hasan, Zoya and Ritu Menon. 2004. *Unequal Citizens: A Study of Muslim Women in India.* New Delhi: Oxford University Press.
Hashia, Haseena, ed. 1998. *Muslim Women in India since Independence: Feminine Perspectives.* New Delhi: Institute of Objective Studies.
Heredia, Rudolf C. 2012. *Taking Sides: Reservations and Minority Rights.* New Delhi: Penguin.
Howlett, Michael and R. Ramesh. 2003. *Studying Public Policy: Policy Cycles and Policy Subsystems.* Oxford: Oxford University Press.
Huntington, Samuel P. 1996. *The Clash of Civilisations and the Remaking of World Order.* New York: Simon & Schuster.
Immergut, Ellen M. 1992. 'The Rules of the Game: The Logic of Health Policy-Making in France, Switzerland, and Sweden.' In *Structuring Politics: Historical Institutionalism in Comparative Analysis*, edited by Sven Steinmo, Kathleen Ann Thelen and Frank Hoover Longstreth, 57–89. Cambridge: Cambridge University Press.
Jacobs, James B. and Kimberly Potter. 1998. *Hate Crimes: Criminal Law & Identity Politics.* New York: Oxford University Press.
Jaffrelot, Christophe. 1996. *The Hindu Nationalist Movement and Indian Politics, 1925 to the 1990s: Strategies of Identity-Building, Implantation and Mobilisation (with Special Reference to Central India).* London: Hurst.
———. 2003. *India's Silent Revolution: The Rise of Lower Castes.* London: Hurst.
———. 2007. *Hindu Nationalism: A Reader.* Princeton: Princeton University Press.
Jain, Ranu. 2012. 'Policies for Muslims in India: Locating Multiculturalism and Social Exclusion in the Liberal Democratic Framework'. In *Lives of Muslims in India: Exclusion and Violence*, edited by Abdul Shaban, 66–87. London: Routledge.
Jairath, Vinod K., ed. 2011. *Frontiers of Embedded Muslim Communities in India.* New Delhi: Routledge.
Jalal, Ayesha. 1995. *Democracy and Authoritarianism in South Asia: A Comparative and Historical Perspective.* Cambridge: Cambridge University Press.
Jenkins, Laura Dudley. 2003. *Identity and Identification in India: Defining the Disadvantage.* London: Routledge Curzon.
Jenkins, Richard and John Solomos, eds. 1987. *Racism and Equal Opportunity Policies in the 1980s.* Cambridge: Cambridge University Press.
Kapur, Devesh and Pratap Bhanu Mehta, eds. 2005. *Public Institutions in India: Performance and Design.* New Delhi: Oxford University Press.

Kelly, Paul, ed. 2002. *Multiculturalism Reconsidered: 'Culture and Equality' and Its Critics*. Cambridge: Polity Press.
Kepel, Gilles. 2004. *The War for Muslim Minds: Islam and the West*. Cambridge, MA: Harvard University Press.
Khalidi, Omar. 2006. *Muslims in Indian Economy*. Gurgaon: Three Essays Collective.
———. 2010. *Khaki and the Ethnic Violence in India: Army, Police and Paramilitary Forces during Communal Riots*. Gurgaon: Three Essays Collective.
Khan, Jawed Alam and Pooja Parvati. 2013. 'Government's Commitment towards Development of Muslims: A Post-Sachar Assessment of Uttar Pradesh and Haryana'. In Council for Social Development's *India—Social Development Report 2012: Minorities at the Margins*, edited by Zoya Hasan and Mushirul Hasan, 250–262. New Delhi: Oxford University Press.
Khilnani, Sunil. 1997. *The Idea of India*. London: Hamish Hamilton.
Klausen, Jytte. 2005. *The Islamic Challenge: Politics and Religion in Western Europe*. Oxford: Oxford University Press.
Klein, Rudolf and Theodore R. Marmor. 2006. 'Reflections on Policy Analysis: Putting it Together Again'. In *The Oxford Handbook of Public Policy*, edited by Michael Moran, Martin Rein and Robert E. Goodin, 892–912. Oxford: Oxford University Press.
Kohli, Atul, ed. 1988. *India's Democracy: An Analysis of Changing State-Society Relations*. Princeton: Princeton University Press.
———, ed. 2001. *The Success of India's Democracy*. Cambridge: Cambridge University Press.
———. 2006. *The State and Poverty in India: Politics of Reform*. Cambridge: Cambridge University Press.
Kumar, Hajira. 2002. *Status of Muslim Women in India*. New Delhi: Aakar Books.
Levy, Jacob T. 2000. *The Multiculturalism of Fear*. New York: Oxford University Press.
Lukes, Steven. 2005. *Power: A Radical View*. Basingstoke: Palgrave Macmillan.
Mackay, Fiona and Kate Bilton. 2000. *Learning from Experience: Lessons in Mainstreaming Equal Opportunities*. Edinburgh: University of Edinburgh, Governance of Scotland Forum.
Mahajan, Gurpreet. 1998. *Identities and Rights: Aspects of Liberal Democracy in India*. New Delhi: Oxford University Press.

Mahajan, Gurpreet and Surinder S. Jodhka, eds. 2010. *Religion, Communities and Development: Changing Contours of Politics and Policy in India*. New Delhi: Routledge.
Mahoney, James and Daniel Schensul. 2006. 'Historical Context and Path Dependence'. In *The Oxford Handbook of Contextual Political Analysis*, edited by Robert E. Goodin and Charles Tilly, 454–471. Oxford: Oxford University Press.
Mahony, James and Dietrich Rueschemeyer, eds. 2003. *Comparative Historical Analysis in the Social Sciences*. Cambridge: Cambridge University Press.
Mason, David. 1990. 'Competing Conceptions of "Fairness" and the Formulation and Implementation of Equal Opportunities Policies'. In *Race and Local Politics*, edited by Wendy Ball and John Solomos, 45–61. Basingstoke: Macmillan.
Mathur, Kuldeep. 2013. *Public Policy and Politics in India: How Institutions Matter*. New Delhi: Oxford University Press.
Mathur, Kuldeep and James Warner Björkman. 2009. *Policy-Making in India: Who Speaks? Who Listens?* New Delhi: Har-Anand Publications.
Mitra, Subrata. 2005. 'The NDA and the Politics of Minorities in India'. In *Coalition Politics and Hindu Nationalism*, edited by Katharine Adeney and Lawrence Sáez, 77–96. London: Routledge.
Modood, Tariq. 2005. *Multicultural Politics: Racism, Ethnicity and Muslims in Britain*. Minnesota: Minnesota University Press.
Moore, Barrington. 1967. *Social Origins of Dictatorship and Democracy: Lord and Peasant in the Making of the Modern World*. Harmondsworth: Penguin Books.
Narula, B. C. 2012. *The Other Side of UPA-II: An Analysis of the Second Innings of the Government of World's Largest Democracy*. New Delhi: Orange Books International.
Nussbaum, Martha C. 2007. *The Clash Within: Democracy, Religious Violence, and India's Future*. Cambridge, MA: Belknap Press.
Osuri, Goldie. 2013. *Religious Freedom in India: Sovereignty and (Anti) Conversion*. London: Routledge.
Peters, B. Guy. 2005. *Institutional Theory in Political Science: The New Institutionalism*. London: Continuum.
———. 2013. 'Institutional Theory: Problems and Prospects'. In *Debating Institutionalism*, edited by John Pierre, B. Guy Peters and Gerry Stoker, 1–21. Manchester: Manchester University Press.

Pettigrew, Joyce. 1995. *The Sikhs of the Punjab: Unheard Voices of State and Guerrilla Violence*. London: Zed.
Phillips, Anne. 1995. *The Politics of Presence*. Oxford: Clarendon Press.
Pierre, Jon, B. Guy Peters, and Gerry Stoker, eds. 2013. *Debating Institutionalism*. Manchester: Manchester University Press.
Pierson, Paul. 2016. 'Power in Historical Institutionalism'. In *The Oxford Handbook of Historical Institutionalism*, edited by Orfeo Fioretos, Tulia Gabriela Falleti and Adam D. Sheingate, 124–141. Oxford: Oxford University Press.
Pierson, Paul and Theda Skocpol. 2002. 'Historical Institutionalism in Contemporary Political Science'. In *Political Science: The State of the Discipline*, edited by Ira Katznelson and Helen V. Milner, 693–721. New York: American Political Science Association.
Rehman, Mujibur, ed. 2016. *Communalism in Post-Colonial India: Changing Contours*. Abingdon: Routledge.
Robinson, Rowena. 2010. 'Indian Christians: Trajectories of Development'. In *Religion, Communities and Development: Changing Contours of Politics and Policy in India*, edited by Gurpreet Mahajan and Surinder S. Jodhka, 151–172. London: Routledge.
Roy, Olivier. 2004. *Globalised Islam: The Search for a New Ummah*. London: Hurst.
Rudolph, Lloyd I. and Susanne H. Rudolph. 1987. *In Pursuit of Lakshmi: The Political Economy of the Indian State*. Chicago: University of Chicago Press.
———. 2008a. *Explaining Indian Democracy: A Fifty Year Perspective, 1956–2006. Volume I: The Realm of Ideas: Inquiry and Theory*. Oxford: Oxford University Press.
———. 2008b. *Explaining Indian Democracy: A Fifty Year Perspective, 1956–2006. Volume II: The Realm of Institutions: State Formation and Institutional Change*. Oxford: Oxford University Press.
———. 2008c. *Explaining Indian Democracy: A Fifty Year Perspective, 1956–2006. Volume III: The Realm of the Public Sphere: Identity and Policy*. Oxford: Oxford University Press.
Sáez, Lawrence and Gurharpal Singh, eds. 2012. *New Dimensions of Politics in India: The United Progressive Alliance in Power*. London: Routledge.
Shaban, Abdul, ed. 2012. *Lives of Muslims in India: Exclusion and Violence*. London: Routledge.
———. 2016. 'Identity, Citizenship and Hindu–Muslim Conflict in India'. In *From the Margins to the Mainstream: Institutionalising Minorities in South*

Asia, edited by Hugo Gorringe, Roger Jeffery and Suryakant Waghmore, 1–30. New Delhi: Sage.
Shani, Ornit. 2007. *Communalism, Caste and Hindu Nationalism: The Violence in Gujarat*. Cambridge: Cambridge University Press.
Shetty, V. T. Rajshekar. 1993. *India's Muslim Problem: Agony of the Country's Single Largest Community Persecuted by Hindu Nazis*. Bangalore: Dalit Sahitya Akademy.
Sikand, Yoginder. 2004. *Muslims in India since 1947: Islamic Perspectives on Inter-Faith Relations*. London: Routledge Curzon.
———. 2006. *Muslims in India: Contemporary Social and Political Discourses*. Gurgaon: Hope India Publications.
Singh, Gurharpal. 2000. *Ethnic Conflict in India: A Case-study of Punjab*. Basingstoke: Macmillan.
Solomos, John. 2003. *Race and Racism in Britain*. Basingstoke: Palgrave Macmillan.
Sowell, Thomas. 2004. *Affirmative Action around the World: An Empirical Study*. New Haven: Yale University Press.
Subramanian, Kadayam S. 2007. *Political Violence and the Police in India*. London: Sage Publications.
Subramanian, Narendra. 1999. *Ethnicity and Populist Mobilisation: Political Parties, Citizens and Democracy in South India*. Delhi: Oxford University Press.
Suroor, Hasan. 2014. *India's Muslim Spring: Why Is Nobody Talking about It?* New Delhi: Rupa Publications.
Talbot, Ian and Gurharpal Singh. 2009. *The Partition of India*. Cambridge: Cambridge University Press.
Thelen, Kathleen. 2003. 'How Institutions Evolve: Insights from Comparative Historical Analysis'. In *Comparative Historical Analysis in the Social Sciences*, edited by James Mahoney and Dietrich Rueschemeyer, 208–240. Cambridge: Cambridge University Press.
Thimmaiah, G. 1997. 'Karnataka Government's Reservation Policies for SCs/STs and OBCs.' In *The Politics of Backwardness: Reservation Policy in India*, edited by V. A. Pai Panandiker, 108–160. New Delhi: Konark Publishers.
Trivedi, Prashant K. 2013. 'Rural Power Structure, State Initiatives, and the Muslims: Divergent Experiences in Four States'. In Council for Social Development's *India—Social Development Report 2012: Minorities at the Margins*, edited by Zoya Hasan and Mushirul Hasan, 222–241. New Delhi: Oxford University Press.

Vanaik, Achin. 1997. *The Furies of Indian Communalism: Religion, Modernity and Secularisation*. London: Verso.
Varshney, Ashutosh. 1994. *Democracy, Development, and the Countryside: Urban–Rural Struggles in India*. Cambridge: Cambridge University Press.
———. 2002. *Ethnic Conflict and Civic Life: Hindus and Muslims in India*. New Haven: Yale University Press.
Veer, Peter van der. 1996. *Religious Nationalism: Hindus and Muslims in India*. Delhi: Oxford University Press.
Verma, Vidhu. 2012. *Non-Discrimination and Equality in India: Contesting Boundaries of Social Justice*. London: Routledge.
Weiner, Myron. 1997. 'India's Minorities: Who Are They? What Do They Want?' In *State and Politics in India*, edited by Partha Chatterjee, 459–495. New Delhi: Oxford University Press.
Weisskopf, Thomas E. 2004. *Affirmative Action in the United States and India: A Comparative Perspective*. London: Routledge.
Wilkinson, Steven I. 2004. *Votes and Violence: Electoral Competition and Ethnic Riots in India*. Cambridge: Cambridge University Press.
———. 2012. 'The UPA and Muslims'. In *New Dimensions of Politics in India: The United Progressive Alliance in Power*, edited by Lawrence Sáez and Gurharpal Singh, 68–78. London: Routledge.
Yadav, Kripal C. and Rajbir Singh. 1994. *India's Unequal Citizens: A Study of Other Backward Classes*. New Delhi: Manohar.

2. Published articles

Alam, Sanjeer. 2010. 'Social Exclusion of Muslims in India and Deficient Debates about Affirmative Action: Suggestions for a New Approach'. *South Asia Research* 30(1): 43–65.
Ansari, Khalid Anis. 2009. 'Rethinking the Pasmanda Movement'. *Economic and Political Weekly* 44(13): 8–10.
Bajpai, Rochana. 2000. 'Constituent Assembly Debates and Minority Rights'. *Economic and Political Weekly* 35(21/22): 1837–1845.
Biggs, Rachel. 2010. 'Community Engagement for Counter-Terrorism: Lessons from the United Kingdom'. *International Affairs* 86(4): 971–981.
Chiriyankandath, James. 2000. 'Creating a Secular State in a Religious Country: The Debate in the Indian Constituent Assembly'. *Commonwealth and Comparative Politics* 38(2): 1–24.

Copland, Ian. 2010. 'What's in a Name? India's Tryst with Secularism'. *Commonwealth and Comparative Politics* 48(2): 123–147.
Denzau, Arthur T. and Douglass C. North. 1994. 'Shared Mental Models: Ideologies and Institutions'. *Kyklos* 47(1): 3–31.
Deshpande, Satish. 2006. 'Exclusive Inequalities: Merit, Caste and Discrimination in Indian Higher Education Today'. *Economic and Political Weekly* 41(24): 2438–2444.
Dev, S. Mahendra. 2006. 'Policies and Programmes for Employment'. *Economic and Political Weekly* 41(16): 1511–1516.
Engineer, Asghar Ali. 1994. 'Communal Violence and Role of Police'. *Economic and Political Weekly* 29(15): 835–840.
Fazal, Tanweer. 2010. 'Between "Minorytyism" and Minority Rights: Interrogating Post-Sachar Strategies of Intervention'. *History and Sociology of South Asia* 4(2): 145–151.
Fekete, Liz. 2004. 'Anti-Muslim Racism and the European Security State'. *Race and Class* 46: 3–29.
Forester, John. 1984. 'Bounded Rationality and the Politics of Muddling Through'. *Public Administration Review* 44(1): 23–31.
Gonsalves, Colin. 2002. 'Institutionalised Communalism in the Police Force: The Breakdown in the Criminal Justice System'. *Article 2* 1(3).
Hasan, Mushirul. 1994. 'Minority Identity and its Discontents'. *Economic and Political Weekly* 29(15): 441–451.
Hasan, Zoya. 2009b. 'Breaking New Ground: Congress and Welfarism in India'. *Asie Visions 20*: 2–19.
Heller, Patrick. 2004. 'Degrees of Democracy: Some Comparative Lessons from India'. *World Politics* 52(4): 484–519.
Jensenius, Francesca R. 2013. 'Was the Delimitation Commission Unfair to Muslims?' *Studies in Indian Politics* 1(2): 213–229.
Jodhka, Surinder S. 2007. 'Perceptions and Receptions: Sachar Committee and the Secular Left'. *Economic and Political Weekly* 44(29): 2996–2999.
———. 2009. 'Institutionalising Equality: Context and Meanings of Equal Opportunity Commission'. *Indian Journal of Human Development* 3(2): 297–304.
Kalam, M. A. 2007. 'Conditioned Lives?' *Economic and Political Weekly* 42(10): 843–845.
Khaitan, Tarunabh. 2008. 'Transcending Reservations: A Paradigm Shift in the Debate on Equality'. *Economic and Political Weekly* 43(38): 8–12.

Kim, Heewon. 2017. 'Understanding Modi and Minorities: The BJP-led NDA Government in India and Religious Minorities'. *India Review* 16(4): 357–376.
Krasner, Stephen D. 1988. 'Sovereignty: An Institutional Perspective'. *Comparative Political Studies* 21(1): 66–94.
Mahoney, James. 2000. 'Path Dependence in Historical Sociology'. *Theory and Society* 29(4): 507–548.
———. 2001. 'Path-Dependent Explanations of Regime Change: Central America in Comparative Perspective'. *Studies in Comparative International Development* 36(1): 111–141.
Mander, Harsh. 2005. 'Resisting State Complicity in Communal Crimes: Missed Opportunities in UPA Bill'. *Economic and Political Weekly* 40(53): 5527–5529.
———. 2006. 'Inside Gujarat's Relief Colonies: Surviving State Hostility and Denial'. *Economic and Political Weekly* 41(51): 5235–5239.
Nielsen, Kenneth B. 2011. 'In Search of Development: Muslims and Electoral Politics in an Indian State'. *Forum for Development Studies* 38(3): 345–370.
Pierson, Paul. 2000. 'Increasing Returns, Path Dependence, and the Study of Politics'. *The American Political Science Review* 94(2): 251–267.
Rai, Shirin M. 2014. 'Political Performance: A Framework for Analysing Democratic Politics'. *Political Studies* 63(5): 1179–1197.
Samad, Yunas. 2013. 'Community Cohesion without Parallel Lives in Bradford'. *Patterns of Prejudice* 47(3): 269–287.
Schneiberg, Marc and Elisabeth S. Clemens. 2006. 'The Typical Tools for the Job: Research Strategies in Institutional Analysis'. *Sociological Theory* 24(3): 195–227.
Spodek, Howard. 2010. 'In the Hindutva Laboratory: Pogroms and Politics in Gujarat, 2002'. *Modern Asian Studies* 44(2): 349–399.
Thelen, Kathleen. 1999. 'Historical Institutionalism in Comparative Politics'. *Annual Review of Political Science* 2(1): 369–404.
Varshney, Ashutosh. 2000. 'Is India Becoming More Democratic?' *The Journal of Asian Studies* 59(1): 3–25.
Wilkinson, Steven I. 2007. 'A Comment on the Analysis in Sachar Report'. *Economic and Political Weekly* 42(10): 832–836.
Zaidi, Naseem A. 2014. 'Muslims in the Civil Services'. *Economic and Political Weekly* 49(3): 23–25.

3. Published reports

Centre for Budget and Governance Accountability. 2011. *Memorandum to Honourable Prime Minister on Key Interventions for Muslims in 12th Plan.* New Delhi: Centre for Budget and Governance Accountability.

Centre for Equity Studies. 2012. *Promises to Keep: Investigating Government Responses to Sachar Committee Recommendations.* New Delhi.

Concerned Citizens Tribunal—Gujarat 2002. 2002. *Crime against Humanity: Findings and Recommendations, Vol .II.* Mumbai.

Khan, Jawed Alam. 2012. *Policy Priorities for Development of Muslims in the 11th Plan: An Assessment.* New Delhi: Centre for Budget and Governance Accountability.

Shariff, Abusaleh. 2012. *Inclusive Development Paradigm in India: A Post-Sachar Perspective.* New Delhi: US–India Policy Institute.

———. 2013. *Six Years after Sachar: Review of Socially Inclusive Policies in India since 2006.* New Delhi: US–India Policy Institute.

Singh, Gurharpal. 2011. 'Religion, Politics and Governance in India, Pakistan, Nigeria and Tanzania: An Overview'. Religions and Development Research Programme, Working Paper 55. Birmingham: University of Birmingham.

U. S. Commission on International Religious Freedom. 2002. *Annual Report of the United States Commission on International Religious Freedom.* Washington, DC.

———. 2003. *Annual Report of the United States Commission on International Religious Freedom.* Washington, DC.

———. 2004. *Annual Report of the United States Commission on International Religious Freedom.* Washington, DC.

4. News articles (electronic edition)

Alam, Aniket. 2004. 'Quota for Muslims'. *Frontline* 21(17), 14–27 August.

Ali, Mohammad. 2013. 'High-Power Panel to Review Sachar Panel Report, 15-Point Programme'. *The Hindu*, 18 February.

Anand, Utkarsh. 2013. 'Gujarat to Supreme Court: Sachar Panel Illegal, Only to Help Muslims'. *Indian Express*, 28 November.

Bhoir, Anita. 2007a. 'Minority Loans against RBI Policy'. *Times of India*, 19 January.

———. 2007b. 'RBI Opposes Priority Loans to Minorities'. *Times of India*, 17 February.

Business Standard. 2013. 'Communal Violence Bill: Congress, BJP Spar over Modi's Critical Letter, Tweets'. 5 December.
Chakrabarty, Rakhi. 2013. 'Jamiat Slams Mulayam, Manmohan for Communal Violence'. *Times of India*, 16 December.
Chishti, Seema. 2011. 'Justice Verma and Srikrishna Red-Flag NAC Draft Anti-Communal Violence Bill'. *Indian Express*, 25 June.
Communalism Combat. 2002. 'Dateline Gujarat'. March/April.
Counter Currents. 2010. 'Proposed Amendments to the Communal Violence (Prevention, Control and Rehabilitation of Victims) Bill, 2005'. 24 June.
Dasgupta, Manas. 2002. 'Gujarat Incidents a Blot: Prime Minister'. *The Hindu*, 5 April.
Dayal, John. 2011. 'Fate of Communal Violence Bill Questionable'. *Beyond Headlines*, 22 September.
Dhar, Aarti and Sandeep Dikshit. 2006. 'Army Gives Data but Does Not Want It Passed on to Panel'. *The Hindu*, 15 February.
Economic Times. 2006a. 'BJP to Fight Religion-Based Quota'. 18 November.
———. 2006b. 'Report Will Create Disharmony: BJP'. 1 December.
———. 2007. 'RBI Widens Priority Sector Lending'. 2 May.
———. 2011. 'No Need for Communal Violence Bill, Says RSS'. 15 October.
———. 2013. 'NHRC's Burden Will Increase if Communal Violence Bill Passed: Justice K. G. Balakrishnan'. 19 December.
Falahi, Mumtaz A. 2010. 'Nitish Government Spends Huge Sum on Bhagalpur Panel, Victims Hapless'. *Two Circles*, 13 July.
Financial Express. 2011. 'Uttar Pradesh Polls Near, PMO Pushes Move for OBC Muslim Quota'. 25 November.
———. 2012. 'Per Capita Income: Chandigarh: 3rd'. 1 May.
Firstpost. 2013. 'Muslim Votes Only if Communal Violence Bill Cleared'. 17 December.
———. 2014. 'Want to Work for Economic Development of Minorities: Najma Heptullah', 27 May.
Ghildiyal, Subodh. 2013. 'Muslims Want Congress to Pass Communal Violence Bill'. *Times of India*, 24 December.
———. 2014a. 'Govt Opposed to Dalit Status for Converts'. *Times of India*, 10 October.
———. 2014b. 'Minorities 4.5 Per Cent Sub-Quota as Good as Dead?' *Times of India*, 28 May.
Gill, S. S. 2006. 'What the Mandal Commission Wanted'. *Indian Express*, 13 April.

Hasan, Zoya. 2009c. 'Muslim Deprivation and the Debate on Equality'. *Seminar*, October.

Hebbar, Nistula. 2014. 'My Most Important Task Is to Create Confidence and Positivity: Najma Heptullah'. *Economic Times*, 27 June.

Hindustan Times. 2011. 'New Drive Launched to Fill Vacant Reserved Posts'. 25 July.

———. 2013a. 'Centre to Take 4.5 Per Cent Muslim Sub-Quota Issue to Supreme Court Bench'. 3 June.

———. 2013b. 'Muslim Body Raps Uttar Pradesh Government for Muzaffarnagar Riots'. 22 September.

IBN. 2013. 'Centre Makes Communal Violence Bill Community Neutral: Sources'. 5 December.

———. 2014. 'Modi's Ministers on Their First Day at Work', 14 June.

India Today. 2011. 'Government to Consider Views on Communal Violence Bill'. 10 September.

———. 2013a. 'Anna Hazare's Hunger Strike Enters Second Day, Government Ready to Pass Lokpal Bill'. 10 December.

———. 2013b. 'Government Prepares to Table Communal Violence Bill in Winter Session of Parliament'. 20 October.

———. 2014a. 'Prime Minister Modi Abolishes All Group of Ministers and Empowered Group of Ministers from the UPA Era'. 31 May.

———. 2014b. 'Telangana Bill: Pepper Spray, Knives Out as Parliament Plunges to Its Lowest'. 13 February.

Indian Express. 2011. 'Ministry Wants 8.4 Per Cent for Minorities in OBC Quota'. 28 November.

———. 2012a. 'Controversial SCs/STs Quota Government Promotions Bill Passed in Rajya Sabha by Huge Majority'. 17 December.

———. 2012b. 'Justify Minority Quota in OBC, Supreme Court Tells Government'. 12 June.

———. 2012c. 'Supreme Court Slams Government Again, Refuses to Stay Quashing of Sub-Quota'. 14 June.

———. 2013a. 'Cabinet Clears Communal Violence Bill, Fireworks Likely in Parliament'. 17 December.

———. 2013b. 'Communal Violence Bill under Attack, UPA Amends It to Include All Religious Groups'. 6 December.

———. 2013c. 'Government Trying to Expedite Muslim Sub-Quota within Job Quota: Rahman Khan'. 23 March.

———. 2014. 'His Hands Tied, Prime Minister Manmohan Singh Surrendered to Sonia Gandhi: Ex-Media Adviser Sanjaya Baru's Book'. 12 April.
Jain, Bharti. 2013a. 'BJP, Non-Congress States to Oppose Communal Violence Bill in Parliament'. *Times of India*, 3 December.
———. 2013b. 'Bowing to Pressure, Government Reworks Communal Violence Bill'. 2013. *Times of India*, 6 December.
———. 2013c. 'NHRC Refuses to Monitor Bureaucrats under Anti-Riots Bill'. *Times of India*, 21 December.
Kashif-ul-Huda. 2009. 'Ali Anwar's Struggle for Pasmanda Muslims'. 2009. *Two Circles*, 17 November.
Manoj G. C. 2009a. 'Diversity Index May Have to Wait'. *Financial Express*, 26 June.
———. 2009b. 'Diversity Index Report Flawed: Central Statistical Office'. *The Indian Express*, 27 June.
Milli Gazette. 2007. 'Communal Crimes Bill 2005 Rejected by Jurists, Academicians and Activists'. 16 June.
———. 2011. '4.5 Per Cent Sub-Quota for Minorities a Grand Betrayal by UPA Government'. 24 December.
———. 2014. 'Kundu Committee Gets an Extension to Present Report on How Much Muslims Benefited from the Sachar Committee's Recommendations'. 20 June.
Mishra, Garima. 2012. 'Revisiting the Sachar Report'. *Indian Express*, 31 December.
Naqvi, Farah. 2006. 'Open a Window'. *Hindustan Times*, 1 November.
NDTV. 2012. 'Centre Moves Supreme Court over Order against 4.5 Per Cent Sub-Quota for Minorities'. 9 June.
———. 2013. 'Supreme Court Declines to Stay Centre's Scheme for Minority Students in Gujarat'. 6 May.
Outlook. 2009. 'BJP Slams Government for Approving Communal Violence Bill'. 4 December.
———. 2010. 'Don't Sleep over the Ranganath Commission Report: Arjun'. 24 March.
———. 2012a. 'Minorities Panel Seeks Investigative Powers Like NHRC'. 26 January.
———. 2012b. 'New Minority Affairs Minister in Favour of Muslim Quota'. 30 October.
———. 2012c. 'Quota Bill Also a Fair Deal to Muslims: Cong'. 17 December.

———. 2013a. 'Government to Try to Convince Supreme Court on Minority Sub-Quota: Khurshid'. 2 June.
———. 2013b. 'Jaya Asks Prime Minister Not to Move Communal Violence Bill in Parliament'. 2 December.
———. 2013c. 'Mamata Slams Centre for Reviving Communal Violence Bill'. 30 November.
Pandey, Sidharth. 2013. 'Supreme Court Does Not Unlock 4.5 Per Cent Minority Sub-Quota'. *NDTV*, 13 June.
Sahgal, Priya. 2011. 'Sonia's New Riot Act'. *India Today*, 9 July.
Sethi, Neha. 2014. 'UPA Policies Have Done Little for Muslim Enfranchisement: Panel'. *Livemint*, 15 March.
Shah, Bhavesh. 2012. 'Banks Fail to Reach Target for Loans to Minorities'. *DNA*, 29 May.
Shaikh, Zeeshan. 2014. 'Bring Law Like SC-ST Act to Protect Muslims, Says Panel on Sachar'. *Indian Express*, 18 March.
Sharma, Kalpana. 2007. 'Muslim Women Criticise Sachar Report for Overlooking Their Problems'. *The Hindu*, 28 January.
Srivastava, Neelabh. 2013. 'Muzaffarnagar Riots: Guilty Will Be Punished, Says Prime Minister'. *Outlook*, 16 September.
Srivastava, Kanchan. 2014. 'Muslims Prosper in Gujarat and Kerala; Uttar Pradesh, Bihar the Worst'. *DNA*, 22 March.
The Hindu. 2011. 'Communal Violence Bill "Not Needed"'. 24 October.
———. 2012. 'Promotion Quota, if Passed, to Be Implemented from 1995'. 9 September.
———. 2013. 'Creating a Robust Accountability System'. 27 December.
Times of India. 2007. 'Report Shows Sachar Findings Manipulated: BJP'. 31 March.
———. 2009. 'Can't Be Mute Spectator: Moily Defends Bill on Communal Riots'. 5 December.
———. 2010a. 'Case for Reservation among Backwards in All Communities: Congress'. 26 March.
———. 2010b. 'Government Considering Reservation for Muslims through OBC Route'. 28 July.
———. 2011a. 'Nitish Kumar Concerned over Provisions of Communal Violence Bill'. 10 September.
———. 2011b. 'Quota for Minorities: BJP Warns of Civil War, CPM Seeks More Reservation; Congress Happy'. 23 December.

———. 2011c. 'Reservation Demand for Muslims Gains Momentum'. 1 November.
———. 2012a. 'Election Commission Stalls 4.5 Per Cent Sub-Quota in Poll States'. 12 January.
———. 2012b. 'Rajya Sabha Passes Promotion Quota Bill'. 17 December.
———. 2013a. 'Bihar Chief Minister Nitish Kumar Supports Communal Violence Bill'. 17 December.
———. 2013b. 'Muzaffarnagar Riot Victims Should Return Home, not Play into the Hands of Rioters: Rahul Gandhi'. 22 December.
———. 2013c. 'Relief for Babus in Reworked Draft of Communal Violence Bill'. 7 December.
———. 2014a. 'Elections 2014: Lowest Number of Muslim MPs since 1952', 17 May.
———. 2014b. 'Muslims Are Not Minorities, Parsis Are: Najma Heptullah'. 28 May.
Wolff, Martin. 2005. 'When Multiculturalism Is a Nonsense'. *Financial Times*, 31 August.
Zee News. 2012. 'Centre Optimistic about Getting Relief on Minority Sub-Quota'. 10 September.
———. 2013. 'Muzaffarnagar Riots: Rahman Khan Meets PM, Calls for Steps to Ensure Safety of People'. 11 September.

5. Unpublished secondary sources

Javid, Hassan. 2012. 'Class, Power, and Patronage: The Landed Elite and Politics in Pakistani Punjab'. PhD thesis, London School of Economics and Political Science.

6. Oral presentations

Manor, James. 2014. 'An Overview of the Campaign and Results'. Roundtable Discussion on the Indian General Elections and After. School of Oriental and African Studies, University of London, 10 June.
Shastri, Sandeep. 2014. '2014 Lok Sabha Elections: Leadership as a Factor in Voter Choice'. Roundtable Discussion on the Indian General Elections and After. School of Oriental and African Studies, University of London, 10 June.

Index

Acemoglu, Daron 28
Acharia, Basu Deb 99
Act Now for Harmony and
 Democracy (ANHAD) 178, 182,
 189, 205
Adivasis (tribal populations) 5,
 44–45. See also Scheduled Tribes
 (ST)
Advisory Committee on Minorities
 (1949) 41
affirmative action 2, 8–10, 31, 34,
 44–45, 66–67, 73, 77, 84–85, 87,
 91, 94, 109, 126–128, 132, 143,
 147, 186, 195–196, 203
Ahmadi, M. 178
ajlaf (commoner) 5–6, 94
Ali, Sabir 180
Aligarh Muslim University Lawyers
 Forum 191
All India Anna Dravida Munnetra
 Kazhagam (AIADMK) 187, 190
All India Backward Muslims
 Morcha, Bihar 66
All India Majlis-e-Ittehadul
 Muslimeen 37, 105
All-India Muslim Personal Law
 Board 189
Anandpur Sahib Resolution 54
Ansari, Ali Anwar 66
anti-communal violence bill 15, 88,
 171; legislation 12, 192;
 law 13
anti-discrimination 17, 72;
 legislation 46, 83; policies 17
anti-federal concerns 190

anti-Muslim riots. *See* communal,
 riots; Gujarat; violence
'anti-national' 3
arzal (degraded) 5–6, 94
ashraf (noble) 5, 94
Assembly elections. *See under*
 elections

Babri Masjid, Ayodhya 55, 67–68,
 181
backward community (-ies) 6, 8,
 57, 106, 146, 196. *See also* Other
 Backward Classes (OBC)
Bahuguna, Vijay 181
Bahujan Samaj Party (BSP) 21, 78,
 122, 125, 175, 182, 199
Bajpai, Rochana 17, 199
Bajrang Dal 55, 67
Banerjee, Mamata 51, 109, 114,
 121–122, 126, 187, 189, 200
Bardhan, Pranab K. 31
Baru, Sanjaya 138, 198
Basic Services to the Urban Poor
 (BSUP) 133, 162, 166
below the poverty line (BPL) 5;
 census 164; list 163–164
Bharatiya Janata Party (BJP) 2, 10,
 13, 25, 37, 42, 55, 64, 66–67, 71,
 78–80, 104, 108, 137, 140,
 146–147, 175, 177, 182,
 185–190, 192, 195–200; and
 Hindutva forces 65, 84, 123; led
 Hindutva brotherhood 91; led
 NDA 15, 55, 66, 90, 195–198,
 200, 202

Biju Janata Dal (BJD) 175–176, 187, 190
Brass, Paul 52–53, 193
Buddhism 6
Buddhists 6–7, 39, 44–45, 51, 74, 112–113, 139, 150, 154, 157

caste: based lobbies 199; based parties 21; and religion, division between 11
Centrally Sponsored Scheme 136, 161, 163
Centre for Budget and Governance Accountability 168–169, 206
Centre for Equity Studies 206
Chandra, Kanchan 50
Chidambaram, P. 148–149, 170
Christianity 1, 6, 45, 74, 99
Christians 3, 7, 9–10, 14, 16–18, 39–41, 44–45, 51–57, 66–67, 74, 77, 80–82, 97, 99–101, 104–107, 112–114, 139, 150, 154, 157, 164, 196, 199; missionaries 55; in the North-east 52; poor as 10, 17, 101, 105, 199
civil services 25
civil society 15, 69, 99, 171, 175, 177–179, 182, 185, 193, 202–203, 205–206
Clash of Civilisations, by Huntington 1
class-based parties 21. *See also* caste, based parties
Communal Violence (Prevention, Control and Rehabilitation of Victims) Bill (2005) 174, 177, 205

communal: conflict 62, 80; incidents 177, 187; riots 53, 76, 132, 171–173, 181, 184, 191; tension 62; violence 6, 9, 12–13, 15, 35–36, 41, 52, 56, 68, 88, 171–178, 180–186, 189–190, 192, 204–205
communalism 18, 184, 186
Communist Party of India (CPI) 21, 37, 177, 182
Communist Party of India (Marxist) (CPI[M]) 22, 99, 104, 122, 149, 175, 177, 187
community development programmes 132
competing equalities 9, 39, 42, 45–46, 48, 50, 56, 63, 72, 78, 82–84, 102, 126–127, 193, 198, 200
composite living spaces 77
Congress 2, 9–10, 14, 16, 17–18, 22, 30, 37, 40, 47, 50, 53–55, 64–65, 67–68, 78, 80, 84, 89–90, 98–100, 107, 124–125, 136, 146–147, 171–173, 177, 180–181, 185, 187–188, 190, 192–198, 207; and coalition 67
Congress–Nationalist Congress Party government 197
Constituent Assembly 30, 40–42
Constitution (117th Amendment) Bill 125
Constitution 6–7, 10, 19, 30, 40–45, 54–55, 68–70, 73–75, 84, 88, 93, 95–97, 101–102, 105–109, 121, 125, 127, 136–138, 166, 179, 182, 185–186, 188–189, 196, 199–200; making 11, 13, 19, 27, 30, 39–40, 44–45, 51–52, 199;

settlement 10–12, 31, 52–53, 65, 73, 97, 101–102, 107, 196, 200
conversion 45, 53, 55–56, 74, 82, 99
counter-insurgencies 64
'cow belt' 4
creamy layer 50, 105. *See also* Other Backward Classes (OBC)

Dalits 5, 47, 64, 82, 122, 193, 196, 199, 205; Christians 67, 81, 99–101, 107, 196; mobilisation of 46; Muslims 6, 18, 66, 81, 99–101, 107; rural 207
Das, Asha 71–72, 74, 102
Dayal, John 187–188
decision-making process 19, 22, 66, 82, 137, 179
democracy 3, 6, 31, 57, 178, 192, 197; liberal 43–44
Depressed Classes 40, 44. *See also* disadvantaged, communities
deprivation 58–59, 61, 73, 76–77, 94, 156–157, 161, 164, 201, 203
development deficit 2, 6, 15–16, 18, 23, 34, 36, 57, 59, 61, 63, 73, 76, 87, 129, 137
Dharam Yudh Morcha 54
dharma 42
disadvantaged 6, 7, 10, 14, 44–45, 50–51, 61, 124, 139 (*see also* discrimination); caste(s) 7, 11, 14, 17, 23, 30, 39, 52, 102, 105, 199–200; communities 10, 57–58; groups 3, 6, 25, 42–43, 45, 63–64; Muslims 6, 32, 65, 74, 96, 132, 169–170; religious minorities/communities 4, 11, 15–16, 45–46, 200, 207

discrimination 2, 6–9, 16–17, 35, 39, 41–46, 52–53, 56–58, 62–64, 69, 72–77, 82–83, 91, 95, 97, 105, 129, 149, 153, 171–172, 186, 197, 200–201; anti-religious 172; institutional 34, 105; systematic 39
Diversity Index (DI) 36, 69, 72–73, 76–77, 82–83, 95

economic liberalisation 5, 59
education 2, 7, 9, 15–16, 18, 35, 44, 46–47, 50–51, 58, 61–62, 64, 66–68, 75–77, 87–88, 90, 93–94, 98, 107, 113, 123, 125, 127–130, 133–134, 137–139, 142, 147–148, 164, 168, 196–197, 199; quotas in 42; reservation(s) in 5, 7, 51, 70, 137–138, 199; underperformance in 129
election(s) 2, 8-9, 16, 20, 24, 31, 40, 54, 64–68, 80, 88–89, 95, 98, 100, 103, 105, 114, 122, 138, 140, 146–147, 166, 179–181, 190–193, 195–197, 201; defeats 67, 197; in 2004 2, 8, 16, 20, 24, 31, 64–68, 192; state 100, 122, 179, 190, 197; 2014 Lok Sabha 147, 191–192, 195, 197, 201, 206; Lok Sabha 65, 68, 80, 89, 179, 181, 193, 197, 206; state assembly 138, 140, 197; 2017 UP state assembly 197
employment 2, 4–7, 12, 14, 16, 24, 34, 42–44, 46, 50–51, 59, 65, 67–68, 71, 73–74, 76–77, 87–88, 90, 92–95, 97–98, 102–103, 109, 113–114, 121–126, 132,

147, 153, 163–164, 168–169, 185, 193, 196–198, 203–204; data of central government 111–112, 121; in government 59, 61, 67, 70, 87, 90, 96, 105, 110, 196–198, 201; Muslims and 9, 11, 13–14, 23, 36, 57–62, 67, 70, 80, 88, 93–94, 96–98, 105, 107, 109–110, 113, 122–123, 201; reservations/quotas in 2, 7, 9, 16, 42, 44, 46, 51, 67, 98, 164, 193
Engineer, Asghar Ali 187
Equal Opportunity Commission (EOC) 36, 69, 72–73, 76–77, 82–83, 95
Equal Opportunity Commission Bill 200
equal opportunity policies 75, 93, 99, 127, 198, 205
Equality Act (2010) 9
Equality and Human Rights Commission 9
equality of opportunity 2, 6–9, 13, 16–18, 31–32, 34–35, 38–39, 42-43, 45–46, 64–68, 72–73, 76–77, 91, 170, 192, 197–200, 202–203, 207
ethnic/ethnicity 5, 9, 35, 39, 51–54, 75–76, 93, 127, 171, 180, 197, 205; cleansing 56; and religious violence 54
ethno-regional struggles 52
ethno-religious: communities 65; demands 54
evaluation 12–13, 15, 17–18, 23–24, 32, 35, 65, 89–91, 96, 109, 111, 135, 137, 142–143, 148, 155, 161, 166–167, 169, 197–198, 201–204, 207
exclusion 3, 6, 16–18, 31, 44–45, 57, 65, 72, 93, 97, 105, 131, 157, 162–163, 190-91; of Muslim localities 157; of non-Hindu minorities 57

fear psychosis 196. *See also* Islamophobia
15-Point Programme (PM's 15PP) for minorities 24, 48, 69, 71, 75–76, 87, 90, 97, 132, 136–137, 140, 149, 167, 169–170, 201
Five-Year Plan: Eleventh 75, 99, 109, 132, 136, 139, 143, 156, 162, 165, 167, 170; SCs and STs in 75; Twelfth 109, 165, 167–170
Forester, John 21
Freedom of Religion Bills 55

Gandhi, Indira 87, 132
Gandhi, Rahul 90, 194
Gandhi, Sonia 78, 90, 194
Gayer, Laurent 4
Gehlot, Thawar Chand 196
ghettoisation 58, 62–63, 73, 173
Glazer, Nathan 3
Golden Temple, storming of 54
Gopal Singh: committee 202; Panel Report 57
Gujarat: anti-Muslim violence 56; bill against forced conversion 56; communalisation in 55; riots (2002) 2, 14, 46, 56, 64, 66–67, 172, 178, 184

Hasan, Z. 18, 95, 105, 136, 167, 194
Heptullah, Najma 195
Hindu: caste groups 7, 10, 14, 45; majoritarian sentiment 14, 42; majoritarians 42; nationalism 53, 55; right 3, 19, 42, 46, 53–55, 64
Hinduism 5, 42, 44, 55–56, 196
Hindu–Muslim: conflict 66; riots 53, 171
Hindus 5, 18, 39–41, 44, 53–55, 64, 74, 172
Hindutva 10, 55, 65–66, 78, 84, 91, 123, 195, 197–199; forces of 10, 55, 78, 199; agenda 55; allied forces of 10; and global 'clash of civilisations' 66; mobilisation of the forces of 55
Howlett, Michael 22

identity 2, 6, 9–10, 13, 39, 42, 51, 53, 56–58, 62, 64, 66, 72, 74, 129, 167; politics 1, 3, 66
implementation 13–15, 18, 21–25, 32, 36, 46, 50, 65–66, 70, 75, 80, 83–85, 87–92, 96–99, 102, 104, 107, 109–110, 123, 126–127, 136–137, 141–143, 146–148, 150, 153, 156–157, 161, 167–171, 185–186, 192–193, 196, 198, 201–204; problems of 22; Rajinder Sachar Committee's recommendations 24
inclusion 18, 51, 64, 67, 78, 81–82, 84, 99–100, 105, 107, 161, 164, 170, 177, 191; Buddhists in 51; of Dalit Christians and Dalit Muslims 81, 99, 107, 123; of disadvantaged 77; in Kerala 46; of religious minorities 67, 78, 121; social 72; in the SC category 67, 107
inclusive growth 157, 207
Indian Administrative Service (IAS) 25, 57, 114
Indian Foreign Service (IFS) 25, 57
Indian Muslims 3, 6, 9, 18, 61; as outsiders 3
Indian National Congress (INC) 2, 30, 180
Indian Police Service (IPS) 25, 57, 60, 114
Indira Awaas Yojana, (IAY) 133, 162–164, 167
Indo-Pakistan war 2. *See also* Kargil war (1999)
Inequality (-ies) 13, 16, 18, 63, 71, 102
insecurity 57, 62, 129, 173
institutional: resistance 10, 12, 18, 24, 32, 38, 73, 137, 147, 154–155, 170, 199; structures 10–11, 26–27, 31, 34
institutionalisation 14, 45–47, 50, 52, 56; of riot system 52, 193; of state policies 78
institutionalism 10–11, 18, 27–28, 32; historical 11–13, 18, 26–29, 32, 34, 37–39, 198, 200, 203
institution(s) 5, 9–12, 14–15, 17–19, 24–32, 34, 45, 51–52, 61, 63, 65, 76–78, 85, 87, 98, 103, 123, 128–129, 138, 143, 169, 179, 191, 200–201, 204–206; deprived of educational 61; elite education 128; Political 28, 204
insurgency (-ies) 54, 64

Integrated Child Development
  Services (ICDS) 164, 167
Integrated Housing and Slum
  Development Programme
  (IHSDP) 162, 166
Islam 1, 5–6, 18, 55, 66, 74, 99;
  equate Islam with violence 66
Islamic law 18
Islamophobes 1
Islamophobia 66

Jaffrelot, Christophe 4
Jains 39, 57, 74, 112
Jaitley, Arun 182, 185–186
Jalal, Ayesha 31
Jamiat Ulama-i-Hind 191
Jammu and Kashmir 4, 52, 54–55,
  57, 68, 177, 196; conflict in 18;
  killings in 54
Janata government, formation of 54
Jawaharlal Nehru National Urban
  Renewal Mission (JNNURM)
  162–163
JD(U) 177, 187
jihadis 1
Jinnah 41

Karat, Brinda 149
Kargil war (1999) 2, 66
Kashmir. See Jammu and Kashmir
Khalistan 54
Khan, Jawed Alam xiv, 162
Khan, K. Rahman 24, 90, 103,
  106–108, 190
Khurshid, Salman 82–83, 100, 103,
  106, 108, 167, 186
Kohli, Atul 32
Krasner, Stephen D. 27

Kumar, Nitish 187, 191
Kundu, Amitabh 201

Left Front 122
Legislature(s) 5, 7, 25, 27, 40, 42, 44,
  46; quotas in 44; reservations in
  7, 46
Liberhan Commission Report 181
linguistic minorities 2, 9, 67–68, 70,
  127, 182–183, 190
literacy rate among male Muslim 5
Lok Sabha elections. See under
  elections
Lokpal and Lokayuktas Bill 190
lower castes 5, 7, 44, 57, 138
Lukes, Steven 21

madrasa 128; education 5, 18, 129;
  modernisation programme for
  164
Mahmood, Tahir 71, 99
Mandal Commission (1978) 46–47,
  57, 64, 104, 199; debate on
  (1990) 31; Mandal I 50, 52;
  Mandal II 50, 52, 125, 199;
  Pre-Mandal period 46, 105, 147;
  recommendations/report (1990)
  31, 46–47, 50, 52, 57, 64, 66–67,
  104, 106, 125, 199
Manor, James 207
marginalisation 16, 62, 199. See also
  discrimination
mass conversions 55. See also
  minorities, religious violence
  against
Mayawati 187
media, as pro-BJP 79

migration 41, 53. *See also* communal, riots; Partition
militant Hindu groups 53
minority (-ies) 1–19, 21, 23–26, 30–32, 34–42, 44–46, 48–59, 63–80, 82–85, 87–93, 95–109, 111–114, 121–127, 129, 132–143, 146–150, 153–157, 161–173, 178, 181–183, 185–187, 189–190, 192–207; appeasement 79–80; BJP-led NDA's approach towards 196; identity 53; religious violence against 52; rights 7, 13, 34, 38–40, 42, 44, 51–52, 63, 65, 75, 107; UPA's policies on 10, 12, 23–24, 34, 84, 87, 90, 121, 124, 198, 201; political leadership of 41
Minorities Commissions, state-level 75
Minority Rights Sub-Committee Report, by Sardar Patel 40, 42
Misra, Ranganath 107
missionaries, violence against 67
mobilisation: of Dalit communities 46; religious minorities 31, 46, 54; forces of Hindutva 55
Modi, Narendra 146, 178, 187, 190, 195–196, 198
multiculturalism 1
Multi-Sectoral Development Programme (MSDP) 15, 76, 87, 103, 127, 132, 136–137, 141–142, 156–157, 161, 163, 165, 167–169, 201
Munshi, K.M. 41–42

Muslim community (-ies) 2, 4, 5–6, 9, 12–13, 15, 18, 23, 36, 59, 61–62, 65, 69–70, 73, 87, 105, 137, 153, 157, 171, 173, 178, 193, 195, 199, 201–202, 205;
Muslims 1–20, 22–26, 30, 32, 34–41, 44–47, 51–67, 69–77, 79–82, 84, 87–90, 93–101, 103–114, 121–124, 126–129, 132, 137–143, 146–150, 153–154, 156–157, 161–164, 168–173, 178, 189, 191, 193–203, 205–207; in Asia 2; bias on 59; in Bihar 59, 61, 64, 66, 121, 129, 150; geographical divisions of 4; ethnic cleansing of 56; groups 8, 90, 104, 112, 123; in Kashmir 52; as minorities 1–2, 79, 198; NGOs 112; in OBC category 22, 47, 70, 94, 104–105, 163; poor as 23, 39, 94–95, 161, 163, 196; population 4, 53, 58–59, 62, 122, 129, 141, 146, 150, 153, 157, 163; separatism 53; settlements 58, 128–129; of urban 4–5, 52, 59, 114, 157, 162; vote 23, 122, 195; in West Bengal 4, 59, 61, 64, 122–123
Muzaffarnagar: riots 189, 191, 194 (*see also* communal, riots; Gujarat; violence); Rahul Gandhi at relief camps of 194

National Advisory Council (NAC) 168, 179, 182, 184–185, 187–188, 192–193, 206
National Commission for Backward Classes (NCBC) 81, 100–102, 106, 124

National Commission for Minorities
  (1992), (NCM) 51, 71, 82, 88,
  100–101, 104–106, 167, 178
National Commission for Religious
  and Linguistic Minorities 9, 70
National Common Minimum
  Programme (NCMP) 2, 68, 172
National Data Bank 73, 95, 203
National Democratic Alliance 2
National Development Council 79
National Human Rights
  Commission (NHRC) 180, 184,
  191
National Integration Council (NIC)
  68, 186–190, 193
National Minorities Development
  Corporation 68
National Rural Drinking Water
  Programme (NRDWP) 164, 166
Nehru, Jawaharlal 41–42
neo-institutionalism 10–11, 27
non-discrimination 42–43; principle
  of 43
non-governmental organisations
  (NGOs) 24–25, 62, 90, 112, 161,
  201
North-east 52, 54, 57, 187; as
  Christian majority states 54

offence(s) 174–175, 178, 182–183; of
  communal violence 174; sexual
  assault 183
Other Backward Classes (OBCs)
  2–7, 9–11, 22, 25, 44–47,
  50–52, 57, 59, 63–64, 67–68, 70,
  72–75, 78, 81, 83–84, 87–88,
  91, 93–96, 100–106, 112, 114,
  122–126, 132, 147, 163–164,
  179, 196, 199–200, 204–205,
  207; caste based 204; definition
  of 67; as disadvantaged groups
  25; equality and 73–74; Hindu
  4, 57, 59, 94; lobby of 10, 78,
  84, 91, 124, 199; Modi as 195;
  Muslims as 22, 47, 70, 94, 100,
  105, 122, 163; opportunity for
  67–68; reservations/quota for 7,
  11, 44–47, 52, 75, 87–88, 93–96,
  100–106, 122–123, 125, 132,
  164, 199; social backwardness of
  101; social development and 3
Owaisi, Asaddudin 105

Pakistan 2–3, 5, 32, 53, 66–67;
  creation of 40, 44. *See also*
  Partition
Parliament 2, 4, 14–15, 23, 36, 46,
  51, 66, 75, 79–83, 85, 88, 91, 93,
  98–99, 103–104, 114, 122–123,
  126, 137, 166, 170, 174–179,
  181–182, 184–185, 188–196,
  204–206; militant attack on 66
Parsis 57, 74, 112, 150, 196. *See also*
  Zoroastrians
Partition 4, 26, 30, 40, 44, 53–54,
  56, 78, 80, 126, 198; children of
  India's 3; national trauma over
  51; violence of 41
pasmanda movement 6, 66
Paswan, Sanjay 196
Patel, Sardar 40–42
path dependence 7, 11–15, 17, 26,
  28–30, 32, 34, 38–39, 46–47,
  50–52, 56, 63–65, 84, 102, 126,
  170, 193, 198–201, 203–204, 207
Patil, Shivraj 176–177

Patnaik, Naveen 187
Peters, Guy 27–28
Pierson, Paul 29
Planning Commission's Working Group on Empowerment of Minorities 168
pogroms. *See* Gujarat, riots (2002)
political: exclusion 18, 31; Hinduism 55–56; institutions 28, 204; mobilisation 6, 56
Post-Sachar Evaluation Committee 24, 161 201–203; report 15, 90–91, 111, 197, 202
Prevention of Communal and Targeted Violence (Access to Justice and Reparations) Bill (2011) 175, 182, 185–187
Prevention of Communal and Targeted Violence (Access to Justice and Reparations) Bill (2013) 175, 192, 197
priority sector advances (PSA), access to 139, 149, 153–154, 156
priority sector lending (PSL) 139, 141, 149–150, 153–156, 202; provision 150, 153–155
procedural equality 6–7, 9, 43
Promotion Quota Bill (2012) 125–126, 200
proprietary classes 31
Protection of Civil Rights Act (1955) 51, 171
Protection of Human Rights Act (1993) 178, 191
provincial legislative elections 40
public interest litigation (PIL) 23

public policy 1, 10–11, 13, 16, 18-24, 27, 35–36, 50, 57, 77, 198, 204, 206–207; Forester on 21
public sector employment 5, 14, 34, 36, 59, 70, 87, 93–94, 96, 121–123
public sector service delivery 13, 75
Punjabi Suba 53–54

quota(s) 8, 34, 40, 42, 44, 46, 75, 78, 82, 85, 87–88, 96, 100–101, 103–106, 108–109, 122–126, 147–148, 164; in education 42; for minorities 100. *See also* reservation

racial 35, 52, 93, 171
Rajinder Sachar Committee 24
Ramesh R. 22
Ranganath Misra Commission Report (RMCR) 14, 16, 34, 43, 47, 63, 66, 69–72, 74–77, 80–81, 83, 88, 93–102, 104, 106, 108, 123, 128–129, 132, 173, 197, 201, 207
Rashtriya Swayamsevak Sangh (RSS) 188
reassessment 11, 23, 166
reconversion 55
recruiting departments 113–114
relief and rehabilitation 172, 175, 183
religious: community (-ies) 7, 40, 46, 58, 63–65, 73, 77, 111, 153, 174, 202, 207; identity (-ies) 6–7, 10, 39, 58, 74, 167; violence 52, 54
religious minorities 2–4, 9–19, 23–26, 30–32, 34–39, 41–42, 44–46, 50–58, 63, 65–69,

72–76, 78, 82, 91, 95, 97, 101, 105–106, 124, 126–128, 137–138, 141–142, 146–147, 150, 153–154, 163, 166, 169–171, 173, 192–193, 195–203 205–207; institutionalised resistance against 122, 193; mobilisation of 6, 31, 46; policies on 34, 37, 124, 195–198, 200–201, 207; scholarships for 127, 138
representation 5, 10, 14, 18, 34, 36, 40–41, 51, 58–59, 66, 71, 74–75, 77, 80, 87, 93–94, 96, 98–99, 105, 111–114, 121, 123, 125–126, 132, 153, 195–196, 205; communitarian 44; declining 18; equitable 80, 93; of excluded and minority groups 5
reservation(s) 5–11, 14, 16, 18, 29–30, 40–41, 43–47, 50–52, 57, 61, 63–64, 66–67, 70–71, 73–75, 77–78, 81, 84–85, 87–88, 90–91, 93–98, 100–102, 104–109, 112, 121–126, 132, 137–138, 140, 147, 163, 170, 192–193, 196–197, 199–200, 202; abolition of 41; Andhra Pradesh model of 98, 107; for disadvantaged castes 11; in employment 2, 9, 16, 51, 67, 98, 193; to include OBCs 45; in legislatures 7, 46; for Marathas 197; for Muslims 67, 88, 98, 107, 122–123, 197; political 51; right to 51; for SCs, STs, and OBCs 11, 52, 96, 132
reserved constituencies 205
rights: citizenship 52, 56–57; group 7, 42, 45, 63; individual 43, 51;
of religious minorities 14, 17, 19, 30, 39
riots 172–173, 176–177, 181, 185–186, 189, 191; of 2002 2, 14, 20, 46, 56, 64, 66–67, 172, 178, 184, 195
Rashtriya Janata Dal (RJD) 99, 175–176, 187
Robinson, James A. 28–29
Rudolph, Lloyd I. 31
Rudolph, Susanne 31

Sachar Committee 4, 8, 24, 36, 58, 70, 72, 79, 90, 96–97, 146, 203
Sachar Committee Report (SCR) 3–5, 9, 14–16, 34, 39, 57–59, 61–64, 66, 69, 72–73, 75–77, 79–80, 83, 90, 93–95, 97–99, 106, 108, 113, 122–123, 125, 128–129, 132, 137, 139–141, 146, 155, 163, 173, 196–197, 201–202, 206–207; BJP's opposition to 80, 137; Committee's recommendations/ SCR recommendations 24, 79–80, 83, 90, 95–96, 139, 196, 201, 203; for 'equity and inclusiveness' 93
Sachar, Rajinder 24, 70, 95, 178
Samajwadi Party (SP) 21, 37, 78, 80, 99, 104, 175, 182
Sarva Shiksha Abhiyan (SSA) 164, 167, 203
Scheduled Castes (SCs) 2–7, 9–11, 22–23, 25, 35, 41–47, 50–52, 57–59, 61, 63–64, 66–67, 72–75, 78, 81, 83–84, 91, 93–94, 96, 99–102, 104–105, 107, 112, 123–128, 132, 136, 163–164, 170,

179, 182–183, 185, 190–193, 199–200, 202, 204–205; reserved constituencies for 205
Scheduled Castes and Scheduled Tribes (Prevention of Atrocities) Act (1989) 35, 51, 171, 185, 193
Scheduled Tribes (STs) 2–4, 6–7, 9–11, 23, 25, 35–36, 41–47, 50–52, 57–59, 61, 64, 67–68, 72–75, 78, 81, 83–84, 91, 93, 96, 100–102, 104–105, 124–128, 132, 136, 163, 170, 179, 182–183, 185, 190–193, 199–200, 204–205
Schmidt, Helmut 1
scholarship(s) 15, 17, 89, 103, 127, 132, 137–138, 142–143, 146–147, 150, 169–170
secularism 36, 40, 42, 57, 67, 171
securitisation 1–2, 65
security 1, 9, 13, 15, 34, 39, 41, 54, 56–59, 62, 64–65, 87, 92, 129, 163, 171, 173–175, 193, 196, 198, 200
self-employment 128
Shah Bano case 55
Shinde, Sushil Kumar 190
Shiromani Akali Dal (SAD) 54, 187
Shiv Sena 108
Sikhism 6
Sikhs 3, 6–7, 39–41, 44–45, 51–54, 56–57, 74, 104, 112–114, 139, 150, 154, 157; militants 54; political representatives 41; in Punjab 52, 54
Singh, Arjun 100
Singh, Joginder 188

Singh, Manmohan 4, 16–17, 78, 138, 195, 198, 206
Singh, R. K. 187
Singh, V. P. 46-47
Singhvi, Abhishek 100
social: contract 16; exclusion 3, 6, 16, 65, 72; inclusion 18, 72; justice 7, 17, 30, 71, 102, 165–166, 185, 189, 196, 199–200; mobilisation 20; welfare 207
Socially and Educationally Backward Classes (SEBCs) 104, 138
socio-religious communities 77
state policy (-ies) 2, 58, 64; institutionalisation of 78
Supreme Court 45, 47, 50, 55, 81, 87–88, 95, 106–109, 125–126, 146–147, 164, 178, 184, 188, 192, 197
Swaraj, Sushma 177, 186
Swarn Jayanti Shahari Rojgar Yojana (SJSRY) 163–164, 167
Swarnajayanti Gram Swarozgar Yojana (SGSY) 164, 167

terrorism 4
Thomas, K. T. 188
tribes/tribal population. *See* Adivasis
Trinamool Congress (TMC) 122, 187, 190

underdevelopment 2, 4–5, 39, 58, 129, 141, 157, 205–206
under-representation 5, 14, 34, 59, 74, 77, 94, 96, 105, 126; of minorities 34, 123; of Muslims 5, 14, 34, 59, 61, 94, 96, 105

United Progressive Alliance (UPA) 2, 4–6, 8–20, 22–27, 31–32, 34–39, 50–51, 57, 64–66, 68–69, 72, 76–78, 80, 82–85, 87–91, 93–94, 97–99, 104–105, 107–109, 121, 123–127, 132, 137–138, 140–141, 146, 148–150, 153–156, 164, 170–174, 176–180, 182, 186–187, 190, 192–196, 198–207; and 2004 general elections 8, 16, 31, 64–66, 192; development deficit and 2; and equality of opportunity 2, 6, 8–9, 13, 16–18, 31–32, 35, 38, 39, 64, 65–68, 72–73, 76–77, 91, 170, 192, 198–200, 207; policy (-ies) 10–14, 16–20, 22–25, 32, 34, 38, 50, 69, 84, 87, 90–91, 121, 123–124, 126, 198, 201, 205–206; and political coalition 17, 193; and reservations for Muslims 98
United States Commission on International Religious Freedom 172
untouchability 82, 101
UPA II 150, 173–174, 180, 182, 186, 193, 204, 207
upper caste Hindus 5
Urban Infrastructure and Governance (UIG) 162, 166
Urban Infrastructure Development Scheme for Small and Medium Towns (UIDSSMT) 162, 166
US-India Policy Institute 90, 206

Vajpayee, Atal Bihari 66–67
Veerappa Moily, M. 181

violence 53–54; against minorities 2, 52; criminal forces or 175; discrimination and 56; on the Hindu body 53; by Hindu mobs 56; information on 191; killings during 56; legislation against 35; Muslims in 173; of Partition 41, 53; reactions from minorities 53; rehabilitation of victims of 174–175, 177, 205; stigmatisation and 7. *See also* communal, riots
Vishwa Hindu Parishad (VHP) 55, 67
voluntarism 23
vote-bank(s) 8–9, 50, 79–80, 89

weaker section(s) 140–141, 153. *See also* disadvantaged; discrimination; marginalisation
West Bengal State Higher Educational Institutions (Reservation in Admission) Act 123
women 18, 43, 62, 89, 95, 132, 177–179, 205; Muslim 18, 62; and Islamic law 18
Worship (Special Provisions) Act, 1992 68

Yadav, Devendra Prasad 99, 176
Yadav, Mulayam Singh 80, 99

Zoroastrians 40, 139, 154